Heritage Interpretation
Volume 2

Heritage Interpretation
Volume 2
The Visitor Experience

Edited by
David L. Uzzell

Belhaven Press
A division of Pinter Publishers
London and New York

© The editor, editorial board and contributors 1989

First published in Great Britain in 1989 by
Belhaven Press (a division of Pinter Publishers)
25 Floral Street, London WC2E 9DS

Reprinted in 1992

Belhaven Press in association with the Centre for Environmental Interpretation and the
Society for the Interpretation of Britain's Heritage.

British Library Cataloguing in Publication Data

A CIP catalogue record for this book is available from the British Library

ISBN 1 85293 077 2 (Volume 1 only)
ISBN 1 85293 078 0 (Volume 2 only)

Library of Congress Cataloging in Publication Data

Heritage interpretation / edited by David L. Uzzell.
    p. cm.
    Includes indexes.
    Contents: v. 1. The natural and built environment – v. 2. The
visitor experience.
    ISBN 1-85293-077-2 (v. 1) – ISBN 1-85293-078-0 (v. 2)
    1. Historic sites – Interpretive programs.   2. Parks – Interpretive
programs. 3. Tourist trade. I. Uzzell, David.
CC135.H46   1989
363.6'8 – dc 20   89-6668
          CIP

Filmset by Mayhew Typesetting, Bristol, England
Printed and bound in Great Britain by
Biddles Ltd, Guildford and King's Lynn

Contents

Volume 2: The Visitor Experience

List of Figures

List of Tables

List of Contributors

Val Beswick
L & R Leisure Group, 127 Albert Bridge Road, London SW11 4PL, UK.

Richard Broadhurst
Forestry Commission, 321 Corstorphine Road, Edinburgh EH12 7AT, UK.

Alan Capelle
John Veverka and Associates, Minnesota, Michigan, Ohio, USA.

Dr Neil Cossons
Director, Science Museum, Exhibition Road, London SW7, UK.

Antony E.C. Eastaugh
Public Attitude Surveys Research, Rye Park House, London Road, High Wycombe, Buckinghamshire HP11 1EF, UK.

Jenny L. Feick
Chief of Interpretation, Extension and Cooperative Activities, Western Region, Canadian Parks Service, 457 Main Street 3rd Floor, Winnipeg, Manitoba, Canada R3G2M1.

Professor David Lowenthal
Department of Geography, University College London, 26 Bedford Way, London WC1H 0AP, UK.

Alan Machin
Public Relations and Marketing Officer, Calderdale Inheritance Project, 4–8 Old Arcade, Halifax, West Yorkshire HX1 1TJ, UK.

Marc Mallam
Professional Development Services, 98 Stephenson Terrace, Deepdale Road, Preston, Lancashire PR1 5AP, UK.

Dr Paulette M. McManus
Communication Consultant, 4 Gills Hill, Radlett, Hertfordshire WD7 8BZ, UK.

Peter Middleton
L & R Leisure Group, 127 Albert Bridge Road, London SW11 4PL, UK.

Gary Moore
Naturalist Co-ordinator, Metro Parks, Columbus and Franklin County, Ohio, USA.

Ian Parkin
First Interpreters Ltd, Unit 46, Barclays Venture Centre, University of Warwick Science Park, Sir William Lyons Road, Coventry CV4 7EZ, UK.

Dr Paul H. Risk
Parks, Recreation & Tourism Program, University of Maine, 247 Nutting Hall, Orono, Maine 04401, USA.

Terence W. Robinson
Countryside Commission, John Dower House, Crescent Place, Cheltenham, Gloucestershire GL50 3RA, UK.

Dr Terry Russell
Centre for Research in Primary Science and Technology, University of Liverpool, Liverpool, UK.

Harris H. Shettel
Museum Consultant, 14102 Artic Avenue, Rockville Maryland 20853, USA.

Professor Roger Silverstone
Museum Research Group, Centre for Research into Innovation, Culture and Technology, Brunel University, Uxbridge, Middlesex, UK.

Stuart B. Smith
Director, Ironbridge Gorge Museum Trust, Ironbridge, Telford, Shropshire TF8 7AW, UK.

Dr Terry R. Stevens
Director, Centre for Tourism and Recreation Management, West Glamorgan Institute of Higher Education, Loughor, Swansea, West Glamorgan SA1 6ED, UK.

Professor Dr Jerzy Swiecimski
Polish Academy of Sciences, Institute Systematic Experimental Zoology, Krakow, Stawkowska 17, Poland.

Raymond S. Tabata
University of Hawaii Sea Grant Extension Service, 1000 Pope Road, MSB 205, Honolulu, Hawaii 96822.

Dr David L. Uzzell
Department of Psychology, University of Surrey, Guildford, Surrey GU2 5XH, UK.

Dr Gail A. Vander Stoep
University of Massachusetts, Amherst, Massachusetts, USA.

Michael D. Watson
Chief of Interpretation, United States National Park Service, PO Box 37127, Washington DC 20013-7127, USA.

Nicholas Weiss
English Heritage, Keysign House, 429 Oxford Street, London W1R 2HD, UK.

Dr Robert C. Wendling
Department of Health, Physical Education, Recreation and Safety, University of East Carolina, Greenville, North Carolina, 27858, USA.

Martin Westwood
Manager, Warwick Castle, Warwick, Warwickshire CV34 4QU, UK.

John Veverka
John Veverka and Associates, Minnesota, Michigan, Ohio, USA.

Acknowledgements

The publishers wish to thank Chapel Music for permission to reproduce a verse from the song *Meet Me on the Corner*, and to Intersong for permission to reproduce a verse from Van Morrison's *Tore Down a la Rimbaud*, which appear in Chapter 12 of this volume.

1

Introduction: The Visitor Experience

David L. Uzzell

Heritage Interpretation: Volumes I and II is based on papers delivered at the Second World Congress on Heritage Presentation and Interpretation at the University of Warwick in September 1988. The two volumes attempt to provide a comprehensive 'state of the art' review of current interpretative philosophy, theory, practice and research.

The papers in Volume II focus on the promotion, marketing and funding of interpretation, identifying and responding to the needs of visitors and the infrastructural facilities and services required to complement interpretive facilities, and current research on visitors and the effectiveness of interpretive provision. This volume also includes a number of the invited keynote papers at the congress along with David Lowenthal's closing address which, as ever, provides a highly stimulating commentary on contemporary heritage interpretation (Chapter 24).

The order of the chapters in this volume has been largely determined by these groupings. However, the collective theme of the chapters, as reflected in the subtitle of this volume, is the notion that the visitors' needs and interests should be at the heart of interpretive provision if such provision is to be effective. One might see marketing, research ar.d ..itegrated heritage management as three aspects of and perspectives on one important issue: visitor satisfaction. And, of course, each perspective will be suggestive of different approaches, problems, opportunities, constraints and actions.

The Use of Interpretation

Traditionally, interpreters have focused their attention on the resources to be managed, marketed and interpreted, whether in the natural or built environment. This has not been surprising since the initial motivation for interpretation emerged out of conservation goals. Interpretation has been seen as both 'hard' and a 'soft' management tool for controlling and educating visitors' use of heritage sites in order to conserve historic buildings or fragile ecosystems.

But the rationale and motivation for interpretation has changed over the years and it now has to be seen in a much broader context than simply as one aspect of conservation management. Interpretation is now considered to have a much broader role to play within the recreation and tourism industries, as well as in urban countryside and regional planning.

It is possible to identify four principal uses to which interpretation has been put:

(1) Interpretation as 'soft' visitor management
(2) Interpretation as 'hard' visitor management
(3) Interpretation as propaganda
(4) Interpretation as a value-added product of the tourism industry

There are other uses such as interpretation as an aid to the economic regeneration of declining areas, and interpretation for the protection of newly created landscapes. These are discussed in detail elsewhere (Uzzell, 1988).

Interpretation as 'Soft' Visitor Management

Here the visitor to the countryside or the town is informed and impressed by the specialness of upland wilderness or low-lying wetlands and the fragility of their ecosystems, or the threat posed to listed buildings. Once the visitor understands and stands in awe of such marvels, then it is seen as a short and automatic step to creating a change in the visitor's attitudes and inducing thoughtful and considerate behaviour. Interpretation is aimed at making the countryside recreation experience more enjoyable and rewarding, resulting not only in visitors' eyes being opened to new environments, but familiar environments being seen anew. This perspective is best illustrated by an example from one of the stated objectives in the Interpretive Plan for Risley Moss, Warrington New Town in Lancashire:

to use the interpretive process to make visitors aware of the value of the site and the consequences of their actions; to influence their behaviour so as to reduce management problems. (Warrington New Town Development Corporation, 1977)

Interpretation as 'Hard' Visitor Management

Interpretive techniques such as guided walks and way-marked trails can be used to shepherd the public away from heavily eroded or fragile environments to areas which can withstand greater visitor pressure. Again this can be illustrated by reference to the 'visitor management' objectives in the Risley Moss Interpretive Plan:

to restrict public access on the more sensitive areas of the site by means of careful design of paths and access points, by locating the majority of the visitor facilities within the woodland zone, and by the use of interpretation . . .

to control access on to the whole site by channelling visitors through one entrance point where interpretive facilities are located. (Warrington New Town Development Corporation, 1977)

Interpretation as Propaganda

More controversially, interpretation can also be used for public relations or, more provocatively, as propaganda. Large landowning organizations may use interpretive techniques to put forward the land management policies of their organization which may or may not be conservation oriented. The aims of farms open days, for example, have been defined as 'to increase the visitor's understanding of farming, leading to improved standards of behaviour and a greater respect for the farmed countryside, with a greater awareness of the importance of farming as an industry'. (Countryside Commission, 1977, p. 3).

Farm open days often serve to extol the virtues of the agricultural industry and, paradoxically in interpretation terms, unblushingly demonstrate the anti-conservation production methods of modern factory farming (Lee and Uzzell, 1980).

To this category one might also add the kind of interpretation that is provided as an adjunct to industrial tourism. The interpretation of 'extinct' industry is commonplace. However, thriving industry has also seen an opportunity to promote itself through interpretation. The heritage of the product – its constituent properties and its manufacturing process, along with the philosophy and ethos of the company and the industry – are increasingly regarded as marketable commodities like the product itself. The funding of this interpretation is likely to come under public relations, marketing and advertising budgets.

Interpretation as a Value-Added Product of the Tourism Industry

Interpretation can be used as an additional product in tourism provision. Tourist attractions have come to realize that the natural and built environment is of interest and concern to the public, who wish to be more informed about it. Some tourism attractions have realized that the heritage itself can be promoted and marketed as a tourism product while others have attempted to make visitors more aware of the heritage if only in a superficial way as part of a wider tourism product. The Wedgwood company, for example, has a small display on the heritage of Wedgwood china at Alton Towers, the largest theme park in Britain: its function is clearly to add 'weight' to the commercial product and attract the visitor to the shop which he/she passes through at the end of the Wedgwood exhibition. The exhibition is informative and of high quality, but the real job of the space given over to Wedgwood is to sell Wedgwood products. While this may be anathema to some interpreters and conservationists, it is difficult to dispute that it may at least confront various groups in our society with a conservation message to which they might not otherwise be exposed.

There are also examples whereby visitors are encouraged to visit the countryside for various events and activities which may have little to do with the countryside, heritage or conservation. The function of these events is to act as a catalyst to encourage visitors to take an interest in the heritage of the town or countryside and perhaps be attracted to more systematic interpretive programmes. The extensive events programme at Queen Elizabeth Country Park in Hampshire provides an example of this type of approach, where the intention is to attract visitors to the park for 'popular' events in order to make them aware of both the beauty of the park and park values. Having visited once, it is hoped that they will return on a future occasion, when the park is less crowded, and become involved in more specific and overt interpretive programmes.

These 'uses' of interpretation are neither mutually exclusive nor incompatible. It is possible for 'hard' and 'soft' interpretation to exist on one site and for the interpretation to have a propagandist function as well. However, it is worthwhile distinguishing between these applications because not only do they reflect shifts in both the use of interpretation over the past two decades and the type of professionals and organizations who now look to interpretation as part of their tool kit, but it is also suggestive of the potential use to which the set of techniques that interpreters have developed might be put in future.

Resource or Market Led?

One consequence of the lateral expansion of the 'terms of reference' of interpretation is that the goal of interpretation is no longer solely to encourage pro-conservation behaviour. The rationale and *raison d'être* of interpretation is now more extensive and complex.

Secondly, there has been a shift from seeing interpretation as a resource dominated activity, to recognizing the need to incorporate visitor needs into the equation. This reflects, in many ways, the concerns of the tourism industry which is necessarily market-oriented and marketing conscious. As Robinson (Chapter 6) points out, marketing is a set of techniques that discipline the operators to match what they can offer to what people want. Furthermore, it is not only about increasing numbers: it can also be about limiting numbers to ensure that the capacity of a site is not exceeded with consequential irreparable damage. Robinson, in a review of a study carried out on behalf of the Countryside Commission for England and Wales which examined the importance and management of visitor centres, found that the standards of environmental care of sites and visitor centres were generally first-rate; however, there was a much wider variation in the attitude of staff towards members of the public. This is a reflection of a traditional resource-management bias. The need to effect a balance between the capacity of the resource and the needs of the visitor is illustrated by Tabata's paper (Chapter 8) which discusses the marketing of special interest tourism in Hawaii to promote, interpret and protect a fragile marine resource.

A third consequence of broadening the scope of interpretation is that the practice now involves professionals from a much wider range of specialisms and disciplines. This should be seen as highly beneficial. There are those who would argue, though, that interpretation and its goals is in danger of being appropriated by groups whose interest in the original concerns of interpretation are marginal, if not non-existent.

Interpretation Matters

At one level, interpretation could be seen simply as a set of communication techniques of varying degrees of effectiveness in varying situations which can be used to get particular messages across to particular groups of people. Given this definition, interpretation becomes an adjunct to the communications industry. Some might go further and argue that, given the type of communications techniques used, it should be seen as part of the entertainments industry. Does this matter?

There is a risk, of course, that the medium will become the message. How far off is the day when, while queuing to enter the most newly opened heritage experience – 'All Muck 'n' Brass' – you overhear the following conversation:

Charles: 'Did you go to *"Baldrick's Saxon Village"*? I thought that the twenty-track stereo and laser light show in the hunting scene was good. Amanda and Henry really liked it too.'

Tim: 'It wasn't as good as the guillotine scene at the *"Best of Times, Worst of Times"* exhibition. Did you know that they employ 1,000 unemployed youngsters on a Training Agency scheme to play the part of the revolutionary crowd? The smell was so authentic – you would have thought they were real French peasants.'

Charles: 'Yes, but what about *"The Miners' Experience"*? You travel on these heritage coal trucks down a long dark tunnel passing scenes of the working lives of miners. Then you come to the coal face on which is shown a film about the decline of the coal industry. The last scene is a picture of the pithead, with that wheel-thingy not going round – just silence, except the Buggleswick Colliery Band playing "Jerusalem" in the background. Then the coal face wall slowly rises and the heritage coal trucks take you through into this real identical industrial scene of the present day.'

With apologies to Roger Silverstone (Chapter 17), the Ojibwe Indians and St Marie-amongst-the-Hurons, this blurring and lack of definition is identified by Silverstone, who writes, 'the heritage industry is in the business of mass communication and that the boundary between museums and media, and that between reality and fantasy, between myth and mimesis in both sets of institutions and practices is becoming increasing blurred, increasingly indistinct.'

Volume I of *Heritage Interpretation* contains a number of papers which critically analyse as well as defend the 'heritage industry'. There is now little doubt that the interpretation of the heritage, while in some settings has remained cosy, home-spun and non-commercial, in other settings has become an important income generator and valued-added product of the tourism industry. However, there has been a free trade in innovations and ideas. Free trade, of course, has to be a two-way process and one consequence of the interaction between tourism and interpretation/heritage management is that the everyday techniques of the tourism industry have been imported into interpretation. Some, including Stevens (Chapter 12), would argue that heritage has been sucked in by tourism, public relations and marketing professionals, redefined, reconstituted and repackaged to become an exercise in trivia – part of what has been recently referred to as 'the three-minute culture'. As Stevens writes, 'Technological wizardry, media consultants, innovative presentations, audio animatronics – these are the buzz words to switch on the lights in tourist board offices around the world.' Arguably, the backlash at the 'heritage industry' is precisely because of this.

Telling the Truth

It is noteworthy that at least two of the contributors (Swiecimski, Chapter 23; Cossons, Chapter 2) use a rather old-fashioned word these days – truth. Swiecimski discusses seven different interpretations of the meaning of truth in a museum context. Cossons argues that one of the functions of heritage managers is to offer 'truth' to the visitor, but questions whether truth can survive the power of the tourism industry and the pressure of the disposable income economy. The consumer in the future is going to bear more and more responsibility for funding the conservation and presentation of the heritage as public sector support is reduced and the mythical 'freedom to choose' philosophy gains ascendancy. Is user choice compatible with the survival of truth, or does it mean provision at the level of the lowest common denominator? But Cossons reminds us that public funding is not, and has never necessarily been, synonymous with the guardianship of truth. Despite the fact that the visitor will increasingly be paying for the heritage at the point of consumption rather than through taxation, Cossons believes that there is still a role for government in the funding of the heritage: it is, though, a changed role and relationship leading to a public/private mix with defined responsibilities for each sector, offering more flexibility for interpretation and perhaps even ensuring the maintenance of truth.

The public/private mix is an avenue down which many public sector organizations, responsible directly or indirectly for recreation and interpretation, are now travelling. Broadhurst (Chapter 4) describes and details the philosophy and way forward for the Forestry Commission in ensuring that its recreational and interpretive activities are optimally funded.

Stuart Smith, the Director of Ironbridge Gorge Museum, sees the decline in public sector subsidy and support as cause for celebration (Chapter 3), since it will force 'such organizations to become more visitor-oriented and therefore provide a better service for the public'. Some might see this on the one hand as too simplistic and on the other as an unjustified criticism of the pioneering work of the public sector in heritage interpretation. Ironbridge Gorge Museum is outside the public sector, and while it does receive support from government, over 90 per cent of its revenue costs come from admission charges. Such a high reliance on one source of income has led the museum to diversity its sources of revenue, and Smith reports on the imaginative ways in which they have gone about this.

The papers by Cossons and Smith in this Volume, and a number of the papers in Volume I, highlight the potential conflict between what has been called 'earning and learning', and the need to ensure that we are not caught up in the contemporary *zeitgeist* of knowing the cost of everything and the value of nothing. Smith does not mention 'truth' in his paper. However, being responsible for a World Heritage Site, he is only too aware of the need for a balance between the conflicting demands of commercialization and scholarship. Perhaps he would argue, following Cossons' conclusion, that one can provide a thrill as well as authoritative interpretation based on sound scholarship: it just won't be a cheap thrill.

Marketing Heritage

Marketing is often misunderstood and thought to be a brash and hard-sell set of persuasion techniques which encourage people to buy something that they do not want. The main body of Robinson's (Chapter 6) paper concentrates on the need to identify what the market wants from a recreational service and, indeed, who is the market? Very few managers of visitor centres studied sought to collect, analyse and use information about their existing and potential audience. It is a hard lesson to learn, but there is more and more competition for the recreation pound and it is vital that heritage facilities develop, promote and market their services and facilities to encourage new and repeat visitation, as is exemplified by Eastaugh and Weiss's work for English Heritage (Chapter 7). It is only in this way that a conservation message will be put across to a broader cross-section of the public. Almost without exception, commercial enterprises set targets to which to aspire. Although the conventional indicators of the market place, such as profit, are not necessarily present or appropriate to provide a measure of success (and failure) of interpretive performance, this is no reason why public sector or non-profit-making facilities cannot equally set measurable targets. It is noteworthy that Robinson concludes by arguing that a visitor-centred approach is vital to ensure the survival of the resource.

The responsibility for conserving and interpreting much of our heritage is in the hands of the charitable and voluntary sector. These bodies are not immune to the same competitive pressures which are being exerted upon both the public and private sectors. Mallam (Chapter 5) argues that these bodies are now having to learn how to become professional, how to borrow and capitalize their organizations and how to compete for the leisure pound if they are to survive financially. Yet many of these organizations have an entirely different culture to their competitors in the public and private sector. As a consequence there is a danger that these charitable and voluntary bodies will tear themselves apart as the demands of competition and the high-level commercial orientation required will be at variance with the volunteer culture which has often been the foundation for their development and support.

It is a paradox that it is often difficult to get funding for interpretation yet we are witnessing a booming tourism industry. One reason for this is the need for more research on both the markets for interpretation and the interpretive product itself. Some would argue that we have to go much further than this: we have to understand the interpretation business in its larger tourism context and more fully than at present. It often has a poor image, poor presentation techniques, inadequate organization, poor research, poor planning. Providers cannot decide whether they want to be in competition with or co-operate with other heritage attractions, and the tourism infrastructure, such as the environment around attractions, is often very low grade. In short there is a need to be more professional.

Caring for the Visitor

There has been a recognition that if interpretation is to be effective and successful, then attention needs to be paid not simply to the interpretive media but also to the infrastructural base and recreational context of interpretive provision. This is the subject of the paper by Parkin, Middleton and Beswick (Chapter 13), who argue that it is essential to have an integrated approach to heritage management. In essence, this means that all aspects of the visitor's experience of a place should be carefully planned to ensure that from the moment visitors set out to visit a heritage attraction to the time they leave, everything is of the highest professional standard. Parkin's view is informed by a 'post-Disney' philosophy of the *total visitor experience*, and incorporates the disciplines of landscape architecture, urban and transport planning, architecture, marketing, education and others. In short, the authors make a case for integrated heritage management. This means that the signing to and around visitor facilities, car parking, refreshments, souvenir shop and all the other requirements that families have when they are visiting places as part of a recreational experience should be of the highest quality. Unfortunately, many providers of interpretive facilities have failed to recognize that the best interpretation in the world will not compensate for dirty, poor-quality facilities, taciturn staff and a grudging service. However, first-rate facilities will add considerably to the enjoyment of the visitor. Parkin et al. argue that if visitors leave satisfied, they will stay longer, spend more, return at a later date and recommend a visit to friends and relatives.

Parkin et al. express a more significant message than one of simply saying that we must ensure that the lavatories are clean and the tea hot, important though this is. Based on their experience of working in Calderdale, Cumbria and Portsmouth, the authors argue the case for a visitor management strategy which sets the interpretive provision in its town or regional context. This view is echoed in Capelle et al.'s paper (Chapter 14), although they concern themselves solely with a regional interpretive strategy to ensure coherent and non-overlapping interpretive experiences.

The papers by Watson (Chapter 9), Westwood (Chapter 10), Feick (Chapter 11), Stevens (Chapter 12), Parkin et al. (Chapter 13) and Risk (Chapter 15), all have one thing in common. They are all about 'service' and recognize that interpretive provision should be visitor-oriented. The papers range from Mike Watson's account of the research undertaken by the United States National Park Service into visitor needs and how these get fed into a visitor services programme at a national level, Jenny Feick's paper which examines the six-stage planning process which makes up an overall service strategy in the Canadian parks, through to Martin Westwood's 'nuts and bolts' account of managing an eleventh-century castle to ensure that not William the Conqueror but rather the customer is king. Inevitably, there is also overlap between these papers and the chapters on training in Volume I. For example, Paul Risk's exploration of the role of non-verbal communication in generating a rapport with visitors is essential to a friendly and caring service and clearly also has important training implications.

Research and Evaluation

The third theme, which also relates to the emphasis placed in this Volume on the visitor and his or her needs and experiences, is research and evaluation. Marketing obviously relies on research. Typically though, research of this kind is concerned with the demographic characteristics of visitors, market segmentation and visitors' preferences for and levels of satisfaction with different types of facilities, services and experiences. The research which is reported here is of a more fundamental kind, drawing on the theories and conceptual frameworks provided by academic research in psychology, sociology and linguistics. Silverstone (Chapter 17) cites Popper's argument that is impossible to observe, describe or analyse outside a theoretical framework, if only because observation is always selective. This is an apposite point given the wide range of theoretical and methodological approaches which inform the chapters on research and evaluation.

Despite the use of a profusion of technologies to enhance visitor under-standing and enable learning, it would seem from research on the effec-tiveness of exhibitions that visitors to museums actually do not learn very much (Shettel, 1968; Borun, 1977; Screven, 1975). Is this because of the inherent deficiencies of the interpretation or does it reflect a defect in the research methods used to assess learning and attitude change? Indeed, are we asking the right questions? It has to be questioned whether the metho-dologies currently used to assess learning and understanding are sensitive enough, ecologically valid or even appropriate to the variety of settings in which interpretation is found? Many of the research and evaluation papers attempt to answer these questions.

A Brief History

A historical perspective is always both fascinating and instructive. Shettel's (Chapter 16) historical analysis of assessment and evaluation studies reveals that the 1980s saw an explosion in the number of such studies undertaken in museums. Out of 384 publications between 1916 and 1988, 58 per cent were published between 1980 and 1988, and 94 per cent between 1965 and the present day. Shettel relates the growth in evaluation studies to larger movements within the social and governmental programmes of the times. Too often it is assumed that new developments emerge somehow out of the ether, outside of any larger political, social, cultural or economic context. Furthermore, what seems like a factor bringing about change is simply a small part of a larger social process. One can cite many examples. The success of a number of environmental pressure groups in conservation campaigns in the mid-1970s was possibly due to the efforts of those pressure groups themselves; but it was also due to a stagnation in the world economy with the consequent depression on the developments which placed environ-ments and the heritage at risk. These were therefore economic forces outside the control of individual or group agency.

Shettel points to some seminal examples where evaluation has been an essential part of a museum's development work, but laments that it is the exception rather than the rule. It is noteworthy that exhibitions are now costing a great deal of money, and yet museum boards are usually unwilling to spend even 1 per cent of an exhibition budget on formative and other evaluation in order to ensure the effectiveness of their exhibitions and level of visitor satisfaction. Russell's study (Chapter 22) examines a range of formative evaluation techniques that can be used to reduce abortive exhibi-tion design work and discusses their respective value. It is paradoxical that at a time when there is more and more competition, not only for the leisure pound but, as Cossons points out, leisure time (that is, it is disposable time not income which is becoming a critical factor in determining leisure consumption) museums and those responsible for displays are unwilling to spend a tiny fraction of development costs on ensuring that exhibits are effective. The value of Shettel's arguments in support of evaluation is that they are pertinent, not just to the design of exhibits, but to visitor provision at heritage facilities and museums generally.

It has been an unquestioned implicit assumption of much research that the major portion of the variance of visitor learning is attributable to the exhibition material itself. More recent research evidence suggests that social interaction mediating the visitor/exhibit relationship is more critical to the process of cognitive learning and attitude change (Gottesdiener, 1988; Uzzell and Blud, forthcoming) than the direct effects of the exhibition material itself. Research has largely been confined to the investigation of adult visitors *as individuals*. However, the two main groups of visitors to museums are school groups and family groups (Laetsch et al., 1980). Very little research has investigated children's learning in museums. In particular, little is known about learning in either school groups or family groups. Research indicates that most people visiting a museum see it as primarily a social event, rather than an educational trip (e.g. Borun, 1977). Yet there has been a failure to investigate the implications of this for exhibition design or visitor learning.

The emphasis must now be on establishing a social psychological framework for evaluating informal learning in museums, so that the focus is shifted from individual cognitive processes to the social and interpersonal aspects of learning. McManus (Chapter 19) describes a study she undertook which is both informed by such a social approach and provides another example of the diversity of research methodologies now being used in museums. McManus used the analysis of discourse acts to understand and illustrate the surface features of visitors' interactions with exhibits. Transcripts of visitors' conversations, recorded as they stood in front of four exhibits in the British Museum (Natural History) were analysed qualitatively to demonstrate that they are 'learning conversations' and to show that visitors deal with exhibit communications as a social unit. Data from the linguistic analysis of forty-one conversations conducted in the museum illustrate quantitatively the ways in which language is used as a vehicle for thought in museum communications. McManus suggests that a continuum of communicative control is expressed through the form of exhibit presentations with traditional, object-orientated displays being at the weak end of the continuum.

Turning on to Heritage

Silverstone provides a critical analysis of museums and heritage, and places this analysis within the 'contemporary culture' mode of analysis, relying on semiology, literary theory and ethnography. He goes on to argue the case that museums, heritage displays and television all share a number of common attributes, not least of which is that they are all constructions. That is, they are designed and created to approximate reality and be read like reality. They are texts with varying degrees of clarity or opaqueness. Silverstone uses the word 'text' in a semiotic sense, i.e. as a system of signs: 'at the heart of any act of communication is a discrete organization of signs – words, images, sounds, objects – that in their ordering lay claim to meaning. The work of design and production is oriented solely to the creation of a text in this sense; the work of the visitor is that of deciphering and recreating the text for him or herself.' Those unfamiliar with this type of analysis might be interested in the work of Roland Barthes (1973; 1977) who provides numerous examples of the coding and decoding of images. This approach to evaluation is extremely powerful but, as yet, rarely explored in a museum or heritage setting. The value of Silverstone's work is that while it is theoretical, it is nevertheless directly applied to the design and day-to-day management of museums and is therefore 'a major route into the study of the mechanisms of an exhibition's effectiveness'.

Silverstone, however, goes further than the pragmatic, arguing the case that museums and the heritage industry are a fundamental part of contemporary (communication) culture and therefore should be studied as such. It is therefore interesting that this is precisely the conceptual framework which informs Machin's paper (Chapter 18). Machin asserts that interpretation should be used as a tool for social development at a community level. One means of achieving this and reaching a home-based audience is to work with and through the mass media and education, and thereby influence popular culture. Machin's ideas are formulated in the context of a social helix model of social change which comprises four elements: discovering, understanding, decision-making and reaction.

Gail Vander Stoep (Chapter 21), in a paper which again reflects the diversity of approaches and techniques being used to understand visitor behaviour, uses three observation methodologies to assess depreciative behaviour: the analysis of behaviour or physical traces (that is, those physically observable pieces of evidence providing signs of past behaviour); personal observation; and mechanical observation. The latter technique involves the use of time-lapse photography, which is traditionally used for studying wildlife and visitor movement. The strengths and weaknesses of each of these techniques is assessed and Vander Stoep finds much to recommend time-lapse photography as a research tool.

Changing Attitudes and Behaviour

One set of questions of particular interest to the psychologist concerns the degree to which interpretation is effective. Does interpretation change attitudes and behaviour? We are spending millions of pounds and dollars each year on interpretation: are we getting a return on the investment in terms of a more enlightened and caring public? Presumably this is, or should be, of fundamental concern to heritage managers, conservationists and inter-preters as well.

Tilden's oft-stated dictum 'through interpretation, understanding; through understanding, appreciation; through appreciation, protection' (Tilden, 1957) has at its root a psychological model of attitude and behaviour change which has been the subject of intense debate and research in psychology over the past sixty years. This model postulates that information leading to increased understanding of an issue will lead to attitude change and then, as a consequence, to behaviour change. While this model has appeal, if only through its intuitive logic and simplicity, more thoughtful consideration will suggest that it is problematic. If attitude change were simply a question of giving people information which makes the case for a particular position or cause and which exhorts people to support something because it is a good thing, then presumably anti-smoking campaigns and other preventive health programmes be more successful: all the more so as they are obviously directed towards self-interest. We know, however, that the effect of these programmes is not immediate, direct or even necessarily in the direction intended. Indeed they have only a limited effect in bringing about behavioural change. Therefore, what chance do issues have which are not immediately within the domain of our own everyday experience or affecting our self-interest — issues such as the destruction of the tropical rain forests and the ozone layer?

The role of interpretation in changing attitudes and behaviour remains one of the critical areas necessary for fundamental research. After all, it is essential that we know whether interpretation works. Critical indicators of this are the answers to such questions as: do people change their attitudes as a consequence of interpretive programmes? Does this lead to a change (or reinforcement) in behaviour? What attitudes are changed, and in what direc-tion? What is the time span required for attitudes to change? Does it require repetition, elaboration and reinforcement of the interpretive message, or is one exposure enough? Who changes, under what conditions and why? Wendling's study (Chapter 20) is the only one to address the issue of attitude change, although the focus of his study is on the value of field trips rather than the effectiveness of interpretation *per se*. Nevertheless, his study is an interesting one: he found that participation in a field trip increased learning about ecology, and reduced ethnic differences in environmental attitudes.

The lack of papers examining the effectiveness of interpretation in chang-ing attitudes and behaviour is perhaps not surprising since psychologists have had considerable difficulty in specifying the links between attitude and behaviour change. That being said, however, it still remains a fundamental area for research, and perhaps ought to dominate our research interests over the next few years. After all, it should be of vital concern to heritage managers, conservationists and interpreters because at the end of the day, whatever criticisms are levelled at the 'heritage industry', unless our work is more effective and attitudes and behaviour are changed there will not be a heritage, or even a heritage industry, to be critical about.

Acknowledgements

The task of editing and preparing this book was undertaken by an Editorial Board comprising Graham Barrow, Gillian Binks, Malcom McBratney, Dr Roger Miles, Ian Parkin and Dr David Uzzell, who were originally responsible for organizing the six theme groups of the congress. I am very grateful to all of them for their hard work over an exceptionally short period of time to ensure that this book would be published within a year of the Second World Congress. I would also like to express my sincere gratitude to Mrs Rosalind Gilbert for undertaking a great deal of the administration and typing that a project such as this requires. The speed of publication to ensure that the book is, rather than was, the 'state of the art' is also dependent upon a highly professional publishing staff who at one and the same time know when to 'crack the whip' but who are also sensitive to the pressure of work faced by editors. Iain Stevenson, Patrick Armstrong and Sara Wilbourne of Belhaven Press fulfilled this role admirably.

References

Barthes, R. (1973) *Mythologies*, Collins, London.

Barthes, R. (1977) *Image-Music-Text*, Collins, London.

Borun, M. (1977) *Measuring the Immeasurable: A Pilot Study of Museum Effectiveness*, Association of Science-Technology Centres, Washington, DC.

Countryside Commission (1977) *Farm Open Days*, Countryside Commission Advisory Series No. 3, Cheltenham Glos.

Gottesdiener, H. (1988) 'Visitors' interaction in front of a computer game in an art exhibition', paper presented in the symposium 'A Social Approach to Exhibition Evaluation', British Psychological Society London Conference, (20 December).

Laetsch W.M. Diamond, G.J.L. and Rosenfeld S. (1980) 'Children and family groups in science centres', *Science and Children*, March, 14–17.

Lee, T.R. and Uzzell, D.L. (1980) *The Educational Effectiveness of the Farm Open Day*, Countryside Commission for Scotland, Battleby.

Screven, C.G. (1975) *The Measurement and Facilitation of Learning in the Museum Environment: An Experimental Analysis*, Smithsonian Institution Press, Washington, DC.

Shettel, H.H. et al. (1968) *Strategies for Determining Exhibit Effectiveness*, American Institute for Research, Pittsburgh, PA.

Tilden, F. (1957) *Interpreting Our Heritage*, University of North Carolina Press, Chapel Hill.

Uzzell, D.L. (1988) 'The interpretative experience' in Canter, D. Krampen, M. and Stea, D. (eds) *Ethnoscapes*, Gower, Aldershot.

Uzzell, D.L. and Blud, L. (forthcoming) 'Vikings! Children's social representations of history', in Breakwell G. and Canter D. (eds) *Empirical Approaches to Social Representations*, Oxford University Press, Oxford.

Warrington New Town Development Corporation (1977) *Risley Moss Interpretive Plan*, Warrington New Town DC, Warrington.

2

Plural Funding and the Heritage

Neil Cossons

By the end of the century the world's manufactured goods will be made in the Far East, its food grown in North America, and Europe will have become one vast open-air museum. Our economy will be locked into the treadmill of tourism which for some countries, Britain included, may be the largest single foreign exchange earner. Heritage tourism is the major sector of that market and one that we will increasingly be pushed towards serving.

If this is to be our future it presents dilemmas that we are only now beginning to perceive; of reconciling conservation with access, the use of history with its survival. For the tourism industry, while espousing quality, measures its achievements in quantity. Numbers through the door are the measures of its success, superlatives are the terms by which it sells itself. And the experience of tourism, like pornography, goes in only one direction. Those who were satisfied with a well-turned ankle yesterday, want thighs today.

The future promises to be exciting. Those of us whose job it is to be guardians or interpreters of that heritage, whether that be part of our natural or historical environment, have to survive within that sort of society and that sort of economy. The future will see greater disposable time, disposable income, and mobility. These will have a powerful and increasing influence upon the economy. That will not just be a national economy but an international one. The strength of the 'disposable income economy' and its rate of growth will make the Industrial Revolution look like a brief flicker across the economic landscape of the eighteenth century. It will be a worldwide revolution, not one just confined to a few Western nations. Indeed, as the power of the wealthy nations increases disproportionately to that of the poor, some of those underdeveloped countries will skip the process of industrialization and go straight from subsistence agriculture to serving the pleasure-seeking populations of the rest of the world. How far will their cultures survive this process?

The Economics of Truth

Our job, whether we are preserving or interpreting the heritage, stems primarily from a range of qualitative values which have their roots in scholarship and manifest themselves, from the consumer's point of view, in terms of truths. We are credited, as national parks officers or museum curators, as historic house owners or interpreters, as yeoman warders at the Tower of London, zoo keepers or tour guides, with offering a commodity which has 'truth' as one of its primary components. How far we deserve this accolade is a separate issue, for debate elsewhere. But can truth survive the pressures of the disposable income economy and the power of the tourism industry? Both generate wealth but, equally, they challenge those who aspire to purvey truth. Some will say that truth will simply wither away when the user pays; that the lowest common denominator will always apply. A cheap thrill will be more tempting than authoritative interpretation based on sound scholarship. And cheap thrills are also cheaper to provide.

That there will be increased emphasis on the user paying seems inevitable. In the Western world in general the boundaries of the public sector, in which taxpayers' money is spent corporately by the state, are being rolled back. The philosophy is that if money is not taken in taxation, then it remains in the pockets of people who can exercise personal choice on how it is spent. It would be wrong to think that availability of personal disposable income is new, a product of the 1980s. On the contrary, a century ago, disposable income, coupled with a rapid increase in disposable time, gave birth to the English seaside resort, ably exploited by railway investors. And for much of this century it has led to the growth of the holiday market, the day out, the trip to the country − first by charabanc, then in the family car.

In the future there will be a greater growth in the ability of people to spend money than in the growth of their time. If we look, for example, at the British economy in the last decade, we see increased spending power − certainly of those who are employed − being a major factor in the economy. Those people, generally speaking, work hard for their money; in other words they only have a modest growth in their disposable time but, relatively speaking, a much greater growth in the cash that they can spend in that time. The determination of choice as to how people spend their disposable *time* will become more critical to them than how they choose to spend their money in that time. People will be more anguished at having wasted valuable time than they will at having wasted less valuable disposable cash.

If I am right, and we are going to see a greater emphasis on user choice, is that incompatible with truth surviving? We must of course remember that in the past, full public funding has not guaranteed the survival of 'truth'. The visible decay of some of our great collections and the buildings that house them is a monument to years of public neglect, and this has compromised the values we all wish to promote at least as much as have the pressures of the market economy in which we now live. The only realistic way forward is to find the right mix of public and user funding; to take advantage of the positive benefits of both.

Owning the Heritage

What have we got now? Throughout the world the large part of the financial responsibility for both maintaining and interpreting the heritage has been borne by the taxpayer. The general assumption is that the heritage lies within the public domain, that the public owns it and has a right to it. The people whose job it is to deliver the heritage to the customer are, generally speaking, employed in the public sector. There are of course notable exceptions. One thinks of the great wealth of English country houses, many still in the ownership of their original families, and open regularly to the public at large. There are also organizations that fall between the public and private sectors, such as the National Trust, one of the largest membership-based conservation and interpretation organizations in the world. Here is an organization that is not directly supported by government but which has used a combination of endowment, subscription income, entrance fees and commercial activities to preserve and present for the public at large an illustrious heritage of landscape and great buildings.

But the bulk of what most people perceive to be the heritage lies firmly in the public sector. Most of our great museums are run directly or indirectly by central or local government. So are our ancient monuments, most parks, and many historic houses. In the case of all of these the bulk of the cost of conservation and interpretation falls upon the taxpayer. Although many museums are free, an increasing number are beginning to charge; ancient monuments have always levied a charge, so too have many historic houses. But in almost all cases the income generated directly from the visitor makes only a modest contribution towards the costs of upkeep. This pattern, generally speaking, is typical throughout the world. The United States National Parks Service and Parks Canada, and their smaller state and provincial equivalents, are firmly in the public sector.

The nature of the dilemma, of where the balance lies between public and private interest and funding, is highlighted in Britain's national museums. All are funded by grant-in-aid from government and run by boards of trustees. The large majority provide free admission to their visitors although in the last five years a number have begun to charge. For most of them 90 per cent or more of the direct operating costs are paid for by the taxpayer. Very little capital is available for redevelopment and much of what is obtained is coming from commercial sponsorship. Because many of them live in buildings that are over fifty years old they are beginning to accrue major costs of maintenance.

Furthermore, the public perception of museums is changing, to a great extent as a result of what many of the new museums of the last twenty years have provided. No longer is the word 'museum' a synonym for dust and decay. In the minds of many people it symbolizes sparkling displays in which outstanding collections are presented in high quality galleries. In short, our national museums are wearing out at a faster rate than they are being renewed, at a time when they have never been more popular, when demand for them is growing. That demand is coming from an increasingly sophisticated and discriminating public. But these museums are also facing increased competition from well-capitalized, highly commercial attractions that know how to market themselves well and will command more and more of people's precious disposable time.

The difficulty is one of forging a link, from which the museums can benefit, between the increasing number of users and their demand for quality and those whose job it is to deliver the museums of today and tomorrow.

Changing the Relationship with Government

Government has got into the habit not of thinking of itself as an investor but as a source of deficit funding for bodies which are perceived to have few financial management skills or commercial ability. In some senses government is right. There has been no need for those of us who have relied to a very great extent on public funding to pay too much attention to our market, to do very much about research into it, or to gain a detailed picture of those people we serve or the way in which we serve them. Government is now withdrawing and leaving us in a curious and very unsatisfactory form of limbo. The inherent instability of this position is further heightened by the efforts that government, to its credit, is making to allow museums to help themselves. Our national museums now have their budgets allocated on a three-year rather than an annual cycle, the trustees and directors have full responsibility for their buildings rather than relying on the government's Property Services Agency and there are now greater freedoms to operate in a businesslike manner and retain the income that they earn rather than return it to the Treasury. In another sense too, the British national museums are in a fortunate position because the concept of the 'arm's length relationship', in which government devolves virtually all the financial and management decisions to the museums' trustees and directors, really does leave them substantially free from political interference. These museums suffer little of the political interventionism which is apparent in some other countries. Within the monies made available to them they are, generally speaking, left to get on with the job.

But by virtue of being so substantially in the public sector they are uniquely denied access to capital from the public purse and the freedoms to get it from elsewhere. Although earned income and sponsorship will go part of the way to meeting their demands it is by no means the answer. This presupposes that these museums must move away from the limbo position in which they find themselves. One possibility – and I believe a remote one – is for them to return wholly under the protective skirts of government. It seems to me inevitable that by the mid-1990s taxation levels and therefore government expenditure will again start to increase, but this will not provide more than marginal benefits to the great museums. The increase will be the result of the failure in low tax economies to sustain much of the physical infrastructure of society, an infrastructure which can only be supported from the public purse. By then the leisure revolution will have developed still further. Users will increasingly be paying at the point of consumption for their heritage and in some cases, for example, in open-air museums, science centres, some historic houses, the bulk of the cost will be borne directly by the beneficiary. In the case of some museums and galleries, particularly in the field of fine art, endowment, benefactions, property development and subscription income will insulate them from the worst hardships faced in the traditional public sector.

For the rest, however, a new formula is needed. What are the options? If money is paid at the door by the user is to form an increasing part of museum income then a new means of mixing it with public money is necessary. First, I believe, business-style accounting and access to venture capital are essential. The museum's assets should be depreciated in a conventional commercial manner and the income generated through them should be available to service debt. This cannot, of course, apply to the collections; they are inalienable. But much of the investment in modern museums goes into the increasingly complex and expensive hardware of presentation and interpretation. Buildings, displays, audio-visual units, visitor centres, are all part of the working assets of a heritage organization.

At present government pays for the day-to-day running costs but not for the continuing renewal of the plant. This concept of splitting the inalienable assets from the rest might suggest that the financial responsibilities for a museum are similarly split; that government provides core funding to maintain the collections, provides properly environmentally controlled storage for them, and pays the key people responsible for their curation and conservation. In other words, the collections which are the property of the people will be paid for corporately by the people, as taxpayers. This, in theory, ensures that they can be passed on to our successors in no worse a condition than the one in which we inherited them. Those other assets, which are consumed directly today, are depreciated in a normal manner and paid for at the point of consumption by today's public. It would be possible, for example, to float the Properties-In-Care Division of English Heritage as a separate company using the government's grant-in-aid to maintain the monuments and putting the use of those monuments on to a wholly commercial footing. In the case of museums the split might be more difficult, but not impossible. But, I have no doubt, the present arrangements in which museums attempt to raise money by sponsorship and appeal to pay for their depreciation has little to offer the future. If we were to move towards a more commercially responsible mode of operation there would still of course be the opportunity to raise sponsorship monies, but the financial base upon which our great collections were funded and within which our museums would then operate would be a more sensible one. It is important in this context to stress that this approach is not 'privatization'; it is the more efficient use of the taxpayer's money, which would be essential to maintain the collection in perpetuity.

If government was to be the core funding agency, responsible for the well-being of the collections (or the real estate in the case of a national park or historic property) then clearly the museum would have to agree a collecting policy with the government. Some curators might find this restrictive, whilst government, for its part, might be alarmed about the rate of growth of museum collections. Since most museums dispose of a tiny fraction of what they acquire, their collections can only get bigger. These collections might be perceived by government as a liability – which in financial terms they are – rather than an asset of increasing social and cultural value.

But in another sense museums might find themselves less constrained in their interpretation and presentation policies. Money from government and money from sponsors inevitably carries strings. It is a peculiar paradox that money from the user is, in effect, some of the cleanest money on which museums can lay their hands. They deliver a product and sell it in the market place. Where a museum might feel anxious about presenting a politically unacceptable story, or one which would not enhance the image of its sponsors, there is ample evidence to demonstrate that the public are more open minded. Museums should be capable of handling sensitive environmental issues, of becoming forums of debate in which both sides of a social or economic argument can be presented. There is an increasing trend on the part of many museums to tread this path and an increasing demand on the part of their public to see fully rounded stories.

But what of smaller provincial museums run by local authorities? Here the nature of use tends to be quite different. Tourists represent a small or non-existent sector of their users. The majority of visitors and the majority of those who use the collections as an archive are local people who see the museum primarily as the guardian of their own history. Visitor numbers are often small, people drop in for twenty minutes on their way to the shops, the commercial opportunities are minimal, but the museum is often highly valued by the local community. These are the very museums which many local authorities tend to neglect and, when they catch the tourism fever, tend to pass over in order to develop something entirely new and often – in heritage terms – somewhat specious. Their collections must be maintained as part of the archive of the locality and there seems to me little option but to pay for them directly from the public purse.

But when it comes to organization, management, and the overall structure within which these museums operate then, I believe, there are major opportunities for change. The critical mass of many of these museums is so small that they are inherently unstable. Amalgamations and federations might be one way forward, regionalizing the storage, conservation and other essential services to gain greater cost-effectiveness. This implies a degree of co-operation and openheartedness for which local authorities are not well known and a degree of willingness on the part of local communities for whom sovereignty of the collections is often a strongly felt need. There are, however, great opportunities to be taken from the regionalization of small local museums in which the best of local community participation can be combined with the best that could come from the larger financial and organizational base within which each of these small museums would then exist. The number of these museums might well diminish, but their quality could well rise and, in the case of their collections, the essential prerequisites of maintaining them for future generations could be more readily met.

Concluding Interpretation

Tourism will be an almost irresistible economic force from which those of us who have responsibility for the heritage can, if we are careful, benefit enormously. But it can also be a destructive force sweeping all before it, putting impossible pressures upon the environment, and creating irresponsible demands from those public agencies – national, regional and local – who believe that it provides the economic panacea for their futures. Our job is to embrace tourism with cautious enthusiasm but to put much more effort into emphasizing the cultural value of the assets that we interpret and, above all, we must stress that they are inalienable and irreplaceable.

3

Funding our Heritage

Stuart Smith

'Stonehenge for sale!', would be a newspaper headline to cause international outcry. Yet over the last five years the heritage movement in Great Britain has been told more and more by government to go out and find its own money rather than rely on government sources. The Department of the Environment was the government body responsible for ancient monuments and historic buildings. This duty has now fallen to English Heritage, which operates at arm's length from government, although is still subject to government control. One of the consequences of this change of guardianship is that it must raise a considerably higher proportion of its own income. Similarly, many of our great national and regional museums have become governed by boards of trustees and these are now looking to raise a considerable proportion of their income from sources other than central government. Whilst the controversy has raged as to whether such organizations should charge entrance fees or encourage sponsorship, many of us outside the public sector have looked on these changes with a great deal of pleasure, as it will force such organizations to become more visitor orientated and therefore provide a better service for the general public.

Another way in which the government has been attempting to lessen its own responsibilities has been the establishment of private trusts such as the historic Chatham Dockyard Trust. This Trust has taken over a complete eighteenth century dockyard, has been given a £9 million endowment by the government and told to get on with it. A similar approach is being taken at Ironbridge, where the government is handing over many responsibilities previously undertaken by Telford New Town (and therefore centrally government funded) to the Ironbridge Gorge Museum Trust in exchange for which the museum will receive a one-off payment.

It is all very well for government to decentralize and to pass responsibility to other organizations, but how do such bodies which have been traditionally funded on an annual basis endeavour to raise a considerable proportion of their own revenue costs? This paper attempts to explain a few of the ways that are possible without compromising the scholarly, academic and curatorial standards which we all must achieve. It is not the intention of this paper to attempt to cover fund raising for capital projects or sponsorship, which is a completely different area of activity and expertise.

How Do You Pay

Apart from the government, the largest landowner in Great Britain with a phenomenal number of historic houses, castles and sites, is the National Trust. A private body established by act of parliament, the National Trust has been active since the beginning of the century and is actually modelled on an American example which has not grown quite so rapidly!

Currently the National Trust has a membership of over three million and it is largely the income from that membership, together with the correct management of its estates and investments, that allows this body to continue to expand without recourse to government funding.

Some bodies do not approve of charging for culture and therefore ask for voluntary donations. This is not a very effective way of raising money. Neither is it fair nor does it appeal to the general public. It certainly causes embarrassment and it always seems necessary to chain down the collecting box! This is not to say that voluntary collections for the purchase of specific works of art or similar items are to be discouraged.

In most instances, however, the organization will feel that there is no real alternative to charging admission and this is where museums and heritage organizations have a lot to learn from private enterprise. The public want to feel that they have value for money and this means that they expect good service in return for their entrance fee. They do not expect, as at HMS Victory until only recently, to have to queue in the rain outside the ship. They need to have their expectations raised, and from the time that they know they have to purchase a ticket, they should be looked after, cared for and encouraged to return. The admission price should be a true reflection of the value of the exhibits or site. It should not be a token charge, as people will only expect a meagre experience if they are charged a small amount. It might be worthwhile evaluating museums on the principles of the cinema, where one expects to have a certain number of hours of pleasure for a certain fee. For some of our larger institutions where one might expect to return on frequent occasions I have suggested elsewhere (Smith, 1987) that some form of plastic culture credit card could be obtained and used for multiple visits even to several institutions. The technology already exists in the form of the telephone card: it only requires the will to apply it.

At Ironbridge we rely on visitor admission charges for 90 per cent of our income. This is obviously an enormous achievement, but is dangerous as it places far too high a reliance on the vagaries of the English weather and other external factors which can affect visitor numbers. We do, however, place a great deal of emphasis on selling people the correct ticket for the sort

Figure 3.1 The Ironbridge in Ironbridge Gorge.

of visit they would wish to make. Before leaving the car park there are large signs indicating that you will have to pay an entrance fee, but that this fee will cover a visit to all of the various museum sites, whether made on that day or on a subsequent visit. After entering the welcoming entrance building, one is clearly directed to the reception area where one sees the admission prices concentrating on the passport ticket. This gives comprehensive visiting and clearly is at a major discount over individual prices of site admission. All this is also explained by a cheerful, welcoming receptionist who will describe the other facilities to be found on that particular site. If this transaction can be made easier by the use of a cheque or a credit card this will allow the visitor to have more disposable income to use during the rest of their visit. It is also important to point out that this is a comprehensive charge, with no secondary charging for subsequent parts of the museum. However, there are obviously many other opportunities to spend one's money, once inside a museum site.

Other Sources of Revenue

Many museums now demonstrate craft activities in a period context inside the museum and use this as a most valuable form of interpretation. Few museums, however, directly retail from their exhibits, for a variety of reasons. At Ironbridge, however, we find that retailing inside the museum is a most valuable form of interpretation and frequently allows the demonstrator to make contact with the visitor. The final anachronism has now been removed from Ironbridge, as last year we introduced our own token coinage which represents the pre-decimal coinage in use in Britain before 1900. The exchange rate is forty modern pennies to the old penny and this means that all items inside the museum are at quasi-Victorian prices. The coinage has the look and feel of the old coinage, is of great educational value to our school visitors and over 45 per cent of the coinage goes home as souvenirs, which is almost entirely profit!

Some of our exhibits involve the manufacturing of items which are intended largely for sale outside the museum. This particularly applies to our working foundry, which sells cast iron products not only through our shops but also by mail order, and will apply next year to our wrought ironworks now completed but not yet fully commissioned. This will almost entirely be selling wrought iron to people on a worldwide basis but through an iron and steel stockholder.

Museum Retailing

Museum retailing is often seen as a matter to be relegated to a rather junior member of staff. For most people a visit to a heritage attraction is not complete until they have bought a guidebook, had a cup of tea and taken away a souvenir. For this reason we place a great deal of emphasis on the correct management of our shops. This year we have spent a considerable amount of money on redesigning our entire house style and corporate identity, which has been led by the need to re-package items and market them more attractively. By a curious quirk of fate it was as a result of discussions about the image of our retailing establishments that we actually entered into lengthy discussions on the philosophy and objectives of the museum itself. The result of which is that we chose a much harder retailing image than our designers had previously suggested.

Retailing at Ironbridge is carried out through a subsidiary company, the Ironbridge Gorge Trading Company, so that our charitable status is not prejudiced. However, retailing must be seen primarily as a visitor service rather than a source of revenue. It must be borne in mind that profits from tickets are virtually 100 per cent whereas one will be doing extremely well to manage a gross profit of 40 per cent from retailing. We endeavour to load as many museum costs as possible against our retailing operation so the net profit shown is extremely small. By the sales of commemorative china and other high quality products both over the museum counter and by mail order we manage to fund a substantial publications programme. It has to be stressed, though, that publications are produced because the public want them, rather than because they happen to have been written by a curator who wishes to see a publication in print!

Attractions should also think hard as to how they can capitalize on the

Figure 3.2 Coalport China Works Museum, part of the Ironbridge Gorge Museum complex.

historic aspects of their area even if they are not mainstream history. Whilst Ironbridge is known worldwide for its industrial archaeology it is also known to a lesser number, but probably an equally influential band, as the home of some of the best soft toys in the world. Since 1930 Merrythought Toys have manufactured a whole range of teddy bears and other toys in premises previously used as a foundry. Until recently their products were exclusively retailed through some of the top shops in the world, such as Harrods, but after initial trials of selling their products through our own shops we then determined to take matters further. So, we now operate, as far as I know, the only teddy bear shop and museum in the world with displays of historic teddy bears going back to the 1930s and a very large range of modern soft toys. A recent introduction is our own Ironbridge teddy bear complete with our own label and, of course, our own silk bow tie with the Ironbridge motif. It is all part of the corporate house style and identity, which won our designers this year one of the highly acclaimed London Docklands design awards.

Other sources of income that the heritage attraction might consider are catering and accommodation. Once again catering should really be seen as a visitor service which should return a small profit. However, its most important effect is to lengthen the visit being made and to put people in a more receptive frame of mind. For the same reason the provision of accommodation is an area which museums should continue to explore. Several American museums have their own hotels and hostels. We at Ironbridge have successfully operated a youth hostel for several years and are now moving into the field of providing holiday accommodation. Whilst there will obviously be income from this operation, the largest benefit will be to make people stay longer in the area and therefore spend more money on museum admission, catering and souvenirs. For too long heritage attractions have gone for maximum numbers, when they should have been looking for optimum numbers. The long-stay visitor provides the maximum benefits, not just to the heritage attraction but for the area in general. It has been calculated that the average schoolchild visiting an attraction might spend £3 on admission and £2 on souvenirs. Compare this to a married couple spending a weekend at your attraction, who could be spending upwards of £100 in the locality.

There is, perhaps, a mercenary tone to this paper, but if we are spending millions of pounds on the development of our heritage, then surely we are entitled to some of the benefits.

Reference

Smith, S.B. (1987) 'Admission Tickets', *Museums Bulletin*, 28 (5).

4

The Search for New Funds

Richard Broadhurst

Background

The present comprehensive policy for forestry in Britain has its origins in the early years of this century when the forest resource, decimated during the Middle Ages, the early industrial revolution and the First World War, began to be restored. The difficulties of timber supply during the first war led to the report of Sir Richard Acland's Committee, the creation of the Forestry Commission and a far-seeing initial programme of afforestation. (Forestry Commission, 1987)

The initial objective of the Commission was to build up a strategic reserve of timber. In 1957 the government accepted recommendations that the future objectives should be of a commercial and social nature. Indeed in 1935, the Commission had designated its first national forest park in Argyll, some nineteen years ahead of the national park legislation in Britain. The Countryside Acts of 1967 and 1968 recognized the increasing contribution of forests to recreation and granted the Commission powers to provide facilities such as camp sites, picnic places and visitor centres. There has been a steady increase over recent years in the allocation of Treasury funds for recreation, now approaching a net £7 million per annum of subsidy. With income running at approximately £1 million per annum this provides about £8 million for initial input. The overall expenditure of the Forestry Enterprise is £121 million, which is funded by £34 million from Treasury and £87 million from the sale of timber and other items (Forestry Commission, 1988, pp. 47–72). As the overall forest estate matures so the timber revenues will reach a level which will considerably reduce the call on government funds. The growing dependence on the sales of timber in world markets as a source of income will increase uncertainty about income streams, as these will be volatile and subject to changes in exchange rates and other factors outside the Commission's control.

As Forestry Enterprise the Commission has a number of objectives which concern not only timber production but protecting and enhancing the environment, providing recreational facilities and stimulating and supporting local employment. These latter objectives are very important indeed, but are to a large extent dependent on the Commission managing its forest estate. For these reasons timber production is indeed the core activity and as such one might expect that during periods when revenues are lower than expected, other activities' budgets would be vulnerable. It is prudent therefore to develop an approach which will reduce dependence on a single or limited number of sources, and broaden the field of funding by developing a portfolio of funding sources, in particular for recreation and heritage projects. A second more widely applicable reason for developing such a portfolio is merely to explore the full potential of funding arrangements for resource planning.

The economist's traditional view of the three classical factors of production is a useful starting point for considering the Commission's resources:

Land

The Commission manages the best part of 5,000 square miles (actually 1.181 million hectares) of land throughout Great Britain, much of it in the uplands and in relatively remote areas, but with some notable forests close to towns, for example the New Forest, Forest of Dean, Thetford, Cannock, and Queen Elizabeth Forest Park.

Labour

Field staff locally based in fifty nine districts are well placed to identify the needs of the community as well as of visitors. Automation and increases in productivity have naturally reduced the numbers of staff. This has made it more difficult to provide recreation services and to maintain the existing recreation estate. Coincidentally additional opportunities have been created for local residents to become involved in providing service. Recent levels of unemployment have provided a further source of labour through Training Agency schemes and training initiatives.

Capital

There has been steady growth in recent years in the allocation of funds for recreation; this now stands at a net £7 million per annum.

Aspirations

Estimates suggest that there are well in excess of fifty million visits

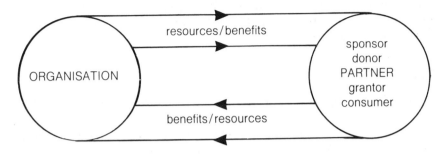

Figure 4.1 Exchange – the basis of all funding.

made each year to the forest. In 1985 it was estimated that there were eight million visits to the New Forest alone. Survey work carried out during 1987 for the Commission indicated that for many it is still the wildlife and the landscape which are the major attractions. Nevertheless, to enjoy this requires the provision of basic facilities for access – roads, car parking, walks, trails and, on occasion, toilets and other services, camp sites and cabins. There is also a general requirement for information. Recognizing the importance of recreation and rural tourism to the national economy, and its social value, there now exists a perceived gap between the aspirations of the visitor (and Commission staff) and the funds available. Currently the Commission is engaged in a recreation planning exercise to quantify this gap and to arrive at a strategy to deal with it. One of the factors which limit the possibilities for action is the available funding.

The Funding Portfolio: Options

There are many options available in organizations in any country. A useful survey has been prepared in relation to the USA (Howard and Crompton, 1980), which is helpful in suggesting new ways of looking at old problems. In developing a framework for identifying opportunities for the Commission a distinction has been drawn between those traditional (internal) funding options which rely on an exchange of a product or service for monies and over which the organization has much control, and those (external) funding options where the basis of the exchange is less tangible and where control might be considered to be exercised more by another party. It is important to remember that despite this possibly artificial distinction, all funding has as its basis an exchange (see Figure 4.1).

Internal Options

These are largely concerned with the development of service, delivery and pricing. In essence, these options are about following good marketing practice, and developing the optimal mix of product, price, promotion and place. Opportunities identified include:

Forest Holidays

A sophisticated approach has been taken to the marketing of forest holidays for a number of years, with computer booking of cabins and cottages, variable pricing to take account of seasonal demand and adequate supporting promotion. With the market currently undergoing something of a restructuring and a reduction in the profit margin over the last few years obtained from Forest Holidays, there may be scope for some adjustments in this area.

Merchandising

The Commission has a number of shops at camp sites and at visitor centres. Some of these are managed directly by the Commission, some by contract and others by lease or franchise. In essence the Commission is sitting on a potential chain store operation, albeit of suitably modest and usually rural proportions. The potential, whilst not as great as that for the National Trust or English Heritage, nevertheless warrants further work. An initial study by a postgraduate business studies student pointed out areas for further investigation, which are being explored with the help of a consultant.

Pricing

The Commission has an open access policy which encourages free access by visitors on foot to all forests wherever legal and operational issues allow. This policy is central to the Commission's recreation strategy and for access of that kind there is therefore no intention to introduce any charge. Recent work carried out by by the author for a dissertation towards an MBA has identified considerable scope for charging which it would be sensible to explore. There is evidence that the resistance to charging as expressed by managers is generally much greater than that expressed by the public (see also Clawson and Knetsch, 1966, p. 316).

The study, which looked at the preferences and attitudes of consumers to pricing for different forms of recreation, identified two very different groups of attractions: those destinations which included open space – hills, loch sides and beaches – for which there was a marked antagonism for any charging; and a second group, which included traditional heritage attractions such as castles, folk museums and historic sites. For this second group, in a comparison of the mean perceived reasonable charge and the mean actual charge, there was only one example where the actual charge exceeded the perceived reasonable charge. This suggests that consumers base their perception of reasonableness on the level of existing charges or the 'Expected Price

Threshold'; or that providers have judged what the market will bear and have retreated a little from the optimum solution. The former seems more likely, given the comments made in a consultant's report (Coopers and Lybrand, 1981, pp. 220–1) in relation to the generally poor knowledge of the market. There are certain facilities such as country parks which fall between the two groups most probably because, like forests, they do not represent a single product but more a portfolio of recreation opportunities.

Some of these opportunities are concerned with activities for which charges have been acceptable for a long time, and others are related to open access, for which the opposition to charging seems to be fundamental. The Commission provides for a wide range of activities many of which attract no charges, like walking and cross country skiing. Some such as orienteering or horse riding, attract a notional charge, and others, such as stalking, bear a full commercial charge. Certain non-charge activities can be enhanced by the provision of information which may be chargeable, such as wayfaring packs. Ways of approaching pricing rationally are covered in many basic texts (Kotler, 1984) but in order to make the best use of pricing it is important to consider the human implications (Crompton, 1982). The opportunities in the Commission's management of recreation to align charging more closely to objectives, whether to raise revenue, ration use or determine consumer preferences, are being explored in a review of pricing.

External Options

In exploring external options the basis of the exchange must be clearly identified. Even in the most basic transaction or fund raising exercise the 'donor' will seek one or a number of benefits. With the trends of privatization and individual enterprise which are evident in the Western world, the political, economic and social climate encourages all of us to seek support in the market place. Initially it seems a very novel approach, but the more one recognizes the basis of the exchanges sought, the more apparent it is that the ground rules are simple. It is merely the mechanisms that are new. The main options being explored by the Commission are listed below.

Sponsorship

The benefits available to would-be sponsors are a green, caring and healthy environmental image and local outlets (forests) throughout Great Britain, reaching an audience which makes in excess of fifty million visits each year. The potential for all conservation projects is high amongst those who wish to project their responsible caring and concern for the environment and also amongst others who have similar objectives in respect of conservation. Many of the projects are small in themselves but in sum extremely valuable.

The Commission is currently considering how best to pursue sponsorship.

In developing its policies it has made use of a sponsorship consultancy and many lessons have been learnt from successful projects such as the Kylerhea Otter Haven project with the Vincent Trust, a classroom hide project in Wyre with multiple sponsorship, and the production of many leaflets with various sponsors including oil companies. The principal lesson is that success is more likely where a clear link exists between the would-be sponsors, their products or services and the objectives of the project. Would-be sponsors can therefore be targeted more accurately. As yet no single large sponsor has been sought but as the opportunities become clear and a recreation strategy is brought forward, such projects will doubtless be explored. The success of English Heritage and Historic Scotland in enjoying the support of a major supermarket chain points to some of the possibilities. Exciting projects are being devised which, if the Commission were to implement them, sponsors would find irresistible.

Bequests

Bequests are a form of sponsorship which until now have not been actively sought by the Commission. The option arose, whilst funding policies were being reviewed, through an enquiry by an undertaker in the Highlands on behalf of a client who had a particular favourite walk.

Donations

These are a little like sponsorship but usually given by individuals. In the case of government departments they are not usually a major source of funding. It does seem likely that people will give more readily to specified causes and projects with which they can identify than to organizations. At a number of visitor centres donation boxes are regularly filled by grateful visitors. In some instances substantial gifts have been made. One of the greatest examples must surely be the David Marshal Lodge, centrepiece of the Queen Elizabeth Forest Park in the Trossachs. The building was given to the Commission by the Carnegie (UK) Trust.

Grants

The list of potential sources of grant is enormous, ranging from the European Regional Development Fund, all the national agencies including tourist boards, development agencies and commission, the Countryside Commissions, sports councils and arts councils through to all the grant-making trusts approximately 2,500 in number and catalogued elsewhere (Charities Aid Foundation, 1985; FitzHerbert, 1986) and local authorities. It has been generally considered that government grants are not available from one government department to another. This seems to be an incorrect or out of date view and a more pragmatic approach seems to be the rule. If the net effect is in support of government policy then such a grant may be possible. In any event most of the above sources of grant would be available to potential partners of the Commission in pursuit of a common goal.

Lotteries

As a source of funding, lotteries have been limited in the UK by act of parliament to local authorities and to charities. Nevertheless, substantial sums have been raised by certain local authorities, in one instance approximately £0.6 million over a few years. The success of the Republic of Ireland and many of the European national lotteries has drawn attention to the massive fund raising potential. In the UK there has been considerable interest in the possibility of a 'national' lottery, to be arranged by linking several lotteries together. For whatever reason, the first attempt failed but it is indicative of the competition for funds which is under way that this should have been contemplated. There are attractive theoretical possibilities for a series of lotteries linked to co-operating agencies or trusts in conjunction with the Commission, but the ramifications need careful exploration, as the National Health Service lottery example shows.

Friends Organizations

There are many successful examples of organizations who, in exchange usually for concessions on admission charges, use of special facilities or services and information in the form of a newsletter, raise not only sums of money from individuals but a great deal of goodwill too. Amongst government agencies or quangos, English Heritage and Historic Scotland are good examples. Most organizations in the voluntary sector have had such arrangements for many years and some are still growing at considerable rate, for example the RSPB. Many of these voluntary organizations start with a considerable advantage in terms of appeal (animals and birds particularly in Britain), but as they have deployed the skills and good practice of marketing and management the advantage has increased. The Woodland Trust is an example where speedy growth followed the injection of business skills into an organization hitherto run principally by tremendous commitment and energy. There are 'Friends' type organizations in a number of forests and these have made an enormous contribution to the provision of facilities and services, for example by pulling in additional sources of funds and manpower. The Grizedale Society in the south Lakes has been instrumental in developing the connection between Grizedale Forest Park and the Arts. Extra funds, and manpower too, have been brought in from North West Arts. The management of the Theatre-in-the-Forest together with the sculpture residencies and other activities in conjunction with the forest provide added funds in kind.

Treasury

Other than timber sales, the Treasury provides the main source of funds for the Commission. In respect of forest recreation and amenity there is a net subsidy of £7 million per annum. As with other sources of funding there is a basis to the exchange and in this case it is the value to society of the conservation and recreation objectives. In a previous cost-benefit study the notional social value of a visit to the forest was assumed at 20p (HM Treasury, 1972, pp. 24 – 7), a figure which has been subsequently updated to 30p to allow for inflation. Recent exploratory work conducted for the Commission indicates that the values of society may have altered a good deal since that earlier study. The figures arrived at now would seem to indicate values in the range of £1.50 or £2.00 or more depending on the particular forest. On that basis alone one might consider that an increase in the subsidy could be justified. Further work will be carried out in preparation for the next triennial budgetary period. It is noted that in the past both the Countryside Commission for England and Wales, and the Nature Conservancy Council have consistently obtained increases where appropriate programmes and policies have been advanced under suitable conditions.

An Integrated Approach

In searching for 'new' funds, or in seeking to achieve more, there are three main approaches. These are outlined in the following pages.

Importing Funds into the Organization

The approach outlined above has described some of the options available.

Pursuing Efficiency and Effectiveness

In recreation terms it is often easier to add a new facility or add a new service. Much more rarely are under-used or no longer appropriate facilities or services abandoned. The example of museums in this respect is pertinent. It is said that in the UK alone some fifty new museums open each year. Until recently it has been suspected that very many fewer museums close. There are of course problems with definition but those who are involved in the management of interpretation or recreation facilities may like to consider their own particular market segments. Policy appraisal and evaluation (HM Treasury, 1988) will be valuable tools to all policy makers and managers concerned with ensuring an optimal allocation of resources. But many questions need to be asked. What is the objective of the facility or service? What would have happened if it was not provided? What has happened? What are the side effects? There are many examples of effective management (Peters and Austin, 1986, pp. 48–9) which clearly indicate that this area pursued vigorously may for many organizations yield 'new' funds on a magnitude which would be very much more difficult to obtain by importing funds. In forest recreation terms it seems likely that there will be many picnic sites, car parks, trails and particularly signs which are no longer required. The cost of maintaining these must obviously divert resources from necessary new projects or spread resources so thinly as to result in a reduction in the standards of maintenance. The Commission is encouraging all managers to look very closely at existing facilities and to devise systems of monitoring. No facilities or services should be introduced without some, however basic or informal, system of monitoring.

Exporting Objectives, Working Through Others

There are many ways of achieving the objectives of the organization working in harmony with other organizations, agencies and individuals. The recent trends in the political, economic and social environment have concentrated efforts to achieve more using less.

Strategies

One of the best ways of doing this is simply by publishing the objectives of the organization or the programme. There has been a spate of strategies published by the major national agencies in the UK, such as the Countryside Commission's *Enjoying the Countryside – Recreation 2000*, the Sports Council's *Sport in the Community – into the 90s* and the English Tourist Board's rural tourism strategy *Visitors in the Countryside*. This ensures that there is scope for goal congruence. Furthermore, the consultation process encourages discussion and communication which leads to the identification of opportunities for resource pooling in order to reach superordinate goals.

Joint Ventures

There are many examples of joint ventures within the Commission. This could take the form of partnerships with local authorities. Often the local authority will provide a visitor centre and staffing, whilst the Commission will manage the adjacent forest for recreation; this occurs at Afan Argoed in Wales. A more complex partnership with several public agencies exists at the Sir George Staunton Country Park near Havant in Hampshire. There are also partnerships with voluntary organizations such as that with the Royal Society for the Protection of Birds at Symonds Yat in the Forest of Dean.

There are also such group partnerships as the English Tourist Board's

'Tourism Development Action Programmes' where several adjacent organizations and neighbours fund joint projects. In the Commission's case, this occurs at Kielder Forest (in the core of the Border Forest Park) and the Forest of Dean, and in time we hope in other areas as well. In all partnerships it is necessary to consider any possible negative effects including the dilution of the organization's goals or divergence of objectives of different organizations over time, and to take appropriate counter-measures.

Joint Marketing

There is much scope for developing products or services by what marketing people call 'positioning'. This, to a large extent, requires information to be prepared and targeted to enable would-be consumers to perceive the service in a particular way. In effect there are many ways in which the recreational and interpretive opportunities in an area may be packaged. In the New Forest the Commission has worked with others in presenting information in a joint package both with the New Forest Centre and Museum under the aegis of the New Forest Ninth Centenary Trust at Lyndhurst, and in leaflet form. There is potential at many forests for joint marketing with other providers not only of attractions but also of related services and accommodation. Activity holidays provide an example where the Commission could play a major role.

Managing at Arm's Length

Franchising, leasing and managing by contract are all ways of providing services whilst making use of others' resources. To do this effectively without losing control of the situation requires support. The Commission is looking at ways of achieving more through arrangements of this kind in the field of recreation.

Adopting Sites or Services

Arrangements in which private individuals or organizations take over the provision of a service or the management of a site is an area which should be explored further. If the Commission seeks to dispose of a wood as part of its rationalization programme there is an arrangement by which if the relevant national agencies, Countryside Commissions or Nature Conservancy Council have certified that the area is of particular recreational or conservation importance, the wood may first be offered to a trust or charitable organization. The Woodland Trust is one of the main organizations to benefit from this policy. There are other less formal arrangements such as at Whitwell Wood near Worksop which is of particular interest to a local naturalists group which effectively wardens the area and thereby involves the community.

The Integrated Approach Process: Summary

Stage 1: Identifying Opportunities and Resources Required

Objectives must first be clearly established as far as possible in specific, measurable and achievable terms consistent with the overall aim. Then the resources required to achieve the objectives must be identified. It is probable that in most cases the objectives can be reached using different blends of resources – more labour and less capital, or vice versa. Figure 4.2 shows a way in which one might seek to identify the possible resources which could be applied.

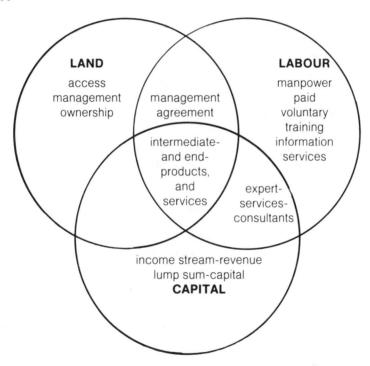

Figure 4.2 Identifying the possible resource mix.

Stage 2: Identifying Resources and Benefits Amongst Potential Partners

Different opportunities will apply in each case, but there are usually organizations and individuals at hand who have some resource or commodity in apparent excess. Table 4.1 gives an idea of possible starting points. It is important to identify clearly the benefits which would accrue to partners. There are some publications which will help in this process (Allen, 1988;

Table 4.1 Seeking resources − some starting points

Resources	Private Sector	Public Sector	Voluntary Sector
Land	Large estates Private individuals Chartered surveyors Pension funds Forestry companies Water companies	Forestry Commission Local authorities Water authorities	National Trust Woodland Trust RSPB RSNC
Labour	Secondments Large companies (sometimes through intermediaries e.g. Association for Business Sponsorship of the Arts) Information services or channels Contract services	Employment training NACRO Military Assistance for the Civil Community Information services or channels Contract services	Task orientated BTCV Scottish Projects Trust Large untapped resource: would-be volunteers through 'Friends' organizations Information services or channels Contract service
Capital	Sponsorship Companies Patronage: Company charitable trusts Donations Bequests Rentals, leases contracts	Grants European Regional Development Fund Countryside Commissions Sports councils Arts councils Development Commission and agencies Local authorities Lotteries Treasury Rentals, leases contracts	Grant-making trusts 'Friends' organizations Donations Bequests Lotteries Rentals, leases contracts

Norton, 1981, 1986). In the case of the Commission, the benefits on offer have been summarized (Table 4.2) as an example.

Stage 3: Identify Suitable Mechanisms for Service Delivery

In selecting the form of management − direct, franchise, lease, contract − consideration should be given to how the strategic environment of the organization and of any partners will change and whether this will affect the proposed service. In joint projects a committee, a trust or a company may be the appropriate vehicle.

Table 4.2 Some benefits on offer to those associating with the Forestry
Commission

Image building	The Commission has a strong developing corporate identity associated with the environment, enjoyment and the healthy outdoors.
Access to 50 million visits nationally	To advertise product, brand, company or organization name, services.
Local outlets throughout Great Britain.	To enable local targeting.
	To enable involvement with local community where company/organization has an interest.
Specific market segments	To enable association of product or organization with a range of particular activities from land management to conservation to recreation, from angling to mountain biking.
Access in a range of situations	To enable direct sampling in visitor centres or more subtle approaches through printing trail guides or forest park videos.

Conclusion and Summary

The search for new funds must begin within any organization, as here it has most control. Thereafter, there are many ways of importing funds from outside or exporting the objectives. All arrangements are based on the principle of perceived equity of exchange no matter how tangible or intangible the benefits. The particular mechanism chosen will reflect the needs of all those party to the arrangement and should be selected with an eye to possible future developments. Perhaps the greatest single area which remains to be explored for organizations seeking new funds is that of information (see Figure 4.3). The encouragement of flows of information from the consumer in market research or to the consumer in promotion is a major factor in increasing effectiveness. Really effective marketing has come late to recreation and interpretation. In addition, providing would-be partners, such as donors or perhaps potential small businesses, with the information about the potential for benefits, whether gratification or future income streams, may be an important conceptual form of vertical integration.

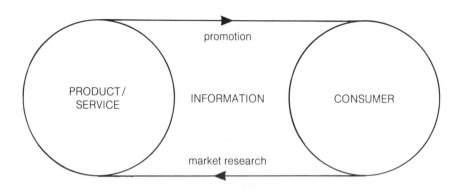

Figure 4.3   Information – the bridge that creates service.

Figure 4.4   Recreation in the forest.

References

Allen, S. (ed.) (1988) *The Sponsorship Yearbook*, Hobsons Publishing, London.
Charities Aid Foundation (1985) *Directory of Grant-making Trusts*, Charities Aid Foundation, 48 Pembury Road, Tonbridge, Kent.

Clawson, M. and Knetsch, J.L. (1966) *Economics of Outdoor Recreation*, Johns Hopkins University Press, Baltimore, Maryland.

Coopers and Lybrand Associates Ltd (1981) *Service Provision and Pricing in Local Government*, HMSO, London.

Crompton, J.L. (1982) 'Psychological dimensions of pricing leisure services', *Recreation Research Review*, October.

FitzHerbert, L. (ed.) (1986) *A Guide to the Major Grant-making Trusts*, Directory of Social Change, London.

Forestry Commission (1987) *Forestry Facts 1: Forestry Policy Since 1919*, Forestry Commission, Edinburgh.

Forestry Commission (1988) *67th Annual Report and Accounts 1986 – 1987*, HMSO, London.

HM Treasury (1972) *Forestry in Great Britain, an Interdepartmental Cost/Benefit Study*, HMSO, London.

HM Treasury (1988) *Policy Evaluation: a Guide for Managers*, HMSO, London.

Howard, D.R. and Crompton, J.L. (1980) *Financing, Managing and Marketing Recreation and Park Resources*, Wm C. Brown, Dubuque, Iowa.

Kotler, P. (1984) *Marketing Management: Analysis, Planning and Control*, 5th edition. Prentice/Hall, London.

Norton, M. (ed.) (1981) *Industrial Sponsorship and Joint Promotions*, Directory of Social Change, London.

Norton, M. (ed.) (1986) *A Guide to Company Giving*, Directory of Social Change, London.

Peters, T. and Austin, N. (1986) *A Passion for Excellence*, Fontana/Collins, Glasgow.

5

Can Heritage Charities be Profitable?

Marc Mallam

Introduction

This paper comprises a critical analysis of some of the main characteristics of many heritage-based charities which should be clearly understood when working with or within them. In particular, they should be borne in mind *prior to* their creation for any given heritage development situation. The comments made should not be construed as an inherent criticism of these charities or, indeed, of their great relevance to many heritage situations.

The Heritage and Charities

Heritage organizations can exist within the public sector, private commercial sector, or private charitable sector of the economic community. They can even be a mixture of all three.

For many reasons, the 'independent' sector of heritage-based organizations has recently been growing significantly, and many if not most of these, I would suggest, have taken the form of charities (often now companies limited by guarantee). There is a strong case for believing that the national or local heritage belongs to the community. Whilst a specific property may be owned privately, its history and that of its previous owners or creators cannot be 'owned' at all. Thus, for many years now, the natural guardian of our heritage has been the public sector. Recently, however, a combination of the realization that heritage is a potential tourist attraction of great value, and restraints on the ability of the public sector to invest in such a politically low priority issue, have meant that ways of returning heritage to the private sector have been sought to earn income from the tourist industry. To privatize heritage completely is often unacceptable, especially if it might entail a commercial risk. The charitable 'formula' therefore becomes an obvious solution with many instant advantages to offer all parties.

Four main advantages immediately come to mind:

(1) Charities are by definition *good things*. Their motives and those of the people within them are exemplary. They cannot be accused of promoting the self-interest (at least financial) of their members. The very concept of 'heritage' in particular tends to evoke non-private ownership of the various assets in question (cf. Hewison, 1987). Charities are a socially acceptable means of non-politically controlled, publicly accountable, private ownership. Charities have become so respectable that they are the only acceptable form of direct royal involvement in economic affairs. Royalty's involvement can often provide a useful spur to patronage by others seeking public recognition for their efforts through civil honours.

(2) Charities provide a possibility of raising free investment capital, without the need to provide any financial return to 'investors'. There is often the need to make sure these 'investors' get their return in other forms though, as money rarely comes without strings.

(3) Tax concessions are given to charities by national and local government, and discounts given by private sector suppliers of products and services. These same organizations also sponsor charitable events and activities.

(4) Charities have the advantage of independence. They are relatively free of political and bureaucratic control, as well as from the commercial constraints of shareholders. To large organizations with commercially or politically difficult heritage situations, charities can be an acceptable means for the disposal or privatization of their heritage 'liabilities' into separate accounting centres in which they can retain a means of influence through the membership or trustee system.

These are all very real advantages and should not be underestimated.

But the actual practice of charities is necessarily very different from both public or private sector organizations, mainly because of the assorted and sometimes obscure (to outsiders) motivations within charities, and the particular charitable culture that has grown up with their practice over the years. What are the characteristics of charities that make this distinction?

It is often said, as a rule of thumb, that there are only five acceptable general objectives of an organization that can give it potential charitable status:

(1) Relief of poverty and deprivation.
(2) Relief of suffering through disease, ill health and/or disablement etc.
(3) Pursuit of acceptable religious beliefs.
(4) Education and recreation of the public.
(5) Provision of funds to pursue other charitable objects, such as those above.

Most, if not all, heritage-based projects (whether natural or manmade) will come under the 'Education and recreation' objectives. These will therefore provide the founding motivation for the organization.

However, all charities also work within a very strict and often restrictive moral culture going considerably beyond the powers and limitations imposed upon them in writing in their memorandum and articles of association. Much of this may be the remnants of a Victorian value system and ingrained tradition, when charity was the most important, if not the sole, form of social welfare.

Charities: Who Owes Whom a Living?

To be blunt, charities, almost by definition, often feel the world owes them a living. Unlike commercial concerns who have to earn their living from *the market*, charities perceive themselves as deserving continuous support from *the community*. Thus, as a consequence, they have often exhibited a tendency towards paternalism or rather maternalism – 'Nanny knows best'. This, in a consumer society where the market and the community are very closely interlinked, can easily seem outdated, insulting and irrelevant.

There can also be echoes of guilt assuagement in charities dominated by a few, very wealthy, benefactors. Thus, there may be a consequent need to demonstrate such benefactors' value to the community, over and above their own commercial interest and success, through the operation of the charity and its good works, which have gained the benefactors' special support. Indeed, whilst the benefactor may contribute financially in the form of a gift (i.e. there is no expected financial return), the so-called gift is rarely without strings attached and can still be seen as a form of investment requiring a direct return in various non-financial forms.

These comments are not made in an attempt to criticize charities, but to demonstrate the complexities of motivation that inevitably grow within them. Unless these are clearly understood by those both inside and outside charities, relationships can become frustrated and awkward. Certainly what is important is to realize that there is no one overriding motivation such as profit or political power that dominates their existence, in the totally understandable way of the commercial or public sectors. The prediction of attitudes within charities that may influence decision-making can, therefore, also often become a problem from both within and outside.

Management Style

All of this leads eventually to a totally different management style within charities. Expenditure of its monies becomes an ultra-sensitive issue, especially non-productive expenditure on administration, staffing, interest charges etc. The traditional moral assumption can also require that bought-in products and services should be heavily discounted or provided free of charge. Cheapness is often a substitute for value for money. This can even apply to staff, who are expected to work longer hours at no extra reward or even to work on a voluntary basis or at below market salary rates.

Such attitudes can significantly warp the value system of the whole organization. How can value for money be compared or performance assessed? What incentives can be offered by the organization to increase efficiency and performance when normal commercial incentives may not apply? The importance of interpersonal relationships can become exaggerated within the organization because of an unreasonable if not perverted value system towards personnel. Are two inefficient but free volunteers worth more or less than one expensive but competent salaried staff member?

Indeed investment itself, or at least the assessment of a proper level of investment, can become a real problem attitudinally. Charities find the concept of investing to make a return a difficult one to accept. Shouldn't others do the investing on behalf of the charity, only allowing the charity to reap the benefits of such investment? Why, if many charities have considerable investment and borrowing powers in their deeds, are they so loath to use them effectively in business terms? First of all, some charities cannot make the requisite level of investment to secure their future, even if they wished to do so, because their assets are, by definition, not usually available to act as security for such a financial risk. Secondly, the concept of making an investment in order to gain a reward remains distrusted by many charities as a commercial approach inapplicable to their own affairs. Yet, paradoxically, charities can often take non-financial risks that commercial or public bodies could never contemplate (for example, the raising of the *Mary Rose*). They can thus become extremely adroit at financial risk avoidance, often to the extent that it almost becomes an object of the organization itself.

These attitudinal confusions serve to demonstrate how different the world of charities is from, in particular, the commercial world. If they weren't different, of course, there would be no need for their existence. Yet charities work best when there is strong leadership or a powerful charitable object that drives the motivation of the organization to such an extent that the various 'warp' factors in the style of management are quickly forgiven for the immediate benefit to the cause. This could be defined simply as team spirit. It is, however, likely to be fairly short lived, related as it is to a particular individual, group of individuals or a specific accomplishment.

It is important to distinguish between heritage-based charities and others. Charities with objectives of furthering good health or the relief of human suffering and poverty have a naturally greater interest in the community, since such problems relate to all human beings directly, regardless of special interest or background. Heritage causes are often very specialized indeed appealing directly to only a small minority of interests, yet they may still retain a fairly wide 'passing interest' by the public. Thus it is usually easier to make a case for heritage charities in near crisis conditions on a once and for all basis such as to 'save this unique property' or to preserve that priceless object'.

Unlike Oxfam, Save the Children and other major international charities which have an obvious continuous need, heritage charities go through very definite and different phases in their life cycle. First there is usually the initial development phase, where the preservation, conservation and presentation of the property, artefact(s), or environment are of paramount importance to the organization. This is often the most exciting part, and the easiest for a charity to manage (at least in theory) being oriented directly to the main charitable object and focus of the whole project. It is also capital intensive: although it is increasingly more difficult to raise capital in the heritage charitable finance 'market place' because of enormous competition, it is certainly easier than the continuous provision of charitable revenue support. At least the benefactors get a direct physical return on the investment of their cash – the continuing survival of the central object of the cause.

Heritage and Tourism

Heritage sites are not increasingly dependent on the tourist industry for the provision of revenue support. Whilst holding out great opportunities for solving the revenue problems of heritage projects, this increasingly competitive and market oriented industry (given the growth of new attractions and destinations), brings with it the absolute requirement to enter the competitive fray for visitors and their spending money.

Successful competition is only likely to be achieved within this market by emphasizing the 'unique selling proposition' of each project. This should hardly be difficult with heritage-based projects and is therefore one of their great strengths. The maximum development potential of the product also needs to be realized and the management and marketing performance of the project must be up to scratch in terms of the standards and quality of the overall visitor experience and service. The difficult but fascinating challenge of heritage-based leisure projects is the need to perform across the board. A fault in any one area quickly lets down success in others. It is now, therefore, often necessary to make considerable further capital investments in more mundane and less glamorous facilities such as lavatories, facilities that are unlikely to attract direct charitable contributions easily. Likewise, investment has also to be made in less tangible areas like the proper marketing and management of the site. There must be an assurance that there will be a much more performance oriented operational style – more hard-nosed, more demanding and more determined. This will no doubt limit the ability of the organization to accommodate the natural idiosyncrasies of the more traditional charitable approach.

Worse still for the charitable heritage-based project, the private sector is beginning to realize the market potential of the 'education leisure' market itself. It is moving increasingly into a directly competitive role, bringing with it its commercial skills of marketing, management and the vast resources of capital investment from private sources. The private sector is no longer likely to commercially cheapen the product either, since they too have come to realize the value of a heritage-based project's unique selling proposition in marketing terms. To kill off the goose that lays the golden egg makes little commercial sense.

The natural reaction to these forces in the heritage/leisure/tourist market place has been to sharpen up the performance of the charitable organizations where possible. In certain locations it has resulted in the consideration of joining forces with the private sector in joint ventures, or through management contracts. Some of these efforts may be little more than boosting the role of the charity's existing wholly owned trading company running the souvenir shop. Others are investigating more ambitious and complex packages between all the various sectors (public, private and charitable) as I have been doing now for some years for the Portsmouth Naval Heritage project on behalf of the five charities involved. Such complex organizational arrangements require, however, significant sophistication and commitment to a joint approach from all parties. This is necessary in order to break down the cultural boundaries between the very different types of organization and begin to develop a project oriented approach that bridges the divides and builds on the various strengths of each organization. These are potentially very great and combined carefully can minimize the weaknesses of each part of a project for the benefit of the whole. The combination must be very carefully structured from the outset to minimize also the potential of such a venture to split up and revert to traditional organizational value systems.

Conclusions

If heritage projects are to succeed through the harnessing of the potential of the tourist and leisure industries, without unlimited public subsidy, then any heritage charities involved in such a project must learn that they are now becoming part of a very competitive and commercial industry. They will accordingly have to learn the necessary skills of that industry in order to compete successfully within it. However they must at the same time remember to respect their inherent heritage characteristics and qualities and never compromise these to such an extent that the project loses its unique flavour or special ethos, which in the long run will always remain the foundation of any of the project's future 'commercial' success. In order to gain the commercial world's special skills without compromising the very heritage to be preserved, it is possible to consider a form of joint approach between the private sector and a heritage-based charity that can lead to dramatic success. The distinction of roles between the parties is the key to such success and the commitment to a positive, ongoing relationship between them. The public sector can often be a useful catalyst in this respect.

Obviously, it is ideal if a joint approach can be identified as relevant from the very beginning of a project, ensuring the structure and the personalities are co-ordinated from the start. But what is now becoming obvious from our many contacts with clients of heritage-based projects, is that often the first organizational structure that comes to mind for a project is not always the best in the long term, and the whole project and all the many options for its successful realization have to be thought through with the rigorous discipline of the private sector's traditional *business plan* approach. Only then is it possible to be confident that there will be a strong likelihood of continuing success over time matched to each individual project's unique circumstances. It is very difficult to change horses in midstream if the project starts off on the wrong foot.

Likewise, the inherent distinctiveness of each heritage project has to be recognized. Pet formulas do not often work in every situation: the variables are just too great. Each project involves a different location, a different theme or concept, a different context, a different financial situation and, most significantly, different people. However, there is a discernible widespread trend towards breaking down the barriers between the public, private and voluntary sectors. This is possible to achieve, and can usually bring great benefits to a project and most importantly to its visitors, who are now being asked to support it through their enjoyment of a visit.

Reference

Hewison, R. (1987) *The Heritage Industry*, Methuen, London.

6

Marketing in Visitor Centres: A Study

Terry Robinson

Marketing and Interpretation

Marketing is an emotive term in the countryside. Those who work to conserve natural areas or encourage public support for conservation have viewed it with distrust. What, then, is marketing?

Marketing is a set of techniques that discipline the operators of a public service to match what they can offer to what people want. It does not refer to techniques that inveigle people into buying from you things or services that they do not really want.

Marketing techniques are extremely useful in all situations where a service is being provided, not just those where money is changing hands: it is just as crucial to the success of a non-commercial venture as to a commercial one.

Some of the resistance to the use of marketing in countryside interpretation rests on a belief that marketing necessarily means boosting visitor numbers. Many managers see a need to limit or to try and reduce the visitor numbers to sites that are fragile to intensive visitation. It is interesting to note that many of the techniques used to limit or reduce visitor numbers are, in fact, marketing techniques, and indeed marketing can influence visitor use downwards as well as upwards.

To quote from the study on which this paper is reporting;

The philosophy of marketing is relatively simple and characterised by sensitivity to demand, which in turn means a strong emphasis on the needs of the customer and the offerings of competition, in making management decisions. It is not in practice an easy discipline to implement, and relatively few commercial organizations in the leisure field could be said to be strongly marketing-oriented. (Research Bureau Ltd, 1982)

The Countryside Commission and Countryside Interpretation

Most people managing countryside visitor centres and other countryside interpretation facilities will initially have been motivated by a basic interest in managing the countryside itself rather than the people in it. So interpretation programmes tend to be run by nature conservationists, planners, estate agents or others whose prime professional interest is in the resource itself. Not many of these find the necessary public relations skills naturally easy to exercise. Marketing therefore imposes a very apt set of disciplines, based on a sensitivity demand that forces people to think from the position of the audience for interpretation rather than the agency providing it.

Visitor centres interpreting the countryside have been developed by a wide variety of providers and there are about ninety open to the public in England and Wales. Grant aid and professional support from the Countryside Commission has been provided for most of these because the Commission sees interpretation as a prime method of marrying its two objectives – of promoting the conservation of the countryside and its enjoyment by the public.

The Commission has been concerned that the success of the centres it has grant aided has not matched initial ambitions to attract a target audience and put across an interpretive message.

The Study

In 1981, the Countryside Commission appointed Research Bureau Limited, a marketing consultancy, to study countryside visitor centres and report on their effectiveness and marketing. The Commission emphasized that its main concern was the capability of the centres to convey countryside interpretation messages.

The objectives of centres to interpret the countryside were therefore taken as read and immutable: it was not open to the study to find that interpretation was the wrong business for centres to be in. It is easy to indicate more profitable enterprises than interpretation in the countryside. Profitability however, was not of prime interest to this study.

The objectives of this exercise were to give the Commission advice on good practice in visitor centre management and to devise criteria for visitor centres for successful marketing within the field of countryside interpretation.

The study looked in detail at two contrasting centres, Brockhole in the Lake District National Park, a major visitor centre in a very popular tourist area, and Tintern Station, a small wayside centre in a picnic site in the Wye Valley, a less popular but just as intensively used tourist area. Both centres are run by local authorities and both were thought to do a creditable job at interpreting the countryside. However, they are different in terms of level of investment made in them, the level of management devoted to them and the size and orientation of the audiences they seek. The national park centre aims to give people enjoying several days' stay in the Lake District a good introduction to and explanation of the area. In contrast, Tintern Station aims to convey a sense of place for that particular location to more casual day visitors and some long-distance walkers. The study involved intensive inspection of the management of the centres, visitor surveys, market surveys in nearby towns and centres of interest and intensive interviews with managers.

The two centres were selected as good examples so secondary studies took place at another five centres to include some representative problems of countryside centres. Consultants undertook visits to a further twenty-two centres at the outset of the study.

It should be noted that this study was one of a number undertaken on behalf of the Countryside Commission to assess the effectiveness of marketing and interpretive provision (Coopers Lybrand, 1979; Dartington Amenity Research Trust/University of Surrey, 1978, Stansfield, 1982).

Performance of Visitor Centres

Interpretation

From the broad sample of centres, the consultants reported a number of findings disquieting to people interested in the success of visitor centres. One concern of the Countryside Commission that led to the study being undertaken was that many centres looked and felt the same no matter what part of the country they were in. When one of the main purposes of interpretation is to convey a sense of place, this uniformity of feel is to be avoided. Much of the cause appears to lie in the lack of a sharp, carefully worked theme of true local significance. Messages came across to the consultants as repetitive, predictable and unimaginative at a broad variety of centres. Standards of design were generally high but scripts were badly written and were too long and not aimed at the casual visitor.

There was also a failure to orient the visitors on arrival and make clear where they were, what they could do and how they could use the interpretive facilities. Not all centres had events programmes organized at them. Those that did were generally performing better.

In general, then, the centres appeared to be stodgy and lack-lustre, thereby attracting less of the audience than might be hoped for, and consequently damaging their effectiveness. They also failed to get clear messages across to visitors, wasting a valuable opportunity to communicate information about and encourage an appreciation of the countryside.

Management

The consultants were concerned that the lack of financial objectives for the centres induced an approach to management that made it difficult to cater for visitors' needs efficiently. As the demands to save money in publicly funded agencies has grown, so a number of those than run visitor centres have attempted to raise more income for the centres from their visitors. Where financial objectives have been tacked on in this way they have often limited the ability of the centre to achieve the objectives with which it was set up.

In centres run by non-profit organizations there was an overwhelming concern to limit spending. These centres often tended to be under-funded to an extent that damaged their performance enough to severely limit their income-raising ability.

The standards of environmental care of the sites open to the public and the centres themselves were superb. This reflects the resource – management bias of the people running the centres, as does the reported variation in attitude of staff to the public. Some centres appear to discourage the public; others have a very welcoming feel. The performance of the centre in this regard depended wholly on the attitude of the manager, who sets the tone of the whole place. For those who lack the necessary instinct or skills, there is little in their management structure or training provision to make staff better at dealing with the public or providing for their needs.

Finally, and perhaps most importantly, the consultants reported the centre managers' almost total lack of any attempt to collect, analyse and use evidence that would inform them better about their existing and potential audience. Most centres lack any performance targets and therefore any ability to measure and judge performance. Many centres failed to publicize themselves either through paid advertising or through opportunities for publicity. Many centres were not signposted from surrounding roads. Of the large variety of simple monitoring and evaluation techniques that centre managers could use to study the effect of the interpretation on the users of the centre, very few were employing these and were therefore ignoring a large amount of useful information that would shed some light on how to get their interpretation across.

Interpretation in the Market Place

Most centres have objectives; a few are drafted to be incisive and clear but the majority are written in rather vague terms. Centres need to have their objectives written so that they are testable and so that they include management and financial objectives. There is nothing wrong with interpretation objectives in themselves but if interpretation is to seek to change people's attitudes and behaviour, objectives have to be drafted to be more than just acts of faith.

When one surveys the public to see what they want, the list of their priorities is in strong contrast to what the centre's objectives aim to provide. It is the requirements of the market that dictate how worthwhile numbers of the public can be attracted to the centre and be engaged with the interpretive message. The mismatch between what the visitor wants and what business the centre believes it is in restricts severely the ability of the centre to cater for the public. Designers and managers of centres need to be prepared to provide for visitors' wants and needs in the objectives for centres.

Failure to do this can only result in visitors going elsewhere: there is plenty of choice. One of the main costs that visitors have to bear in visiting a centre is their own time. If they find it is better spent at some other visitor attraction, they will do so.

Market Research

It is difficult and notoriously expensive to find out what the market requirements are for any recreation service. It requires intensive market surveys both at the centre, in the form of site surveys, and in surveys of the surrounding population either by post, by visit or by street surveys. These are essential to reveal why some people do not visit the centre and whether anything should be done to encourage them.

Whether or not they should be persuaded will depend on whether or not they form part of the target market, which will have been defined within the terms of the objectives for the centre. The market for the centre is almost certain to be divisible into a number of segments. It is important to discern these because they will be attracted, and to a certain extent catered for, by different means. Some well established segments of the market for a centre are local people, small social groups, day trippers, residential holiday makers and organized parties such as those from schools.

Crucial stages in attracting and satisfying an audience exist in the need to make members of the target market aware of the centre, through advertising and promotion. But awareness and motivation to visit are separate and it should be remembered that the experience of others and their word-of-mouth recommendations are most important. Once the target market has been persuaded to visit the centre, there is a need to engage their attention with the interpretation. A measure of success of the second and third of these crucial stages is how far people are persuaded to return to the centre on future occasions.

Financial Management

Two important objectives for a centre will be communication and influencing attitudes. There will also be some financial objectives and there is increasing pressure for centres to at least cover their costs.

The income that a centre expects to earn should be expressed as an objective, and a target should be set. The level to expect will depend on the number of people coming to the centre and their spending habits: it can be expressed as income per person visiting the centre. This, in turn, will be derived from two sources, an admission charge if there is one and the profit on sales made to the visitor from ancillary services such as a restaurant facility or a shop. Attention to these details is important in order to achieve the income target and to ensure that ancillary services form as much a part of the experience as other elements of the centre.

Once a centre is built and running, most of the money has been spent on it. There is normally a comparatively low cost involved in management. The outgoings for a centre are therefore predictable. The income per head can then be set as a target either to cover all or a proportion of the costs, or to make a profit. A few centres which have been the subject of massive initial investment are known to make a profit, but no countryside visitor centres are believed to do so.

Interpreting a Sense of Place

What is important, however, is that realistic and firm targets are set for all aspects of the performance so that keen attention can be devoted to catering for the needs of the public.

Image is all-important in marketing. Interpretation must have a strong image, which is likely to be closely related to the sense of place. From this stem the themes for interpretation; without their clear definition there is no hope of projecting a strong image. Lack of rigour in working up a theme that has real significance to the place itself is almost universal in countryside inter-pretation. It is very difficult to project the local character of a place on the basis of a loose theme, such as 'Man and the Environment' or 'Change in the Landscape', which tend to lead to the bland and universally similar approach reported by the consultants.

Conclusion

In marketing terms, the theme for interpretation is its packaging: it has to hold together a manageable amount of the product (the interpretation) and make clear and attractive to the potential consumer what is inside.

This is just one of a number of marketing concepts that people involved in interpretation would benefit from adopting. The environmental movement generally has been dogged by the presumption, 'when I talk, others will listen'. The few exceptions to this stand out for the effort they devote to converting their knowledge into appealing and graspable concepts and messages: there is no reason why this has to result in any loss of veracity. There is still a tide of goodwill in the developed world for environmental issues; we have receptive public. But this may not last forever. More importantly, time is running out for the environment itself: once that is damaged beyond retrieval, messages that interpreters want to convey will be redundant.

No message has impact if its deliverer is not clear about what he or she wants to say: the lack of clarity in objectives reported by the study is therefore disturbing.

Just as disturbing is the failure to grasp the importance of a public undertaking such as interpretation basing its objectives on an understanding of its audience. If they want 'meaty bite-size chunks' and all they are given is bland, homogeneous fodder, it is not surprising that interpretation attracts little interest or backing. The research revealed widespread 'whistling in the dark', which is a waste of everyone's time and energy.

Acknowledgements

I am indebted to Jon Wilkinson and Mary Short of the Research Bureau Limited, who carried out this study. As at 1 January 1989, the report has not been published but there are plans to do so by the Centre for Environmental Interpretation, Manchester Polytechnic, UK.

References

Coopers Lybrand Associates Ltd (1979) *Rufford Country Park Marketing Study*, Countryside Commission, Cheltenham, Glos..

Dartington Amenity Research Trust/University of Surrey (1978) *Interpretation in Visitor Centres*, Countryside Commission, Cheltenham, Glos.

Research Bureau Ltd (1982) *Visitor Centres Marketing Study*, Unpublished Report to the Countryside Commission, Cheltenham, Glos.

Stansfield, G. (1982) *Effective Interpretive Exhibitions*, Countryside Commission, Cheltenham, Glos.

7

Broadening the Market
Antony Eastaugh and Nicholas Weiss

The Heritage of England

Historians are divided on the details, but by the time of the Roman Conquest in AD 43 the culture of Britain had something like 1,500 to 2,000 years of development behind it. It is this legacy, in addition to the 2,000 years that have elapsed since the early days of Julius Caesar's expeditions, that successive generations have variously been unaware of or ignored, but that they now treasure as a nostalgic link with our origins. It is also a source of commercial activity.

As a tourist attraction, our heritage gives Great Britain a comparative advantage over other countries. Indeed, it is clear from research (English Tourist Board, 1986) and admission figures to heritage attractions that our architectural and historic monuments are a major factor in making this country an attractive tourist destination for overseas visitors.

As an indication of the sheer size of this attractive pull, in 1986 England alone accounted for over a million historic buildings and sites of particular interest or merit, ancient and ecclesiastical monuments, as shown in Table 7.1 (English Tourist Board, 1987).

Creation of English Heritage

If anything, this advantage in number of attractions has strengthened over the last twenty years. There has been a marked increase in conservation activity, as demonstrated by a burgeoning of local amenity societies and official 'listing' exercises. This culminated in a government decision (National Heritage Act 1983) to create a Historic Buildings and Monuments Commission for England, now popularly known as English Heritage which would assume responsibility for some 400 monuments and buildings previously managed by the Department of the Environment. Certain major attractions, for example, The Tower of London and Hampton Court Palace, remained

Table 7.1 Buildings, etc. of particular interest in England

Listed buildings (of particular architectural or historical merit)	395,377
Conservation areas (areas of special architectural or natural interest – largely in rural or smaller urban districts)	5,902
Ancient monuments (structures of national importance)	12,875
Sites of archaeological interest	635,000
Ecclesiastical buildings (including 8,500 pre-Reformation in 16th Century)	16,622
Hotels (of particular historical literary or architectural interest)	5,202

Source: English Tourist Board/British Tourist Authority (1987).

under the aegis of the Department of the Environment. As a consequence, that department continues to be interested actively and in its own right in managing tourist attractions.

The Historic Buildings and Monuments Commission started operating formally as a new entity in April 1984, existing parallel to other non-government bodies such as the National Trust and the Historic Houses Association. Founded in 1895, the National Trust cares for some 190 houses which it opens to the public and over 243,000 hectares of land of outstanding beauty or interest. By 1984 it had already established itself in the public's mind as a leading organization protecting much of the nation's heritage and enabling it to be placed on show.

The Historic Houses Association, on the other hand, represents the interests of owners still living in their properties, a large number of whom have opened their doors to the public.

With the creation of English Heritage came a change of emphasis. Previously Department of Environment policy, as passed down to its site custodians, had been to 'guard [sic] and clean' the properties in their charge – a policy epitomized in the dress issued to site staff. This was a scarcely veiled and modified form of prison warden's black uniform, and open threats of prosecution of visitors who were interested and foolhardy enough to walk upon areas of hallowed grass!

As the 1983 National Heritage Act expressed it, the new organization's responsibility was 'to secure the preservation of ancient monuments and historic buildings in England' but also to:

i   promote the preservation and enhancement of the character and appearance of conservation areas in England, and

ii promote the public's enjoyment of, and advance their knowledge of, ancient monuments and historic buildings situated in England and their preservation.

In other words, the passive role of guardianship was to be cast aside in favour of the active promotion of heritage properties and their preservation.

Initial Development

From October 1983, when the Historic Buildings and Monuments Commission started work, five planning groups concentrated on issues related to

archaeology and ancient monuments;
historic buildings;
marketing and trading;
presentation and interpretation;
education.

The services of an independent market research agency (Public Attitude Surveys Research – PAS) were enlisted to gather basic data about the nature of the existing visitor market and how those in daily contact with it (site custodians) felt about their present and future roles. Specifically, this stage took the form of:

(1) desk research amongst surveys already available from published sources;
(2) extended in-depth interviews with custodians; and
(3) face-to-face interviews with UK and overseas visitors at sites typical of the various types of property in the English Heritage portfolio: prehistorical (e.g. Stonehenge, Grimes Graves), Roman forts, other fortifications (e.g. Carlisle and Kenilworth Castle), religious institutions (e.g. Whitby Abbey) and historic houses (e.g. Audley End and Chiswick House).

This took place over the summer of 1984.

To produce a sense of unity within the Commission and easy recognition by the public, the popular name 'English Heritage' was chosen. This was to be accompanied by an easily recognizable symbol expressive of the organization's identity and purpose.

Marketing to the Visitor

On the basis of this and other work a new face to English Heritage's property was created. In communication terms, it took the form of

- guardianship planks announcing, at each site, English Heritage and its responsibility;
- a range of full-colour leaflets for all but the least significant sites, providing quality illustrations, short historical information and essential details such as opening times, admission prices and how to reach them;
- new uniforms for custodians in soft, but welcoming, tones;
- new enlarged sales points and a wider range of merchandise.

Direct to consumer advertising was geared to the specialist nature of the 'heritage property visitor' which had been identified both through the conventional analyses referred to later in this paper and through ACORN (residential environment descriptions derived from UK visitors' home addresses).

This along with budget constraints, precluded conventional mass advertising in favour of selective campaigns in publications most likely to hit the target market. These included travel guides, such as *Where to Go* and *Historic Houses and Gardens*; the local press; and *Heritage* magazine.

Direct mail campaigns in support of English Heritage membership (see later) were mounted both in specialist media accessed through purchase of specialist mailing lists and lists of holiday enquirers, and interest magazines such as *History Today* and *The Climber*.

At the other end of the spectrum, mass circulation publications such as the *Radio Times*, *TV Times* and the *Mail on Sunday* were used, and advantage was taken of their facility for inserts. Further extensive leafleting (illustrating places of interest in the paths of potential visitors) was directed at hotels, guest houses, and tourist information centres throughout England.

Joining English Heritage

The concept of membership of English Heritage was launched in 1984. In return for an annual subscription members are entitled to:

(1) free admission to properties and sites;
(2) reduced prices at English Heritage events, for example, open-air concerts, re-enactments of battles;
(3) participation in special-interest conducted tours;
(4) regular contact from English Heritage via its publication *English Heritage News*.

Membership has grown from 12,764 in October 1984 to 146,690 at the same time three years later. Membership development, as conceived by English Heritage, is less likely to bring about a broadening of the visitor market than to increase loyalty and visit frequency among a traditional following. Indeed, the age and social class profile of members, as revealed by surveys, displays all the characteristics (above average education, higher social class) that one would expect of visitors normally.

The property itself is unquestionably the most effective source of recruitment to membership, and here a new role for the custodian was devised and introduced via an extensive customer service training programme. This has been based on techniques tried and tested elsewhere in service industries such as retailing and airline travel.

Custodians – the face of English Heritage to its visiting public – have undergone an extensive programme of customer service training. This seeks to emphasize the importance of projecting properties to visitors through the custodians' own interest and concern for them whilst encouraging more regular visiting behaviour through membership recruitment.

Training guides based on distance learning techniques were produced for custodians. The results of this exercise were later assessed by an independent survey of custodians' product knowledge, perceived benefits from training and standards of service to the visitor.

In a total government vote of £64.8m in 1987–8, English Heritage's visitor orientated marketing budget totalled £1.8m, allocated broadly to:

(1) membership scheme development and administration 40 per cent
(2) direct-to-market promotion 25 per cent
(3) staff costs 15 per cent
(4) miscellaneous (consultancies, research, retained services) 20 per cent

Results of Activity

What can English Heritage show for its effort since 1984? Has it improved its position in a competitive market which has been in the doldrums until recently? Has it made any progress towards broadening the appeal of the 'heritage property visit', an objective inherent in the terms of reference of the National Heritage Act?

Changes in the socioeconomic character of the United Kingdom which have accelerated during the later decades of the twentieth century have encouraged the growth of leisure activity. Notable among these influences have been: the growth of personal mobility through increased car usage; greater disposable income, of which leisure is forecast to take full advantage; greater disposable leisure time, whether through unemployment or early retirement; and a slight but nevertheless significant upward shift in social class status towards those segments of the population for which leisure activity have historically been most important.

Against this background, visits to historic buildings and monuments have not fared particularly well. Whilst innovations and improved marketing have made a positive contribution, the historic property 'industry' is very much at the mercy of extraneous economic and natural influences. A period of economic depression from 1978 to 1982 restrained the market but this phase was followed by generally improved over-the-year trends until 1986. It was

Table 7.2 Sightseeing attractions

		1984	1985	1986
Total		2,741	2,918	3,117
Historic buildings		960	943	1,023
	%	35	32	33
Gardens		187	190	204
Museums/art galleries		966	1,048	1,118
Wildlife attractins		138	151	163
Others		490	586	609

Source: English Tourist Board/British Tourist Authority (1987).

then that fears of Libyan terrorism and the Chernobyl disaster brought about a marked fall in visitors from overseas, particularly from the USA.

Returns for 1987 suggest that last year saw a marked recovery from 1986 admission levels, despite indifferent summer weather and the October storms.

Spending by UK residents on entertainment (which includes visits to stately homes, etc.) is forecast to increase in real terms over the remainder of this decade but the number of attractions for that expenditure is increasing year by year, as a glance at Table 7.2 will demonstrate. What is more, the type and character of attractions is changing: historic buildings, whilst still a large proportion of the total, are tending to be proportionally less numerous as they make way for increasingly large numbers of museums and other attractions such as country parks, steam railways and model villages.

Within a market where historic buildings were tending to become less numerous relatively, and certainly less visible in the face of competition from privately owned and operated wildlife and theme parks, government-owned properties had fared relatively badly. Table 7.3 illustrates how this sector's share of admissions had been declining in relation to those of the National Trust. Comparable figures for private properties are not available and so it is not possible to include this sector, but its inclusion would almost certainly exacerbate the trend.

Ironically, this decline took place over the years when government admission prices were not increased in line with inflation, a feature which disappeared in 1985 (Table 7.4).

The impact of English Heritage becomes evident from its increasing share of the market from 1985 onwards, despite increasing admission prices at a rate which outpaced the trend of government properties as a whole.

A Site Case History: Audley End House

Numbers alone do not tell the full story. Reference was made earlier to visitor surveys conducted in 1984: these were repeated in 1987. From the

Table 7.3 Visitor admissions, government property shares 1980–7

	1980	1981	1982	1983	1984	1985	1986	1986
Properties operated by government 1980–7	34	31	29	30	31	32	27	23
Properties operated by government 1980–3; handed over to English Heritage in 1984	34	33	32	31	29	30	34	
National Trust	32	36	39	39	38	39	43	43
Total admissions (000)	12,623	10,956	10,867	11,466	12,889	13,865	12,859	13,481

Source: English Tourist Board/British Tourist Authority (1988).

Table 7.4 Index of Admission Charge *(1982 = 100)*

	1982	1983	1984	1985	1986	1987
Government properties (including those handed over to English Heritage)	100	100	100	123	162	163
National Trust	100	110	123	129	141	151
Private properties	100	110	117	128	137	151
Retail Price Index (inflation index)	100	105	110	117	120	125

Source: English Tourist Board/British Tourist Authority (1988).

comparative results, one English Heritage site serves to illustrate how judicious promotion of a property resulted in

- visitor increases in excess of the overall English Heritage trend;
- increased sales revenue, increased spending per head;
- a popularizing of the visitor profile; and
- increased 'repeat' visiting.

Audley End House is a Jacobean country mansion set in grounds land-scaped by Capability Brown, west of Saffron Walden, an Essex town midway between London and Cambridge. It houses notable collections of contemporary furniture and pictures which visitors come to appreciate as features conveying something of the life and times when the house was lived in by its owners in the seventeenth century.

Not surprisingly, therefore, the profile of visitors in 1984 displayed all the characteristics typical of many heritage properties: a visitor population socially elevated and educated to above average standard.

Widening the appeal of Audley End presented a particular challenge. In the interest of conservation and preserving the lived-in feel of the property, virtually nothing could be done to alter the contents of the house or introduce interpretive techniques which would be out of character. Yet its vast gardens, with their serpentine waters enclosing on three sides and the borders opening out to countryside beyond, afforded an alternative opportunity, that of marketing the property by popularizing the gardens through special events mounted regularly throughout the year.

Typical events are the following, held in 1988:

- demonstration of sheepdog skills;
- re-enactment of a Civil War battle;
- craft festival – held in a marquee;
- open-air concert;
- 'Wheels and Wings' extravaganza;
- national patchwork quilt exhibition.

Shop facilities were also improved and a wider range of merchandise offered for sale.

The impact of these activities has been quite dramatic. They demonstrate how judicious marketing of a property of particular character and arguably limited appeal can broaden a market with no detriment to the intrinsic character of the site and no loss of interest on the part of visitors.

Over the three years from 1984 to 1987 the social class profile of visitors to Audley End has displayed a shift in favour of the middle managerial and skilled manual groups that go to make up social classes C1 and C2 at the expense of the higher social classes (A and B: see Table 7.5).

Table 7.5 Social Class Profile of Visitors to Audley End

		1984	1987
Bases		226	229
Social class		%	%
	AB	43	31
	C1	24	38
	C2	16	20
	DE	16	11

Source: PAS Surveys for English Heritage.

Furthermore, the proportion making repeat visits to the property had increased from 33 per cent in 1984 to 37 per cent in 1987. At the same time the numbers coming through the gate had risen dramatically and certainly far more rapidly than for English Heritage properties as a whole (Table 7.6).

Lest the impression be given that Audley End was the only site to which

Table 7.6 Paid Admissions at Audley End compared with
the rest of English Heritage sites

	1984	1987	
Audley End	44,121	87,499	+98%
Rest of English Heritage sites	3,945,879	4,448,501	+13%

Source: English Heritage.

Table 7.7 Trading revenue and sales per head

	Audley End	
	1984	1987
Trading sales	£8,732	£60,630
Spending per head	20p	69p

Source: English Heritage.

English Heritage devoted so much attention it should be mentioned that events have been mounted at a large number of other properties with encouraging results on admission trends in the long term. Analysing admission figures from six castles, for example, where a programme of events has been held since 1984 against figures for six castles where no events have been held reveals that admissions have been increased by 16 per cent from 1984 to 1987 at event compared with non-event sites.

Trading revenues from the property have also improved dramatically. In 1984 the annual revenue of £8,732 (Table 7.7) was derived from a sales table in the entrance hall generating spending per head of 20p. Improved sales facilities resulted in trading sales rising to £17,603 in 1985, £35,953 in 1986 and £60,630 (69p per head) in 1987.

Summary

The marketing policy adopted by English Heritage has begun to widen the appeal of their heritage properties. Based on the classic marketing approach of identifying customers and their needs, it has shown that treating a heritage property as a product to be 'sold' can be achieved without any loss of the property's dignity or integrity. It can be undertaken in a manner which stimulates interest both on the part of the existing market and those for whom a visit to a heritage property offers the prospect of a new and rewarding experience.

References

English Tourist Board (1986) *English Heritage Monitor, 1986*, London English Tourist Board/British Tourist Authority, London.

English Tourist Board (1987) *Sightseeing in 1986*, English Tourist Board/British Tourist Authority, London.

8

Implications of Special Interest Tourism for Interpretation and Resource Conservation

Raymond Tabata

Introduction

What kind of tourist enjoys rafting down raging rapids? What sort of tourist is willing to travel to the ends of the earth for a once-in-a-lifetime experience costing thousands of dollars? This is the special interest traveller, this growing segment of tourism. Organized tour packages can simplify trip planning for anyone who seeks an unusual, adventurous, or even inspirational vacation. Special interest tourism, however, challenges us to improve interpretive services for these travellers, as well as to pay closer attention to their potential impact on our communities and resources.

This paper will: discuss the significance of special interest tourism; review the impacts of special interest tourism on communities and resources; present a case study of diving tourism in Hawaii; and present some issues which need consideration.

Significance of Special Interest Tourism

The rapid growth of international tourism in the last few decades has made it second only to oil as an item in world trade. In Hawaii, visitor arrivals jumped from fewer than a million in the early 1960s to over six million last year, with projections of ten million by the year 2000. Tourism is more important to the Hawaiian economy than the traditional mainstays of sugar, pineapple and federal expenditures combined.

Bergerot (1979) believed that the growth of international tourism was caused by: (1) increased populations in generating countries; (2) a desire to escape urban areas; (3) improved air service and mass media; (4) more leisure time, longer vacations, and greater income. Mathieson and Wall (1982) also cite higher levels of education which have increased people's desire to see and experience new things, people and places.

A Growing Market

Special interest travel is booming and 'yuppies' are going on longer and more expensive trips (Alpine 1986). A survey of US travel agents revealed that about 15 per cent of bookings involved special interest travel. One agent said that 'people are tired of doing the same old thing, and are interested in action-packed trips such as hiking, biking, and rafting.' Outdoor activities were most popular for adventure vacations including white-water rafting, ballooning, wilderness expeditions, hiking, fishing, biking, scuba diving, sailing, helicopter rides, skiing, birdwatching, and wildlife safaris. Other types of tour focused on history, art, food and wine. Clients are demanding quality in special interest vacations. Another travel agent said, 'people who are serious will spend the money for the extra experience and don't mind the price.' Travellers come from all age brackets and backgrounds, although most are married, between thirty and fifty years old, and professionals. The one thing they seem to share is that 'they crave challenge and diversity in their vacations.'

Who Is the 'Special Interest Traveller?'

It is difficult to classify them neatly as they include a range of tourist types. Smith (1977) proposed seven types of tourists (explorer, elite, off-beat, unusual, incipient mass, mass, and charter). Perhaps the special interest travellers on organized tours could fit several of these categories, such as the 'elite', 'off-beat' or 'unusual'. However, independent travellers who purchase optional tours at their destination from an activities desk (for example, a whale-watching tour) might belong in the 'incipient mass' or 'mass' category.

Cohen (1972) suggested another scheme to segment the vacation market on the basis of 'novelty-seeking' roles. Snepenger (1987) relates Cohen's categories to the novelty of experiences sought (i.e., familiar v. novel) and use of tourist infrastructure (i.e., hotels, tours). Snepenger found that Cohen's classes of 'organized mass tourist', 'individual mass tourist', and 'explorer' could be applied to Alaska visitors. For example, he found that the largest segment travelled to Alaska on an organized tour that minimized novelty and maximized familiarity. The next largest segment was explorers who try to get off the beaten path, but still look for comfortable accommodation and reliable transportation. Finally, the 'individual mass tourist' uses short sightseeing tours and excursions to provide a blend of novelty and familiarity.

In summary, tourist types as proposed by researchers such as Smith, Cohen and Snepenger provide some insights regarding who are 'special interest travellers'. Perhaps more important than describing who they are, however, is understanding to what extent they affect the host community.

Impacts of Special Interest Tourism on the Community

From a tourism development point of view, it may be desirable to attract
travellers who have a greater interest in the local environment and culture.
The special interest traveller wants to experience something new, whether it
is history, food, sports, customs or the outdoors. Many wish to appreciate the
new sights, sounds, smells and tastes and to understand the place and its
people. How do these travellers fit into a community's idea of what is
'appropriate'?

Destination and Community Identity

Tourism based on an area's unique features helps distinguish it from a thou-
sand other competing destinations. For many years, the typical tourist's
image of Hawaii has been Waikiki, Diamond Head, and hula girls. For
anyone who has the interest, however, Hawaii has much more to offer: from
plantation history and the monarchy to volcanic wonders and rare plants.
These parts of Hawaii's natural and cultural heritage, as well as the island
lifestyle, are among the things which are most treasured by residents. By
marketing special attractions, potential visitors will realize that there's more
to a place than merely sun, sea, surf and sex (Uzzell, 1984).

Figure 8.1   Coastal field trips offer residents and visitors a variety of native plants
found only in Hawaii.

Figure 8.2 A walking tour in the town of Koloa on the island of Kauai provides glimpses of a sugar plantation town and its rural lifestyle.

Community Involvement

If residents are actively involved in defining and presenting the distinctive aspects of an area, tourism should cultivate more pride and feeling of 'ownership' in the industry. Gabe Cherem's concept of 'community interpretation' is well suited for identifying a community's tourism resources, and interpreting them to visitors. In the city of Rochester, New York, Cherem helped develop an interpretive master plan which directly involved residents in identifying interpretive themes in their own backyard, then finding innovative ways of making their community 'come alive' for visitors. At two seminars held in 1984, Cherem shared his ideas on 'community interpretation' with people in Hawaii. He said then, 'If the story of a community could be realistically and properly told, residents would gain a renewed sense of community pride, and visitors would gain a far deeper appreciation for the community's uniqueness.' The seminars inspired a small community in Hawaii to develop a visitor centre for a popular beach park. Another group produced a brochure which helps residents and visitors discover a variety of ocean-related activities.

Economic Benefits

Attracting tourists wishing to experience the 'real Hawaii' can be justified in various ways. First, special interest travellers are expected to come back if they are satisfied. Second, being relatively affluent, they are supposed to spend more. Third, they would help boost hotel occupancy and length of stay especially in areas away from the tourist meccas such as Waikiki. Fourth, special interest travellers could help diversify the market and 'hedge' against fluctuations in the world tourism market. Finally, there would be an economic incentive for protecting and more effectively managing our natural and cultural resources.

Impacts on Communities and Resources

On the negative side of the balance sheet, special interest tourism could bring certain types of environmental and cultural effects which must be carefully addressed. First, deterioration of 'authentic' attractions and experiences can be a problem in assuring visitors that they are getting the real thing. As authenticity is sacrificed to dollars, residents begin to develop a negative perception of tourism as being 'too commercial' or 'plastic'.
Figure 8.3

Figure 8.3 Increasing numbers of Japanese tourists visit the Arizona Memorial at Pearl Harbour, Oahu, where the Pacific War between the US and Japan began.

Second, the effort to encourage special interest travellers to enjoy unique experiences will undoubtedly result in some conflicts. They might want to visit less popular areas which might be sensitive to a new influx of people. For example, the Na Pali wilderness area of Kauai became such a popular destination for hikers and backpackers in the 1970s that the government now limits the numbers of users by permit. Such areas can handle only so many people before the environment and experience are degraded.

Dive Travel – a Case Study in Hawaii

Recreational snorkelling and diving are among the most popular activities for tourists. Advertisements lure divers to exotic places such as Palau, Australia, Philippines, and the Red Sea. Major diving destinations such as legendary Truk Lagoon are relying on dive travel as a primary form of tourism (PATA, 1977). Diving is big business. A recent survey of nearly fifty dive shops in Hawaii revealed that they provided nearly 250,000 tours and grossed about $(US)20 million in 1986 (Tabata, in press).

Divers enjoy their sport in almost any body of water including quarries, lakes, ice ponds, kelp beds and caves. The divers themselves are generally well educated, young and financially secure. The sport is also male-dominated, although there are increasing numbers of women divers. The diverse backgrounds and interests of divers challenge resource managers, who must accommodate their varied recreational needs.

What Appeals to Divers?

A *Skin Diver* (1985) survey showed that divers are attracted by features such as reefs, wrecks, lobsters, abalones, shells, 'walls', 'drifts' and caves. In a Great Lakes area study, Somers (1979) found that nearly 40 per cent of respondents enjoyed coral reef diving; they also enjoyed wrecks, underwater photography, ice diving, spearfishing, treasure hunting and cave diving. Matheusik (1983) and O'Reilly (1982) provide detailed analyses of diver preferences for underwater features, including water clarity, geological features, diverse marine life and underwater scenery.

Implications of Divers' Preferences

Understanding diver's preferences for underwater environments can be useful not only in targeting divers as a specialty market, but also for designing experiences for them, including interpretive services. This diversity also means that divers could be segmented according to skill levels and interest in particular attractions. Divers could be dispersed to more sites, each site highlighting something different.

To some extent, this is already happening in Hawaii and elsewhere. On the island of Oahu, for example, certain sites are much more heavily used than others. Interestingly, the single most popular site features a sunken wreck; the second features outstanding underwater scenery. Many of the other sites highlight other unique attractions such as tame eel, fish, resident turtles or a sleeping shark, In a way, the various dive operators are carving out niches in the dive market by 'creating' attractions such as tame eels hand-fed by dive guides.

Off the island of Maui, the state's most popular dive site, Molokini Crater, suffers from overly effective advertising. Every tourist publication singles out Molokini Crater as a 'must'. Dive operators say they are obliged to go to Molokini because their customers demand it. The thirty to forty dive and snorkel operators at Molokini are now complaining that congestion and anchor damage to corals are degrading the visitor experience. Other popular snorkelling places such as Hanauma Bay are also being overrun by tourists. The facilities and services at Hanauma Bay have not kept up with the demands of over a million visitors a year.

Potential for Interpretation

There is tremendous potential for interpreting the underwater environment for divers and snorkellers. Underwater interpretation, such as that done by the US National Park Service in the Virgin Islands, would be a start. New technology, such as tourist submarines, will introduce thousands of non-divers to the underwater environment and perhaps inspire them to try scuba diving. Dive charter operators have a great opportunity to provide interpretation. Hawaii Sea Grant expects to work with the dive industry to incorporate interpretation in their dive tours. Opportunities for self-guided experiences could be enhanced by providing information and interpretation for divers. To help develop these opportunities, Hawaii Sea Grant published a statewide dive guide and installed an interpretive display at a popular snorkelling beach.

Need for Resource Management

The impact of divers on the marine environment must be managed in order to prevent deterioration of the resource. At Molokini Crater, where recreational use is taking its toll on the resource, Hawaii Sea Grant has been working closely with commercial operators and the state government to install specially designed mooring pins which would reduce anchor damage to corals. The Molokini system could be a prototype for a statewide system of day-use moorings. There is also need to educate divers about basic

Figure 8.4 Waimea Canyon on Kauai is a favourite place for enjoying Hawaii's geological wonders and rare native plants.

conservation. Through interpretation, divers can become more aware of how trampling, collecting, touching and breaking harm corals and other marine life.

Some Issues to Consider

Hosts and Guests

The needs of tourists must be carefully balanced with the desires of residents. At a recent conference on interpretation in Hawaii, participants voiced concern that residents, as hosts, should have a say as to what tourists visit and experience. Just as guests in a home are expected to behave in a certain manner, visitors should also behave appropriately in a given setting.

Tourism and Resource Planning

While much of tourism planning focuses on infrastructure (hotels, transportation, airports, convention centres, etc.) much less attention is devoted to the importance of natural and cultural resources which visitors come to see. The national and state/provincial parks model in the US and Canada could be applied to overall tourist planning. There would be better integration between managing both resources and the visitor experience. In Hawaii, a governor's task force is now examining how ocean and coastal resources can be better utilized to support tourism. Several working committees have already expressed interest in managing and interpreting resources more effectively to enrich the visitor experience. They also suggest the development of information centres whose job would be to facilitate experiences and, thereby, better satisfy visitors.

Training Interpreters

As more special interest travellers visit a place, it will increasingly become important for professional interpreters to develop and improve their interpretive skills and subject knowledge. In Hawaii, this could include anyone conducting a wilderness boat ride, dive charter, or a whale-watching tour. If a visitor is to get more than trivia and off-colour jokes, interpreters will need to learn how to inspire and provoke their audience. Several years ago, Hawaii Sea Grant helped start the 'Interpret Hawaii' programme at a community college in Honolulu. 'Interpret Hawaii' now sponsors vocational training courses, informal coffee hours, innovative walking tours for the public, and institutes. Similar programmes are starting on other islands. Hawaii Sea Grant hopes to start working with one of the new programmes to train people in the ocean recreation industry.

Conclusions

Special interest tourism can benefit a community by highlighting the local environment and cultural heritage, and thereby contribute to a positive view of tourism. Tourism planning must recognize that quality experiences depend on the love of residents for their home and pride in their rich natural and cultural legacy. As hosts, they are more likely to protect their legacy and enjoy sharing it with others. Showing visitors around becomes a joy, not just a job. In Hawaii, this attitude of sharing could be called the spirit of 'Aloha'. Aloha comes from the heart, not the mind. This is where special interest tourism can be a powerful concept in a place like Hawaii. Tourist experiences which touch the heart are more likely to leave visitors with a lasting and memorable impression of a place and its people.

References

Alpine, L. (1986) 'Trends in special interest travel', *Specialty Travel Index*, (Fall/Winter) 83–4.

Bergerot, J. (1979) *South Pacific: Guidelines for the Development of Tourism, its Significance and Implications*, UN Development Advisory Team for the Pacific, Suva.

Cohen, E. (1972) 'Toward a sociology of international tourism', *Social Research 39*, 164–82.

Matheusik, M.E. (1983) *Sport Divers and Underwater Parks: a Market Segmentation Analysis*, MS thesis, Texas A & M University, College Station, Texas.

Mathieson, A. and Wall, G. (1982) *Tourism: Economic, Physical and Social Impacts*, Longman, New York.

O'Reilly, M.B. (1982) 'Sport diving in Texas: a study of participants, their activity, and means of introduction', MS thesis, Texas A & M University, College Station, Texas.

Pacific Area Travel Association (PATA) (1977) *Truk: a Study of Tourism Development*, PATA, San Francisco, Calif.

Skin Diver (1985) *1985 Subscriber Survey*, Petersen Publishing, Los Angeles, Calif.

Smith, V. (ed.) (1977) *Hosts and Guests: the Anthropology of Tourism*, University of Pennsylvania Press, Philadelphia.

Snepenger, D. (1987) 'Segmenting the vacation market by novelty-seeking role', *Journal of Travel Research*, 27 (2), 8–14.

Somers, L.H. (1979) *Profile of a Great Lakes Diver*, Michigan Sea Grant Reprint (MICHI-SG-79-301), Ann Arbor, Mich.

Tabata, R.S. (in press) *Statewide Survey of Dive Operators in Hawaii*, University of Hawaii Sea Grant College Program, Honolulu, Hawaii.

Uzzell, D.L. (1984) 'An alternative structuralist approach to the psychology of tourism marketing', *Annals of Tourism Research*, 11 (1) 79–99.

9

An Interpretive Challenge:
The US National Park Service
Approach to Meeting Visitor
Needs

Michael D. Watson

The National Park Service Director, William Penn Mott, Jr, began his administration of the National Park System (NPS) with a special emphasis on interpretation. He and the ten regional directors of the service formulated a far-reaching twelve-point plan for the NPS. Half of those twelve points have broad implications for programmes in interpretation:

- Stimulate and increase our interpretive and visitor service activities for greater public impact.
- Share effectively with the public our understanding of critical resource issues.
- Increase public understanding of the role and function of the National Park Service.
- Expand the role and involvement of citizens and citizen groups at all levels in the National Park Service.
- Seek a better balance between visitor use and resource management.
- Enhance our ability to meet the diverse uses that the public expects in national parks.

To emphasize how important interpretation is to him, a year and a half ago Director Mott recreated an old, but previously abandoned position for interpretation at the Washington level. This position, Assistant Director for Interpretation, oversees the activities of the Division of Interpretation and of the Harper Ferry Center. This is the NPS Interpretive Design service Center that plans and produces interpretive media for all 344 parks in the National Park System – media such as visitor centre exhibitions, wayside exhibitions, audio-visual productions and publications. The Division of Interpretation co-ordinates the person services side of interpretation, including visitor services, training of over 2,000 permanent and seasonal interpreters, volunteer programmes, co-operating associations, and special service-wide interpretive themes. For the first time in nearly twenty years, personal and media services in interpretation are once again under one umbrella in the NPS.

The first priority was to produce a five-year plan for interpretation in the

National Park Service, entitled *The Interpretive Challenge*. This was completed and distributed throughout the national park system in Spring 1988.

We looked hard at the state of interpretation in the National Park Service. We found that existing and new pressures increase the difficulty of meeting our dual mandate, i.e. to preserve the resources of a diverse park system while providing for public enjoyment. We know that interpretation can be a powerful management partner in helping achieve the National Park Service mission. Yet if interpretation – that unique function of NPS operations which interacts between the resource, the visitor and park management is to be effective, it must meet the highest standards of the profession.

Field interpreters and superintendents agree on the organizational and programmatic issues of greatest importance in helping to improve interpretation. The common recurring issues and concerns identified include:

- research, planning, and development for interpretive techniques and programmes;
- the quality of interpretive services and media;
- the role of interpretation in park management;
- interpreter training and supervision;
- interpretive media production and rehabilitation.

The Interpretive Challenge presents a strategy to address and resolve five areas of concern, or 'challenges'. These five challenges are:

(1) Professional excellence
(2) Evaluation
(3) Education
(4) Programme integration
(5) Media.

The first challenge, 'Professional excellence', examines ways to enhance interpretive programme management and staffing, provide research and development, and ensure interpretive professionalism. The second, 'Evaluation', looks at ways to bring interpretive services throughout the NPS to a consistent level of quality. The 'Education' challenge promotes environmental and heritage education, learning opportunities in urban areas, and outreach programmes. 'Programme integration' directs us to find ways to better co-ordinate and champion special interpretive initiatives, to enhance partnerships with other governmental and private sector groups, and to promote leadership in interpretation at national and international levels. The fifth challenge, 'Media', asks us to find ways to upgrade our interpretive media, to evaluate the media's effectiveness, and to achieve quality interpretive facilities and media in all parks.

A companion document to *The Interpretive Challenge*, called *Implementation Strategies*, was also created. It suggests over a hundred concrete strategies for implementing the components of the five challenges outlined above. It will be reviewed and evaluated by park and regional staffs to test its credibility and realism.

Several of the proposed strategies are already being implemented. Under the 'Professional excellence' challenge a technical bulletin for NPS interpreters was commissioned. We have just printed the second issue of *Interpretation*, which deals with the interpretation of critical resource issues. The first issue examined interpretive philosophy in the National Park Service since Freeman Tilden first produced *Interpreting Our Heritage* (1957).

Currently, the most exciting implementation of *The Interpretive Challenge* relates directly to meeting visitor needs. Under the second challenge, 'Evaluation', the plan states:

Interpretation deals with *impact, understanding*, and *goodwill* – impact of programs on visitor values and enjoyment, impact of visitors on resources, impact of interpreters on park management; understanding of visitors, understanding of resources, understanding of the NPS and its goals, and goodwill between people and organizations. The problem is how to measure impact, understanding, and goodwill.

Identifying and responding to the needs of visitors and evaluating the effectiveness of interpretive programmes has always been the 'Achilles' heel' of interpretation. Too often, NPS interpretive programmes have reflected the needs of the staff rather than the needs of park visitors or park management. Park themes sometimes revolved around interpreters' expertise and interests rather than management objectives or visitor expectations.

Freeman Tilden's first principle of interpretation states:

Any interpretation that does not somehow relate what is being displayed or described to something within the personality of experience of the visitor will be sterile. (Tilden, 1957)

It is imperative that we are confident we know what these personalities and experiences are, as well as what expectations our visitors bring to our resources.

And proving that interpretation makes a difference in increasing visitor understanding and appreciation of park resources, in inspiring visitors to formulate a personal ethnic towards the conservation of the areas they visit, and in reaching management goals, is elusive. We cannot ignore the importance of evaluation as we strive to identify and respond to visitor needs.

Field and Wagar (1984) identify several problems that diminish the effectiveness of interpretation:

- *Misallocation of effort.* Do we interpret at times and places suited to our visitors? Do we present the same information repeatedly to the large percentage of repeat visitors?
- *Working against usual behavioural patterns.* Do we utilize intragroup communication or work against it?
- *Inadequate attention to visitor motivation.* Do we consider how interpretation will reward our visitors or only what we think should be communicated and how it should be communicated?
- *Mismatching of messages to visitors.* Do we recognize the diverse ages,

backgrounds, and interests among our visitors or do we aim at a 'standardized' visitor?

- *Not monitoring the effectiveness of our efforts.* Do we clearly state what we hope to accomplish with interpretation? If objectives are clear, what feedback mechanisms do we use to diagnose how well our interpretive efforts are accomplishing these objectives?

A major programme is under way in the Division of Interpretation to try to answer these kinds of question. Called the Visitor Services Project (VSP), it is a programme developed by Dr Gary Machlis at the University of Idaho, A Cooperating Park Study Unit (CPSU) in the NPS. This is a university that has entered into agreement with the NPS to carry on research in areas of benefit to both the university and the NPS. A CPSU normally has an NPS employee duty-stationed at the university. The VSP involves three phases of information useful to park managers: (1) knowledge about the kinds of services, activities, and opportunities available to the public; (2) knowledge about visitors – who they are, where they go, what they do; and (3) understanding of the relationship between services and visitors – are visitor needs being met in the most efficient way while protecting resources?

For five years Machlis has been developing a simple way to survey park visitors that results in valid and reliable information about their habits, their activities, their expectations and their demographics. The system is designed to gather important visitor data on visitors and interpretive services, and how the interpretation serves visitors. It has to be useful, cheap, accurate, efficient, fast and legal.

Nearly twenty parks have participated in the programme to date, with rewarding results. The results have been so well received that an outcry arose to make the programme an operational unit of NPS Interpretation so that it can benefit all parks in the system. Two members of my staff have been seconded to work with Machlis in order to take the programme over in the next two years.

How the 'Visitor Services Project' works is illustrated in Figure 9.1.

A field questionnaire is tailored to a park's programme after the study design workshop. Consistent demographic and park data are present in all studies, however.

Each survey is completed in approximately two to three weeks. After the questionnaires are returned to the CPSU, the data is analysed and a draft report is produced. The findings are presented to the park staff within six months of the survey. Park suggestions are included in the final report, which is in a park's possession in time to utilize for the next visitor season.

The kinds of result being collected are of utmost importance to interpretive services. But many other park operations can benefit as well.

The cost to an individual park for a complete survey is about $7,000. Costs for the university and personnel administrating the programme are subsidized by the Washington and regional offices of the NPS. For a year after the final

Park Selection

Study Design Workshop

Draft Survey

Fieldwork

Data Analysis

Draft Report

Study Results Workshop

Final Report

Additional Analysis

Figure 9.1   How the visitor services project works

report has been presented, a park can ask for follow-up analysis, cross-referencing any of the collected data. After a year, the park is given all the raw data and results to store and perform further study upon.

One of the first tasks undertaken by the two new NPS employees assigned to the VSP programme at the University of Idaho will be to take the twenty park studies which have been completed, and perform an analysis of what common trends can be gleaned from one study to another. From this we plan to produce a comprehensive report which examines all of the results studied so far.

Such an effort will parallel another study in the identification of visitor needs, called the 1985 – 1986 Public Area Recreation Visitor Survey

(PARVS). Briefly, about 6,000 visitors to nearly fifty NPS areas participated in this jointly sponsored survey by the US Forest Service, the US Army Corps of Engineers, the US National Park Service, and a number of co-operating state agencies. The objectives of PARVS are to produce highly credible and broadly comparable estimates of the economic importance of providing recreational opportunities on public lands, and to develop detailed information about recreational users.

Specifically, NPS and The Ohio State University plan to use the PARVS data to generate interpretive participant and non-participant profiles based on a variety of variables for which data was gathered. This study will be conducted over the next two years and should provide interesting comparisons to our VSP programme.

Interpreters are excited about programmes like the Visitor Services Project and are staking a lot on their future. For so many years, we have seen *natural* and *cultural* resource assessments take place with inventories and recommendations about managing them. We are now in the position to perform similar *human* resource assessments through these programmes. Interpretation as a profession is maturing and taking responsibility for its actions.

References

Field, D. and Wagar, A. (1984) 'Visitor groups and interpretation in parks and other outdoor leisure settings', in G. Machlis and D. Field (eds) *On Interpretation: Sociology for Interpreters of Natural and Cultural History*, Oregon State University Press, Oregon.

Tilden, F. (1957) *Interpreting Our Heritage*, University of North Carolina Press, Chapel Hill.

10

Warwick Castle: Safeguarding for the Future through Service

Martin Westwood

This paper discusses how management at Warwick Castle identifies and responds to the needs of visitors. This is a complex and far-ranging subject and the paper provides an insight into how the operation is run to provide the visitors with a pleasurable and satisfying experience. However, like most other people in this business, we are continually learning and striving to improve the facilities and quality of service we offer.

The castle as an enterprise has become increasingly successful in recent years and so we must be doing many things right. At the end of the day we are happy to let others judge and leave the market to decide. However, we have much yet to achieve to produce a totally satisfactory experience and a lot of fairly important adjustments to make in order to make a visit more easy to enjoy.

Warwick Castle, founded by William the Conqueror in 1068, was the sixth castle to be built in this country by the Norman invaders as they travelled north to quell rebellion. Except for the Mound, little remains of the Norman castle so most of what is seen today dates from the fourteenth century but with extensive alterations and additions both inside and out taking place right up to the end of the last century. So much of the original fourteenth century building remains, however, that the castle is described as 'the finest mediaeval castle in England' and few have chosen to argue with that or even with Sir Walter Scott's description as 'that fairest monument of ancient and chivalrous splendour'.

Its owners have filled page upon page of English history, sometimes illustrious sometimes notorious like Warwick the Kingmaker or King Richard III. Often at the very centre of power and intrigue, the name of Warwick was one of the most potent symbols of the middle ages. In 1978 the present Earl of Warwick sold the castle and 100 acres to Madame Tussaud's, firmly believing that the castle's future lay in its potential within the leisure industry and that in this way its preservation would be assured. Naturally there was considerable controversy at the time but Madame Tussaud's, which owns several other very successful tourist attractions in England and one in

Amsterdam, was suitably equipped to manage and market this expensive undertaking.

As part of the Pearson group Madame Tussaud's has injected large sums of money to restore the fabric of the castle and radically improve its services infrastructure so that after ten years what was a moderately successful enterprise to begin with has become a thriving one. It is now in the very top rank of historic attractions in England charging an admission fee and by far the most visited 'stately home' in Great Britain. No longer a military stronghold or family home, it is a place of entertainment offering a gentle mix of leisure and learning in an incomparably beautiful setting.

The new ownership has been quite clear from the purchase that the dignity and perceived beauty of the site should be maintained and enhanced. This year the castle will open its gates to 650,000 paying visitors and it is intended that by 1991 the maximum visitorship of 750,000 will be achieved.

Had you been an unwelcome visitor in the middle ages you might well have had a somewhat hostile reception. In fact, the whole building was designed with the specific purpose of keeping people out. How times have changed. Today we extend a warm welcome to visitors from all over the world. No longer do archers, capable of releasing clothyard long arrows at a rate of seven a minute with astonishing accuracy, line the battlements. The murder holes no longer shower a cloud of burning quicklime as you enter the gatehouse killing ground, nor are piles of boulders stored at high level which when dropped from the towers will ricochet horizontally and catch you under the chin. Things are far more welcoming these days. We even let people know that they are welcome through the simplest of messages which we promulgate far and wide – Warwick Castle opens every day except Christmas Day from 10 a.m. – no doubts, no confusion – no need to check if we close on the third Tuesday after Pentecost or when there's an 'r' in the month. Open every day except Christmas Day tells our potential customer that we shall open to receive him or her and that generates confidence.

Good road signs as the property is approached give a feeling of welcome and care as does ease of parking both for the car-borne visitor or for the coach operator on a tight time schedule who can set down passengers right outside the entry point. Our car parks are attractively landscaped and laid out with good surfaces, with no chance of visitors stepping out into a puddle, sodden grass or the odd rut. We have, however, some serious problems with car parking provision due to the substantial increase in patronage over the last two years so we now are beginning to talk to the local council, who we have no doubt will be helpful, about a visitor car park signing scheme, which should ideally be part of a total 'Welcome to Warwick' visitor management package. Having said this, our on-site parking facilities are adequate for all but the Bank Holiday weekends and the height of the season. If we can take the pain out of parking for our potential customers we go a long way towards putting them in a good frame of mind to buy our entry ticket.

The same is true of having good lavatory provision at the main entry point. Until 1981, when we restored the stables, now our reception area, there must have been many an unfortunate visitor whisked around the state rooms in agony since the only lavatories on site then were literally the last rooms on the tour. It goes without saying that these facilities must be well signed and kept clean, but in our case even more so because they are outside the area the visitor pays to see.

The periphery of the site is extremely important in converting a potential customer into a paying guest. We charge a pay-once inclusive price admission charge. This we hope is the only painful part of a visit and research shows us that the overwhelming majority of our patrons prefer it. Warwick Castle is yours for the day and you can go into as many areas of the castle and grounds as you like as many times as you like. If anything is closed down for repair or other restrictions apply on the day then warning of these is given before you decide to purchase the ticket. When your ticket is checked you will receive a leaflet with comprehensive information about the site facilities and a site plan. This, coupled with the signing around the site and fully informed guides and staff, should ensure that getting around is straightforward and that you are able to make the most of your visit by having the necessary information.

One difficulty we experience at busy times is queueing for one or two areas, which we aim to alleviate by signing other parts of the castle as the first places to visit. This works fairly well and, provided the weather is kind and at very busy times there is a guide on duty outside to generally give guidance and confidence that the end result of queueing is well worth it, most visitors respond positively. If there is an extra entertainment on that day, for example morris dancers, then they will entertain the queue for a period. On Bank Holidays we warn people at the entrance before they pay that we are expecting queues during the afternoon. It is really a matter of trading fairly; it is appreciated by visitors and, candidly, has little effect on turnback. Queue control can also be important for visitor safety and again at busy times the entrance to the Rampart Walk and Guy's Tower is supervised so that the numbers going up do not cause congestion both in the narrow spiral staircase or on the viewing platform on the top.

An ancient castle can be a dangerous place for unsupervised youngsters so we insist on adequate supervision by parents and group leaders in certain areas. Some parts of the castle are also unsuitable for the elderly and infirm and are signed accordingly. Inevitably we have the odd heart attack on site, and other accidents. Because of this many of our staff are trained first-aiders but we are now looking seriously at first-aid facilities on site with fully qualified personnel all year round. With the number of elderly people increasing as a percentage of the population and their disposition to visit places like ours also increasing we can expect more difficulties of the kind described and, therefore, we have to be ready to cope with them for both practical and public relations reasons. In a similar vein we shall soon be creating a mother and baby room to answer a growing need, since babies no longer deter families from visiting us. We have to respond to a proven demand.

Like many similar establishments we offer a comprehensive range of catering facilities and have just invested £750,000 in creating a new assisted service restaurant on the first floor of the eighteenth-century stables and completely refurbishing the restaurant in the fourteenth-century Undercroft of the main castle building. Our aim has been to offer good arrangements to suit most dispositions and pockets in the main trading part of the year. One trend which we may have to recognize is that there is an increasing propensity among visitors, particularly in leisure parks, to take refreshment while walking around. Should we decide to follow through and respond to this it would have to be extremely sensitively handled. At present you may purchase an ice cream or lollipops and that is all there is available to eat on foot. We are awaiting a consultant's report on our catering facilities and it will be interesting to see what is suggested. But of paramount importance to us in this area is clearly maximizing the potential of our existing investment and preserving the character and quality of the site. It may be, therefore, that we have to eschew the obvious benefits which would accrue in terms of spend per head in order to maintain the atmosphere and dignity of the setting. We are, however, prepared to consider the matter but it is clear that the handling will have to be extremely sensitive and the outlets unobtrusive.

We also have three retail outlets, which offer a broad range of items of the souvenir/memento variety but following a recent consultant's report we shall be moving into many new merchandise areas in 1989 and re-equipping one of the shops. The shopping element in any visit has always been a good revenue earner and site operators have always made sure that visitors at some time are directed to it. There is no question that visitors now regard a well stocked shop as part of the visit, and the public's taste has become far more sophisticated with increasing affluence and the resultant disposition to spend on quality merchandise. Part of our strategy in the coming years is to move into more Warwick Castle exclusive items and we have already made a start with items from other Pearson group companies, like the range of Royal Doulton china featuring the Warwick Castle rose. We also sell the rose plant itself which was developed to commemorate the opening of the Victorian Rose Garden by the Princess of Wales in 1986.

Pearson's vineyard interests in France have also produced for us a very fine claret, which we retail in the shop and use of the prestige functions we have in the evenings from time to time.

We regard refreshment and shopping facilities as an integral and important part of the visitor's pleasure. We still have a long way to go to realize more spending potential from these activities and also to fully integrate them in terms of quality with the rest of the experience, but we see them as required and appreciated and certainly from our point of view as increasingly important in terms of profit performance. We shall also be introducing a bureau de change facility coupled with a tourism information office at the stable entrance soon as part of our customer services package, again responding to proven demand.

Having dealt with the basic facilities and services it is important to discuss the preservation and maintenance of the site, which is equally fundamental. Above all our visitors need to find themselves in a pleasant, clean, well main-tained and relaxing environment.

The site of the castle on the banks of Shakespeare's Avon consists of 102 acres about seventy of which are open to the public. The main building is, of course, the castle itself but there are several other large structures, namely the mill, the late eighteenth-century stables which forms the visitor reception area, the late eighteenth-century conservatory currently undergoing complete restoration, the lodge on Castle Hill, not to mention about a half mile of stone walling built in 1796 to encompass the Earl's enlarged grounds. There is also a pair of early nineteenth-century ice houses and a late nineteenth-century boathouse – currently being restored. The grounds consist mainly of landscaped parkland – Capability Brown's first independent work – woodland and two substantial formal gardens, one before the conservatory and the recreated Victorian rose garden. The annual maintenance pro-gramme costs well in excess of £500,000 and is rising!

We believe the access points and car parks should reflect the quality of the site which the customer will pay to see – they are, if you like, our visiting card. They have therefore been attractively landscaped to communicate to the potential visitor the feeling that this site is something special. In the odd place an enticing view has been created by modest tree surgery to add interest, to excite and stimulate conversion. We attempt to keep these areas litter-free by liberal provision of litter bins, regular clearing and maintaining good walking surfaces. The same applies to the castle grounds themselves. The maintenance of the grounds requires an efficiently controlled mowing regime since the grass areas are varied and very extensive. We employ a dozen gardeners and some pretty heavy machinery to carry this out. We know precisely how each particular part of the park will be mown, how it will look, what machine will be needed and how often it will be done. To some extent we can be creative by allowing wild flowers to grow on in certain areas for some of the year or by less frequent mowing of areas which are out of bounds, or by guiding visitors through the tree planting. A problem we have yet to solve is how to stop the wear on some corner areas of the formal lawns in and around the castle. We make fairly extensive use of 'please keep off the grass' signs but this does not altogether answer the problem. Tradi-tional bamboo fencing soon gets devastated and more permanent low fencing is clearly a safety hazard. These areas are re-turfed in the Autumn and usually retain their good looks until June. We pay attention to walking surfaces and from time to time have a major resurfacing programme.

An annual visit is made by our tree surgeons in July and August when there is a major programme of work, as well as subsequent visits when required after winter storm damage or where safety is impaired. Some of the trees in the castle grounds are magnificent and many predate Capability Brown's mid-eighteenth century scheme. We regard trees as very important assets and care for them accordingly. A chance discovery recently revealed many of the signs used to note tree planting by famous and royal visitors to the castle in the last century. These have been reproduced which we hope will be of interest to visitors and give them a feeling for the age of the trees. Sadly, from time to time a magnificent old tree has to be felled. This is part of a policy of creating as safe an environment as possible, which in a place like ours is not easy but is a constant concern.

The same is true of the castle buildings themselves. With this enormous mass of stonework safety repairs take precedence over disruption to rolling programmes. Work to the castle fabric is now an all year round activity except for the depths of winter, when stone is prepared for future use. We endeavour to keep repair work as self-contained and as neat as possible. We know it is a disappointment to visitors when a repair such as that to Caesar's Tower is taking place – rather like the repair of the tower of Big Ben was for millions of visitors to London. It will simply be an eyesore in any photograph. But the work has to go on. We hope, however, to gain some goodwill by explaining what is happening and again by interesting and informing visitors. We go to considerable lengths to match stone when repairing, even on occasion having to acquire stone from the Vosges to get a precise match. At the end of the day it is the castle building itself that attracts the custom and so the very high sums spent on fabric repair are not only an obligation to the future but an investment in the backbone of the business. The high state of preservation is a key factor in our visitors' perception and pleasure. As one old cockney lady remarked to her young charge some years ago 'No dear', she said 'all castles is ruins, this is a good ruin'.

Of course we would like to go faster but the amount of repair is constrained by the financial resources available and the skilled labour supply locally. However, our professional advisers on architectural matters say that most of the serious structural problems have been addressed. In a decade we have turned the corner. Nevertheless we have a classic Forth Bridge type situation and it is unlikely that we shall ever achieve a state of perfect repair. The mouldering hand of time will see to that.

The interiors of the castle and its collections pose no less of a problem – requiring constant cleaning and maintenance. At 7 a.m. sharp every day thirty cleaning ladies and one gentleman move in and prepare the castle for its working day; we open to visitors at 10 a.m. promptly. Much of the cleaning is routine but the continuity is vital in preserving the patinas on furniture, wooden and marble floors, and the gloss on flagstones and quarry tiles. Whilst the gardeners are rendering the car parks and grounds spotless, the lavatories, restaurants and shops are also getting the treatment.

Apart from day-to-day cleaning we have an annual purge throughout the castle during the winter months, when visitors are at their lowest. Since we do not close we have to work in full view of our visitors. On the whole it works pretty well; our visitors realize that such activity has to take place and are often very interested in what is going on. It is not often, for example, that you will have the opportunity to see a 14,000 piece chandelier stripped out on a table, each piece being individually polished. Because visitor numbers are low at that time, guides and cleaners have plenty of time to explain what is going on. The collection of arms and armour, about 1,000 items, is cleaned and oiled. The wax exhibition in the private apartments closes for cleaning during the first week in February, – the quietest week of the year, and the admission fee is substantially reduced to compensate for the disappointment. All major internal repairs are carried out at this time, with minor and remedial work taking place out of hours throughout the year. Restoration and cleaning of pictures, furniture, carpets, curtains and tapestries is handled as and when, also throughout the year, as part of a detailed plan which is laid out four years in advance and updated annually to take account of changing circumstance or conditions.

Underpinning all this activity will be the castle's maintenance department continually addressing the myriad everyday problems and minor damage and mechanical failure occasioned by a throughput of 650,000 visitors – maintaining standards and occasionally backing up contractors who are getting behind schedule.

All this effort has the ultimate purpose of presenting the castle to its paying customers to the best standard ensuring both its preservation and its business success. The latter, however, will not be guaranteed unless our visitors gain pleasure and information from their visit. So what learning and leisure experience does the castle afford? We believe this to be one of its main strengths as a place to visit – the variety in both scope and appeal of its component parts.

First of all is the castle itself – 'the most noble sight in England' as Sir Walter Scott called it. There can be few more splendid arrays of medieval military architecture in Britain, built as it was by the Beauchamps from ransom and loot gained in the Hundred Years War on the remains of a more humble Norman castle, and added to by Richard III who planned a grand artillery fort on the north side which, had he reigned longer, would have been the last royal keep to be built in this country. The setting for the castle is, of course, the lovely grounds landscaped by Capability Brown, with timeless views from the castle mound, gracious pleasure grounds with pretty displays of rhododendrons and roses, the mellow Autumn colours and the tranquillity of Shakespeare's Avon.

Inside are the state rooms – the glory of the castle for 300 years. The chapel, state dining room, great hall, red room, cedar room, green room, Queen Anne bedroom and blue boudoir. 'A Royal Weekend Party, 1898' exhibition by Madame Tussaud's faithfully recreates the colourful life of a great house at the turn of the century, by twenty-nine wax portraits in twelve rooms of the former private apartments. This has won two major awards from the British Tourist Authority, and the Carnegie Interpret Britain Award.

Then there is the Watergate Tower [or Ghost Tower] which leads to the millhouse, the armoury, dungeon – 5-star with *en suite* facilities, a display of torture instruments, the gatehouse, Guy's Tower and the Rampart Walk. All in all there is a lot to take in and we recommend a minimum of three hours to do so properly.

With such a marvellous resource, its history stretching right back to the Dark Ages, getting across enough information to our visitors presents a major problem. We have only begun to scratch the surface of the possibilities. Firstly, the guidebook – an indispensable tool in learning about the castle, its history and contents. Would that everyone bought one and read it. Of course that does not happen, and frankly the majority of visitors rarely glance through it while they are here. Understandably most are here for leisure purposes and are not engaged in a course of study. At the very least it provides them with an admirable souvenir, hopefully promotes reflection on what they have seen, and stimulates interest in other aspects of the heritage when read in the comfort of their homes.

We firmly believe in human contact where possible to inform and entertain visitors and we believe we are doing a reasonable job.

Until 1978 this castle belonged to the present Earl of Warwick. It was his home. It is the place where his family grew up and where he entertained his friends, and so the state rooms are arranged and presented very much as he left them. 'A place', as one writer put it, 'where you really feel that the family has just slipped out for the afternoon'. There are guides in every room to inform you about it or to conduct tours of all the rooms. They are very knowledgeable and where possible are only too happy to share their knowledge.

Pictures are discreetly labelled, for we do not wish to create 'a museum atmosphere'. For the more curious a few minutes spent with a guide can be the most memorable part of a visit. Most of our visitors go round as they please, moving from room to room listening in occasionally to the guided tour of a group on a tight time schedule due to the competitive packaging of their tour operator. But for most this is enough to take in. Our way of guiding in these rooms has evolved according to the demands of the visitors themselves and by and large it seems to work well and satisfy the needs of the different types of interest level. The guides' enthusiasm for their subject is one of our strengths and the curator continually furnishes them with new information to avoid the chance of them developing a stereotyped patter. Guides are also keen to expand their knowledge through their own reading and this helps in achieving a high level of competence which promotes the establishment in the eyes of the visitor.

In the twelve rooms of the former private apartments 'The Royal Weekend Party' evocatively recreates a gathering in the June of 1898, with faithfully reconstructed room sets using many items of furniture in their original positions. Guides are on hand to generally superintend and answer queries, expanding on topics if interest is shown. To most visitors the wealth of detail is so fascinating that the presentation is self-explanatory, visitors are flies on the wall, witnesses to the elegant and colourful life of the aristocracy at a moment in the castle's past.

In the Ghost Tower, in order to vary the experience, the life, times and ultimate murder of Sir Fulke Greville is told in sound. He was granted the castle by James I in 1604 and is an ancestor of the present Earl. The room is thought to be haunted by his ghost – known for generations and evidenced on old key fobs as the Bogey Room. We have also introduced an audio tour of the castle precincts and grounds. It has been well received and is an excellent medium for imparting information in a fairly concentrated but entertaining way about the castle's buildings and history. It usefully covers an area and aspect of the site which it would not be practical to do using human guides.

Parts of the castle have a museum-style treatment, including the armoury and the display of torture instruments. The dungeon with its rudimentary facilities has small descriptive panels, but far more graphic are the pathetic scratchings of its unfortunate past inmates who occupied the cells until the end of the Civil War.

Another approach has been adopted in the gatehouse and barbican where two rooms are presented in conjectural fashion in what was part of the Receiver General's lodgings in the first half of the fifteenth century.

In other areas we rely on sign boards, or on the odd occasion a small plaque will point out some feature of interest.

In the Undercroft restaurant the heraldic quarterings on the banners of the Earls of Warwick from earliest times is explained on the place mats.

Another way of conveying information and adding a touch of spectacle and colour is through the character of Sir William de Beauchamp who patrols the castle precincts during the Summer months. Based on a character from the castle's history, he will be happy to tell you of his exploits with the Black Prince in Spain, how much his chain mail weighs and if he has attended a course at night school.

The same is true of the many different acts who entertain visitors on Sundays throughout the season. Morris dancers perform every Saturday afternoon from Easter to the end of August and on Sundays you may come upon a regiment of the Sealed Knot Society drilling on the green, or the French Imperial Guard – somewhat out of context but beautifully turned out.

We have emphasized the human contact because we are firmly convinced that we are in the people business', and believe that in an age of burgeoning technological sophistication the personal touch will have an increasingly important role to play in our operation by adding to the charm and almost old-fashioned feeling of the place. In this context it is the 250 staff who make our business a success – the people who run it and 'front it up'. Whilst the physical services and facilities we offer are important, far more important is the need to recruit, train and motivate our staff to deliver a satisfactory experience to our clientele. All our staff have to understand that in our business the customer is literally 'King of the Castle', and all approach their tasks with this in mind. Quality of staff makes the difference in any business and as the field in which we operate is becoming more and more competitive it is crucial that our staff commit themselves to a high quality of service.

When we recruit we concentrate less on an applicant's qualifications and more on an assessment of how they are going to interface with the customer. Their appearance must be right, their disposition cheerful and an evident sense of humour is a valuable asset. They are certainly going to need it. Most of our staff come into contact with visitors and in that respect they are all part of the show. Where guides are concerned, proficiency in a major European language is a distinct asset.

Motivating staff to have a positive attitude towards the visitor is a key part of the management of the business. Recently customer service training has become far more in-depth and is recognized as an area where the enterprise can improve and aim to show the competition 'a clean pair of heels'. Well trained and motivated staff enjoy their work more and achieve more job satisfaction, which in turn passes on to visitors in a positive way. We have regular customer care training sessions which are not simply about being polite to people but are intended to convey to all staff that by a positive contribution in standards of performance wherever they are in the organization they will make a difference and they, their colleagues and the customer will benefit. We have much yet to achieve in this area but we have a structured approach and the indications are that results are coming through. At the end of the day we are aiming to have a polite, presentable and helpful staff, who convey warmth and welcome. A lot depends on this being achieved across the board.

But how do we know if we are succeeding from the visitors' point of view? Constant monitoring and evaluation is essential. We use research to acquire statistical information to build up a profile of our patronage – an essential aid in ensuring that our marketing and promotional activity is well targeted and effective. At the same time we solicit criticisms and suggestions for improvement, and ask whether customers thought the admission fee value for money. This provides us with the ability to monitor our activity and to react accordingly. This type of survey has enabled us to engage extra staff at certain times to plug gaps, provide extra facilities or eradicate entrenched malpractice. Some suggestions, however, we decline to respond to like that of installing a lift in Guy's tower!

We also appoint assessors, who come regularly as ordinary paying visitors and who write up a complete survey of the site in all its aspects. The report that follows highlights areas needing attention and recognizes members of staff whose efforts are over and above the call of duty, or below par. All staff throughout the Tussaud's group know that this system is in operation. The value of this type of unprejudiced analysis is that it keeps staff on their toes and gives departmental management an early warning of potential problem areas to be addressed immediately. Good reports are, of course, useful for morale boosting purposes but written complaints are also taken seriously.

The other side of the personnel equation is the excellent help we receive from our professional advisers, who are regarded in every respect as part of the team. We are fortunate in being able to attract some very good people and they are happy to share the commitment and responsibility of our stewardship as well as making a major contribution to our success. We are not shy about paying for expertise and rely to a large extent on their professional judgement. We also engage various consultants on the same basis and the combined effect of this is to maintain and enhance the product we have to sell. All in all we endeavour, with their assistance, to achieve a situation where commerce and conservation are not in conflict.

There is no doubt that to date the Warwick Castle enterprise has been a success. Over the last ten years, since the purchase, over £4 million has been invested in service infrastructure and presentational improvements. In 1980 a footbridge over the river was erected to take in the castle meadow and give visitors the dramatic view of the River Front. In 1981 the car parks were landscaped from a green field site. In the same year the stables were completely restored and have been gradually improved to provide the services available today. In 1982 'The Royal Weekend Party' opened. In 1985 the castle mound was opened to visitors, and in 1986 the recreated Victorian rose garden. In 1987 the formation of the new restaurant in the stables was completed along with the refurbishment of the restaurant in the undercroft.

This large capital expenditure, which does not include the £500,000 spent annually on the upkeep of the building, grounds and collections which is funded from revenue, has been injected by the Tussaud's group and has been funded without any grants whatsoever. As the castle is part of the Pearson group, a highly successful and well diversified international company, the capital has to be paid back by way of return. The enterprise has for several years been making a commercially attractive return on the capital employed in it. It has been able to do this by attracting an increasing patronage and charging an economic admission fee which, incidentally, over 95 per cent of our visitors regard as value for money, and by running its on-site merchandise, guidebook, catering, banqueting and function ancillary businesses at a good profit as well as being innovative in effecting overhead savings by investment where the opportunities have been identified.

So how do we view the future?

Up to now our costs have risen each year and we have raised our admission charges to cover these as well as profiting from the increasing spending on other services around the site. At the same time we have added extra value for the visitor by developing the resource. This policy we believe accounts for the fact that we enjoy 25 per cent repeat visitors from the market within a sixty-mile radius of Warwick and, therefore, we intend to continue this strategy over the coming years.

We plan to open a further section of the wall walk from Guy's Tower into the gatehouse and also to open a room in the gatehouse on the route which will house a large scale model of the castle together with display boards showing the development of the castle from Norman times. This walk will be further extended from the gatehouse into Caesar's Tower when repairs have been completed. We also hope to let visitors on to the lower parapet in due course – our only contribution to the white knuckle industry! Visitors will gain a far greater perception of how the fortification worked. It will add to their experience and create a major loop to spread them out.

We are restoring the boat house in the castle meadow and will install a modest display about the flora and fauna in the grounds. This will also serve as a starting point for a half-mile walk along the castle meadow, which forms an island in the river. The Warwickshire Nature Conservation Trust and the Royal Society for the Protection of Birds are advising and assisting with this project.

The eighteenth-century conservatory is also being restored to look very much as it did in the latter half of the nineteenth century. This will be followed by the creation of a very convincing replica of the famous Warwick vase, which, sadly, was sold many years ago, but was the original reason for the construction of the conservatory.

In 1991 we shall pause for breath, but will be preparing to open a very major addition to the castle's attractions in 1992. We believe we are not making enough of the opportunities that the resource presents so in that year we shall open a presentation on the last fifty years of the fifteenth century, when the castle was at its height in the ownership of Warwick the Kingmaker, the Duke of Clarence and King Richard III, and was for a time prison to King Edward IV. We shall be using the very latest technology, to tell the story of a time when the castle and its owners were at the very centre of this century's affairs.

Having done this, we believe we will have an incomparable product in our niche in the leisure market. However, we are conscious that we shall fail if we do not continue to address ourselves to the needs of our visitors – the lifeblood of our business. The product is strong, the promotion of the product in the market place is strong, but if the handling of our customers is poor then the inestimable benefit that good referral from satisfied visitors gives will be diminished and the enterprise will not maximize its potential.

This business has, therefore, to become thoroughly professional in its commitment to its customers and we constantly need to assess and improve the way we go about servicing them, adopting the kind of positive attitude outlined in this paper. Above all we need to meet the challenge of the 90s with style and enthusiasm, but also with care. This is the principle behind our recently acquired coat of arms, which recognizes that the castle is no longer a military stronghold or a family home but a great monument to the past for all to experience and enjoy.

The motto is 'We safeguard for the future by serving'.

11

Planning to Improve Service to Visitors in Canada's National Parks

Jenny Feick

For over one hundred years Canada's national park system has grown in extent and sophistication. From its initial beginnings as areas of tourism development in a sea of wilderness to its present state as islands of wild landscape amidst an exploited countryside, the Canadian Park Service's policies and ways of planning for public use have evolved.

National parks staff in Canada have excelled in planning for the care and protection of their natural resources in the past twenty years. To balance this, and in order to secure a place in the minds of the voting public, the Canadian Parks Service is turning to a new way of looking at parks – the visitors' perspective.

The 'Visitor Activity Management Process' is exactly that, a process to manage visitor activities which examines what visitors need in order to take part safely in and enjoy an appropriate activity within parks. In many ways, it is a marketing approach, since it examines client needs and wants, and tries to ensure that what parks offer is packaged in such a way as to satisfy its customers.

The first phase of implementing this process involved extensive visitor surveys in Atlantic Canada, and some planning work in national historic parks in the province of Quebec. A pilot service planning project was then undertaken for the western region (Alberta and British Columbia) of Canada's national park system. It involved the preparation of a 'Visitor Activities Service Plan' for Mount Revelstoke and Glacier national parks in British Columbia's interior mountains.

A service plan functions as a management tool. It translates the conceptual directions in the park management plans into how and when to provide services, including heritage interpretation, to visitors. It provides a comprehensive package on how a park can best offer services for its various types of visitors. The plan is a lean, decision-oriented document which links directly to the Canadian Parks Service's approval systems for financial and human resources. It stresses action, is updated annually, and is reviewed every five years.

The superintendent of Mount Revelstoke and Glacier national parks, involved every manager in the development of the plan. A service planning training course was held in March 1987 prior to initiating the project. All park managers, as well as advisors in the regional office in Calgary, Alberta, were consulted throughout the plan's preparation. Involving the managers instead of hiring a planner of consultant, meant reshuffling roles and responsibilities within the organization. As usual, such changes cause some problems and some opportunities for individuals. However, everyone was convinced that the plan, once finished, would prove its worth, and involving managers would ensure greater commitment to the plan's implementation.

The process of producing a service plan involves the following seven basic steps:

Stage 1: Terms of Reference

Stage 1 is to produce a *terms of reference*. This requires a description of what you plan to do and how you are going to do it, and commitment must be secured from other participants.

Stage 2: Review the Current Situation

Stage 2 reviews the current situation and produces the database.

This part of the process can take at least six months, subject to the amount of market information about visitors. Parks that have existing marketing plans and visitor surveys will find this phase quicker and easier.

The team compiled and organized existing socio-economic data developing a market segmentation approach to the visitors, lumping groups with common expectations and activities into six categories which were ranked in order of importance:

Frontcountry users – the largest market of real park users; those who picnic, stop at roadside viewpoints, camp in major camp grounds, walk the self-guiding trails, visit the Rogers Pass Information Centre, drive the Summit Drive to the top of Mount Revelstoke, or who ski or toboggan near the base of Mount Revelstoke. They often have less than a day to spend in either park, and many share concerns about venturing into the rugged wilderness beyond the Trans Canada Highway or Summit Drive.

Offsite groups – this small group uses the park as an educational resource, and supports the educational mandate of the Canadian Parks Service. They request special interpretive programmes outside the parks' boundaries, or written and/or photographic assistance with school projects and research. They may visit the parks as a result of the off-site or extension service provided for them by park interpreters.

Wilderness enthusiasts – this small but keen group loves the challenge of

Figure 11.1   Mount Revelstoke National Park. How do you interpret the rugged
back-country effectively? This is an issue dealt with by the service plan.

hiking, backpacking, mountain biking, ski touring, mountaineering and
caving in the backcountry areas of the wild Columbia Mountains preserved
by Mount Revelstoke and Glacier National Park. They often seek very
detailed information on natural history and skill and equipment requirements prior to their trip. Participants in the all-day interpretive hikes into the
backcountry also form part of this group.

Through travellers – this enormous group of people pass through the two
parks on the Trans Canada Highway, or as passengers on VIA Rail along
the Canadian Pacific Transcontinental Railway. Any interest they take in the
parks is incidental; they are on their way somewhere else. They are usually
in a hurry and dislike sharing the road with tourists slowing down to look
at the scenery or to stop at a visitor facility. They make up the majority of
the people on the highway access into the parks, especially during the avalanche season from November to April.

Waterway users – this tiny group combines the desire for physical challenge
with a short time frame and a front-country venue. The few river experiences
the parks offer canoeists, kayakers and rafters are short and dangerous.

Along with this market segmentation, a visitor survey was initiated to test
how the parks were meeting the expectations of our visitors. This confirmed
many of the staff's gut feelings, but also provided a few surprises. Many
people prayed that the parks would not become another Banff National Park,
with its crowded, commercial areas. They complained about the poor

directional signage, dangerous intersections, the lack of showers and campfire talks in camp grounds, and the weather. They praised the park interpretive programmes self-guiding trails and Rogers Pass Information Centre, the hospitable park staff, the clean facilities and the scenery.

Service planning step number two also meant reviewing the immense database which dealt with the parks' heritage resources, and developing theme statements, park stories and messages – the basis for a parks communications programme. Again, it was necessary to decide which themes and messages had to assume the highest priority, and which were less important to communicate to every visitor.

The park themes developed for the two parks are: hard rock mountains carpeted by lush rain forests and Alpine Meadows (Mount Revelstoke National Park); a wilderness fortress of icy barriers and thundering snows (Glacier National Park).

Themes included both natural and human history topics relevant to each park. Some of these themes, such as 'Rain Forest, Snow Forest, No Forest – the Columbia Mountains Lifezones', applied to both parks, even though this one formed a more significant part of the story of Mount Revelstoke National Park. Others, like 'the Birthplace of North American Mountaineering' or 'Karst Anomaly – the Nakimu Caves Story', applied only to one park, in these two cases, Glacier.

Management messages ranged from explaining the avalanche control programme in operation unique to the Rogers Pass area of the Trans Canada Highway to the changing national stand on forest fire management with national parks. Ensuring that visitors received information on opportunities for recreational and educational opportunities, as well as skill and equipment requirements, and public safety warning were all top priorities.

In the last major part of step number two, it was necessary to clarify the existing visitor provision in the parks (how many picnic areas, how many interpretive exhibits on what themes etc.), as well as what the surrounding region offers to visitors (both complementary services like marinas, helicopter hiking and downhill ski areas, and similar services such as camp grounds and picnic areas). Opportunities that could be developed were listed, such as new hiking trails or a mountaineering ski equipment rental and guiding service. The park wardens helped note any environmental and/or public safety concerns associated with existing or potential services to visitors.

Analyse the Database

The next step is the process of analysing the database and identifying shortfalls, gaps in service and issues to resolve. Not surprisingly hundreds of issues emerged – too many to resolve in the planning exercise. Some issues, such as national policies and fees, had to be 'sent upstairs' to Head Office to deal with. Others were lower priority items which could wait for a few years (nice

Figure 11.2   Glacier National Park. One of the objectives of service planning is to ensure that visitors can travel safely in dangerous areas, like glaciers, by being well informed about skill and equipment requirements before setting off.

to have but not essential according to present statistics and/or safety concerns, for example portages along the Beaver River or Nordic ski trails in Glacier). All service-related issues were organized into categories based on the six visitor activity groups' critical needs within the next five-year time period.

The gap-finding exercise was interesting. This identified that there was not overall orientation to the park story of Glacier National Park at the major visitor focal point, the Rogers Pass Information Centre. The history of Rogers Pass was interpreted well, and through the movie *Snow War* the tale of avalanches was told. An even more serious concern was the fact that there was almost no interpretation at Mount Revelstoke National Park; the information centre and interpretive programmes at Glacier National Park drained the existing resources of the interpretive service. It also became clear that services had been cut back to off-site groups, as resources got tighter. These groups included many local children, who could influence the future of parks as they reached voting age. There was also limited information to waterway users, yet staff participated in a few rescues each year, sometimes involving fatalities. Dangerous intersections, poor directional signage and a lack of key amenities, such as showers in the camp grounds were confirmed as issues to be dealt with.

Stage 4: Develop Measurable Objectives and Goals

The fourth stage is to develop measurable objectives and overall goals for providing services to visitors. This was done in parallel with the listing of shortfalls and issues' taking advice and direction from the superintendent, the draft management plans for the two parks, and regional office specialists.

The objectives provided measurable targets within the basic service areas:

- increase visitation during times of year and in places where the environment could withstand more use without damage.
- promote awareness of the two parks and the Columbia Mountains, a mountain region of Canada much less well known than the Rockies to the east.
- provide excellent pre-trip planning information to potential visitors.
- provide excellent reception, orientation and information on the recreational and educational opportunities available in the two parks.
- provide excellent recreational opportunities appropriate to the rugged wilderness character of each park.
- provide excellent and varied educational opportunities through personal and non-personal means so that visitors could appreciate and experience the park themes and messages.
- provide excellent support facilities and safe access to these opportunities.
- provide opportunities for all users of park facilities and services to give comments and suggestions for improvement of facilities and services.
- provide excellent educational services to off-site groups, especially in the local area.
- provide opportunities for people to volunteer and otherwise co-operate or co-venture with the parks, such as by participating in the Friends of Mount Revelstoke and Glacier.
- integrate and co-operate with the local communities of Revelstoke and Golden, in order to provide a good all-round experience for visitors to the area.

Stage 5: An Overall Service Strategy

Stage 5 is the production of an overall service strategy.

This is the most enjoyable part of the planning exercise – coming up with solutions to problems, resolving issues and developing strategies. Obviously there are differences of opinion regarding which services to assign the highest priority, or which trails should no longer be maintained if or when more budget cuts occur. The end result was numerous flip chart sheets summarizing the basic goals, critical base data and issues related to them, and strategies and implementation/action plans for each issue.

Stage 6: Writing the Service Plan

The sixth stage is the actual writing of the service plan. From day one all the data was gathered on computer file using the word processor as a means of continually updating and revising the draft sections of the plan as it was developed. Thus, a draft plan up to the identification of issues and objectives could be quickly finalized with the material generated from the flip chart sheets.

Stage 7: Review and Assessment

The final stage involves reviewing and assessing the document, making revisions and seeking final approval.

Even in its draft form the service plan has:

(1) helped park managers identify and respond to the needs of their visitors;
(2) provided an integrated approach to planning and delivering interpretation, and other visitor services in a safe and environmentally sensitive manner;
(3) encouraged a team approach to park management;
(4) helped managers make better decisions and assisted them in defending these decisions by justifying and prioritizing them;
(5) allowed them to apply marketing principles and techniques to programme planning;
(6) translated directly into action for annual operational work plans, as well as more long-range funding requests;
(7) helped plan for and manage change in leisure patterns and socio-economic trends.

As this new approach was pioneered growing pains were expected. There were some frustrating moments as things were tried manually, only to discover that they were cumbersome, unnecessary and/or excessively time-consuming. The biggest difficulty was enabling the two key players, both managers, to have sufficient backup staff support to allow them time to contribute meaningfully to the project, and keep the other managers informed and supportive of the project.

The pilot project tested the waters and found them navigable. Several other parks in western region – Kootenay and Yoho in the Rocky Mountains – are near completion with their own service planning projects. They have been able to forge ahead more quickly, applying knowledge gained in the project in Mount Revelstoke and Glacier national parks. Many other national parks, as well as two of the region's national historic parks, are starting service planning. Other regions of Canada, especially Ontario and Prairie Regions, have also embarked up this new, commonsense approach to planning within the Canadian Parks Service.

12

The Visitor – Who Cares?
Interpretation and Consumer Relations

Terry Stevens

Introduction

Probably the most important management fundamental that is being ignored today is staying close to the customer to satisfy her needs and anticipate his wants. In too many companies the customer has become a bloody nuisance whose unpredictable behaviour damages carefully made strategic plans, whose activities mess up computer operations, who dirties displays, and who insists that purchased products should work. (Young, 1980)

This quotation seems particularly relevant to interpretation in the form in which it has been experienced over the past fifteen years. What is of greatest concern, however, is that the message explicit in these words needs to be stressed at all.

That interpretation ought to be close to its customers seems a benign enough message. Why does it need restating? The answer is that despite all the lip service given to market orientation in leisure service provision in general, and interpretation in particular, the consumer is either ignored, considered a nuisance, or is given superficial treatment by market researchers.

The result, at its extreme, is that interpreters force our messages, our stories and our interests down the throats of and into the minds of our visitors. Increasingly we engage modern techniques to create exciting experiences to make heritage palatable and easier to digest.

Interpretation is, today, in greater danger of being hijacked by the designers and media technocrats than ever before. The media is becoming the message.

Technological wizardry, media consultants, audio-animatronics, innovative presentations – these are the buzz words to switch on the lights in tourist board offices around the world. Are we, however, being true to the spirit of interpretation? Are we being true to our profession? Are we paying due regard to the needs, demands, aspirations and sophistications of our visitors?

The new 'designer-led' interpretation is successful. It is only necessary to see

Jorvik, Wigan Pier and others, but take away the novelty elements such as videos, actors and computers and analyse the story, and how well does it stand up?

Interpretation – a Marketing Focus

Freeman Tilden (1957) was, arguably, marketing orientated. Although the resource gave being to his interpretation, the *reason* for this interpretation was people, the consumers of interpretation.

Tilden's six principles of interpretation would sit happily in any discourse on marketing. The principles of interpretation are the embodiment of customer care and give pre-eminence to the consumer.

In leisure services we have traditionally relegated customer care to somewhere in the third or fourth divisions. Generally speaking, it is easy to see why leisure is regarded as:

– a free good;
– not concerned with market loyalty;
– unable or unwilling to identify markets;
– lacking any understanding of marketing;
– involving resource managers to the exclusion of other specialists.

Times are changing. Greater accountability, a pressure to demonstrate economic return, increased competition, enhanced awareness and sophistication in the market place are necessitating change.

Evidence elsewhere in leisure consumer research shows that the perceptions by managers of customer interest, background and tolerances are far removed from the reality of the market place. Interpreters have been using market research rather as a drunk uses a lamp post – for support *not* illumination. The visitor wants the story told well and in an authentic, well managed environment with effective and trained staff. There is clear evidence that superficial presentations of packaged heritage do not sustain interest or gain support. It is logical to suggest, therefore, that our primary concerns and messages are more likely to be effective and well received if we take more time and effort to get to know, to understand and to stay close to our customers.

Because interpretation is elective, it should not be eclectic. Current trends in interpretation are assuming visitors' interest. Presentations are being reduced to the lowest common denominator. Our problem as interpreters used to be with the subject specialists such as archaeologists, botanists or geologists, who would allow no popularization of their subject. Our challenge today is to ensure that interpretation is based upon our understanding of the resource being interpreted, and understanding the character and nature of our customers.

Customer Care — an Attitude Approach

Caring for our customers clearly implies far more than simply presenting an interpretive story that appeals. Indeed, recent research indicates that the interpretation is unlikely to be successful at all, no matter how well presented, if the supporting services are impoverished or poorly managed.

A review of visitor reactions to a variety of heritage properties concludes that 'poor responses' to the sites are stimulated by specific issues and encounters: 'toilets are dirty'; 'tea stewed'; 'guidebook expensive'; 'poor signposting'. These responses will colour the whole experience. They make or break a visit.

A 'good' experience is prompted by general impressions and is summarized by general comments, such as that it is 'clean ... friendly ... nice atmosphere'.

It is important for any interpretive effort, therefore, to get the ancillary and support services correct. Specific negative comments relate to day-to-day management, general comments relate to policy. This means that action can be taken to improve the situation. It also means that action needs to be taken.

Development of interpretive themes, and successfully maintaining the centrality of your presentation to visitor interests, is the interpretive challenge of customer care. Getting and staying close to your visitors and reacting upon the feedback, should ensure increased efficiency of interpretive efforts. This should be relatively easy to achieve because, unlike the marketing of other products or services, the interpreter is working in productive markets. Visitors are generally on your side. The interpreter should act as their 'friend', because visitors are, in the words of the Strawbs, 'in need of a friend'. As the 'friend' and as the purveyor of the story interpreters are in a privileged position. This is a matter of concern, especially as it is possible to misuse this power which has allowed the profession, and our heritage, to be hijacked.

Heritage Illusions

➤ There are also wider concerns of creating the illusion of heritage. This was recently articulated, for example, by Dai Smith, Professor of Welsh History, in relation to the proposed Rhondda Heritage Park in South Wales. He is of the view that history is liberating, heritage interpretation is suffocating.

The interpreter is the *dreamseller* in the tourist's voyage through many different *dreamlands*. Dreamsellers are important and influential people as the rock group Lindisfarne explains,

Hey Mr. Dreamseller Where have you been,
Tell me have you dreams I can see,
I came along just to bring you this song,

Can you spare a dream for me.
You won't have met me and you'll soon forget me
So don't mind me tugging at your sleeve,
I'm asking you if I can fix a rendezvous,
Your dreams are all I believe.
(from: Lindisfarne, 'Meet Me on The Corner')

Since reality does not exist in itself, we create it, with the result that each society and each age has different versions of what reality might be. The interpreter of these interpretations is the interpreter.

Most heritage sites we see are relics of previous declarations of reality – discarded dreamlands which we can never really understand but which have now been turned into dreamlands of another kind (Horne, 1984).

Dominant versions of reality tend to suit dominant groups and are used to uphold certain social and cultural orders. Thus the interpreter, in order to present the truth, is fighting to survive.

Interpreters immediately run the risk of stereotyping our visitors, our storylines, and our heritage. We reconstruct an image of an age in languages of legitimacy. We build images from preconceptions at once compounded and reaffirmed. To modify Horne's comment, 'I like butterfly collecting, interpretation is a mere matter of classification unless we learn how to read at least some of the stereotypes'. Again, as Horne writes,

Would we admire the Parthenon if it was roofed, and repainted in its original red, blue and gold . . . if we re-installed the huge gaudy like figure of Athena. We are likely to undermine and destroy our whole concept of the classical – did the Greeks have bad taste?

It is not the intention to redefine or re-establish the role of interpretation. It seems, however, that the role of the interpreter is to give guidance to his or her customers by stimulating an interest within them, to help them understand the resource which is being interpreted. This essentially means: getting close to your customer; staying close to your customer; and reacting positively to the knowledge gained.

Customer care is an attitude. It is an attitude central to the philosophy of interpretation, certainly as defined by Tilden (1957). Customer care does not mean commercial exploitation. Far from it, customer care programmes in interpretation are more likely to achieve the primary objective of the interpretive effort, namely the creation of discovery and a sense of wonder, as the rock song writer Van Morrison relates,

Gave me pictures in the gallery
Gave me novels on the shelf
Gave me dreams and gave me nightmares
Gave me knowledge of myself
(from: Van Morrison 'Tore down à la Rimbaud)

Conclusion

'We are in a highly competitive business and face a somewhat unpredictable economic climate, and this means that we must more than ever give our customers better service and better value than our competitors' (Peters and Waterman, 1982).

The strength of our business depends on the goodwill of our customers. Service to our customers is influenced more than anything by our attitude to our customers, and the ability to see things through their eyes.

References

Horne, D. (1984) *The Great Museum*, Pluto Press, London.

Peters, T.J. and Waterman, R.H. (1982) *In Search of Excellence*, Harper and Row, New York.

Tilden, F. (1957) *Interpreting Our Heritage*, University of North Carolina Press, Chapel Hill.

Young, L. (1980) 'Views on management', quoted in Peters, and Waterman (1982).

13

Managing the Town and City for Visitors and Local People

Ian Parkin, Peter Middleton and Val Beswick

The essence of the heritage and leisure business is to give visitors a high quality, value for money, memorable and pleasurable experience. It is only by achieving this that visitors will stay longer than they originally anticipated, spend more, leave satisfied, eager to return and, perhaps most important, want to tell their friends. Recent research in Wales suggests that if a visitor is pleased with a facility they will tell four friends it is worth visiting. If it was not a pleasurable experience then they will tell twenty-three! The message is surely well made!

But where and when does the visitor experience start? In many ways, it can be argued, the promotion and marketing to create initial awareness that the facility or attraction exists and to stimulate enough interest to decide to visit is the starting point. This is a specialism in its own right and beyond the scope of this paper. Nevertheless, it emphasizes the importance of a clear, unambiguous concept for the facility which can capture the potential visitor first time through visual images on leaflets, and in the media.

We would argue that the visit starts when the visiting group, whatever it comprises, starts its journey to the facility by whatever means it chooses, whether by car, bus, coach, train or on foot. It is important in trying to cater, or 'care' for the visitor that every step along the way is considered as part of a strategy or *visitor management plan*. Each element is important and a lack of caring, whether it be in the signing, car parking, quality of catering or the cleanliness of the toilets, can destroy the overall visitor experience. It can convert a personal recommendation to a negative response.

This 'visitor ethic', so powerfully demonstrated by the Disney Organization, is increasingly being recognized by providers of heritage, countryside and leisure attractions. At a time when there is increasing competition to attract the leisure pound or dollar, providers need to consider the total 'presentation' of their facility. Issues like a sense of arrival and welcome, friendly, helpful staff and the overall ambience of the site are as crucial as the 'core experience' itself.

We would suggest that whilst many providers in towns and cities are aware of the need to present their facilities to the highest possible standards within their pay boundary, they are not so conscious of the need to consider the 'first impressions' that can so often influence the visitors' overall perception of the place.

A site like Warwick Castle, which attracts 650,000 visitors per year, clearly presents itself to visitors in a highly professional way. However, visitors to Warwick Castle inevitably have to travel through the town to reach the castle. Visitor perceptions of this section of their journey immediately prior to arrival can colour attitudes about the total experience. It is in the interests of Warwick Castle management that this last mile of the visitors' journey is as attractive, pleasant and easy to take as possible. Clean pavements, tree-lined streets, hanging baskets, attractive street furniture and good, clear road signing provide a high quality sense of arrival.

It is also in the interests of the traders, the local authority and the townspeople that such an impression is created. If the town is itself attractive and welcoming then visitors are likely to stay longer to enjoy the streets, shops, churches and museums, and not just the castle. By staying longer visitors will spend more, thereby bringing economic benefit to the town and its people, creating jobs, raising incomes and the general standard of living.

It is therefore important to consider a heritage attraction in its wider context. It is not sufficient any more to provide a quality experience in isolation. We believe that first impressions colour the overall experience. This is particularly important when a facility is within the built fabric of a town or city where car parking is not always within the attraction, and where visitors perhaps have to walk from a station, coach drop-off point or car park to the attraction entrance. In Portsmouth, for instance, the car park and station serving the Historic Dockyard heritage attractions is nearly half a mile away. Assuming the road signing is good enough to ensure that visitors reach the car park without any problems, the walk to Victory Gate becomes an integral part of the total visitor experience. If it is litter strewn, with broken trees, puddles from poor paving, and with a variety of street signs, seats and litter bins, then it will not 'set the scene' for visitors in the way the attractions would wish.

If, however, a tree-lined 'heritage route' is created which is well maintained with attractive paving detailing, a series of interpretive panels introducing the story of the community of Portsea and its relationship to the Dockyard, simple rationalized signing and street furniture, then there is both a sense of 'caring' and of anticipation that the visitor is approaching somewhere rather special.

Both the Warwick and Portsmouth examples illustrate a dilemma. The heritage attractions operate within a discreet pay boundary but the wider environmental considerations are the responsibility of the local authority, the business community and residents. Yet if all parties can be brought together then everyone would benefit. Whose responsibility is this? The local authority which is being increasingly squeezed financially, the Chamber of

Commerce, a local tourism association or civic society? Things are even more complicated when different local authority departments have responsibility to tackle specific aspects of the package, for example signing and interpretation, paving, landscaping, street furniture, but nobody has the overall responsibility. There is a need to break down barriers and bring the different factions together to work together for a common cause.

We would suggest that the problems are not only related to the needs of a single visitor attraction within a town or city. In many places it is the town itself that is an attraction in its own right. People visit York as much for the quaint medieval streets, beautiful buildings and quality shopping as for York Minster, Jorvik and Castle Museum. Yet the same principles of caring for the visitor adopted within a visitor attraction need to be applied to the environmental quality and overall ambience of the wider town. This relates to the streetscape – surfaces, furniture, light fittings, water, art and sculpture, the facades of buildings, the approach to name boards and the overall management. It is an ethic of 'good housekeeping' involving all the senses.

We have devised a series of criteria which can be used to evaluate whether a town has the potential for attracting visitors and to assess what is required in terms of visitor provision to capitalize on that potential. They comprise a mixture of planning and architectural factors related to the quality and strength of the town as a 'visitor resource', the available market and the quality and extent of the themes associated with the town. We call it a *tourism town appraisal*.

Introduction and Background

(1) Is there community interest and involvement?

(2) Which is the local authority?

(3) Does it have a track record for innovation, investment, in-house skills and a commitment to make the most of its area?

(4) On what is the wealth of the town based?

(5) Who are the key employers today?

(6) What is the strength of the voluntary sector? Local civic or amenity groups, interest groups?

(7) Is the town easily accessible to existing visitors in the surrounding area?

(8) What is the quality of the road network? Of rail, seaport, airport transport links?

(9) Does the town have the physical and psychological capacity to accept more visitors?

Existing Initiatives

(1) Is there a 'Town Scheme'?

(2) Are there Conservation Areas, Tree Preservation Orders etc.?

(3) Are there any special designations, e.g. Assisted Area status, Rural Development Area, Less Favoured Area etc.? And if so, what special grant eligibilities apply?

(4) Are there existing interpretive, educational or environmental initiatives using Training Commission, UK 2,000 etc.?

(5) Are there any other injections of mainstream local authority budgets going into the town – highways, pedestrianization, environmental, 'above shop' grants etc.?

'Welcome' to the Visitor

(1) Are there 'welcome' signs at the entrances to the town?

(2) How good is the signposting generally – including to car parks, visitor destinations etc.?

(3) What is the quality of car parking – are the car parks landscaped, surfaced etc.?

(4) Is there visitor orientation at entrance points and disembarkation points, i.e. car parks, bus and coach stops, railway station?

(5) Is there a 'scene-setter' or 'gateway' facility to the town – a small town museum, or anywhere at which the visitor can be introduced to the 'essence of the town'?

The Core Visitor Experience

(1) What is the type and quality of the environmental setting, e.g. hollow, hillside, riverside, forest?

(2) What is the quality of the townscape – any gaps in terrace, ginnels, pedestrian areas, cobbled streets, street furniture etc.?

(3) Are there buildings, terraces, streets, churches of outstanding architectural quality and interest? Listed or not?

(4) Evaluate the landscape quality – open spaces, tree-lined streets, landscape, quality of detailing?

(5) Is there a sense of 'care' and pride – no litter, graffiti, vandalism, empty/boarded-up buildings, empty upper floors of shops?

(6) Is the appropriateness and quality of shopfronts in keeping with the character of the town?

Things to See and Do

(1) What is the level of existing interpretation – orientation, museum, market plaques on buildings, wayside interpretive panels, guided walks, publications, town trails etc.?

(2) Are there stories to tell? What are their strengths, variety, relevance, availability, uniqueness? How important are they – locally, regionally, nationally?

(3) Are there links to other themes or sites in the vicinity which strengthen the heritage appeal?

(4) Does the town celebrate itself already with events, festivals, markets, or allied attractions?

(5) What opportunities are there to develop a heritage centre – available buildings, 'core' local interest, financial resources, a group that could take 'the lead'?

(6) Is there significant educational appeal which could strengthen the product, for example, with a classroom, meeting room, resource centre with seconded teacher etc.?

(7) Are there specific visitor attractions in or nearby the town?

The Visitor Services

All of the following should be considered;

(1) availability of car parks and toilets – well lit and easily accessible?

(2) availability of public transport?

(3) food and drink opportunities?

(4) quality, range and accessibility of shopping – particularly speciality shopping, markets, crafts etc.?

(5) availability of overnight accommodation?

(6) opportunities for evening entertainment? Weather-independent venues?

(7) quality and range of picnic/play area facilities – parks, gardens, riverside walks etc.?

(8) waymarked footpath links to the wider countryside?

(9) waymarked routes, tourist information points, for leaving the town to go on to the next destination?

Using this schedule it is possible to devise a strategy for upgrading the town in environmental terms to relate to the needs of visitors and local people. The involvement and support of local people is crucial; not only does this engender a sense of pride in the town but they become its ambassadors. It is not without reason that tourist towns are embarking on training courses on 'facing the public' and 'customer care' for hotel reception staff, taxi drivers, shopkeepers and publicans. These are 'front line' staff who can make or mar a visitor's perception of a town. Their approach to visitors can influence length of stay and spend in a place.

We would argue that the appraisal and overall philosophy in managing the environment can and should also be applied to our cities. Urban regeneration is all about the revival and reawakening of the decayed, diseased and previously ignored parts of our towns and cities. An enormous amount of practical and financial energy is being focused on these areas, and the effects are beginning to show. Most of the changes, however, are to do with the 'hardware' of buildings and the spaces between them. Rather less attention is being paid to the 'software' of management, environment theming, interpretation and visitor services.

The quality of the hardware itself, within the walls and pay boundaries of commercial developments, retail schemes, visitor attractions and so on, is increasingly high. But the quality of the interconnecting environment – to create the 'total visitor experience' – is frequently poor. Standards of customer care are inconsistent and mediocre; streets and landscaped areas are poorly maintained; signage is not visitor orientated; interpretation is haphazard or non-existent. The result for visitors is a fragmented experience with high standards within facilities simply heightening the contrast outside them.

In short, the whole is not more than a sum of the parts. 'District Neighbourhoods' and 'Quarters of Cities' that are of great appeal and interest to visitors are remembered as a series of poorly connected *events* – not as an orchestrated *experience* of *exceptional quality*.

In cities like Manchester, Sheffield, Coventry, Newcastle, Birmingham and Liverpool massive investment is being channelled by both the private and the public sector into relatively concentrated areas. Some have an area focus because of an Urban Development Corporation, or the activities of organizations such as Pheonix. Others have conceptually declared 'quarters' for example Sheffield's 'Art Quarter', Birmingham's 'Media' and 'Jewellery' Quarters, Coventry's 'Cathedral Quarter' or heritage areas – for example, Manchester's Castlefields Urban Heritage Park. The skills to deliver 'hardware' regeneration are available and increasingly in place. But an appreciation of the equal need for investment in software and a new range of skills for 'quarter management' is much less evident.

The opportunity is there to build on and support the process of regeneration and make it more rounded and whole. The objective is to make our towns and cities more visitor friendly, better places to visit, to live and work in. One of the problems is that local people can easily become anaesthetized to their surroundings and not see the litter and lack of care. It is the visitors who have the highest standards. If we meet their needs we will also meet the needs of local people.

The real problem at the end of the day is the one of responsibility. How can the perceived needs of Portsmouth, Warwick or Manchester be tackled comprehensively? The responsibility for urban management and visitor services are split between numerous organizations with a myriad different objectives, delivery standards and perspectives. The achievement of quality standards, the filling in of gaps in services and the theming and interpretation of the total environment is a complex set of tasks requiring sensitivity, exceptional software management skills and the ability to instil a belief in a culture of excellence.

There is a need to extend the concept of town centre management currently related to retailing to the wider town and city environment. Perhaps a 'heritage area management service' needs to be established – initially local authority led – but with representation and financial support from all sections of the community – Chamber of Commerce, traders' associations, visitor attractions, civic societies etc. There need to be highly professional staff capable of co-ordinating initiatives, raising sponsorship and other funding to 'make things happen'.

The Benefits of This Approach

What are the benefits of this approach?
– Visitors stay longer, spend more, give positive recommendations to others.
– Greater visibility and identity for towns and parts of cities at a level people can respond to.
– Friendliness, brighter, cleaner, more interesting towns and cities.
– A sense of pride and achievement.
– Belief in a culture of excellence.

We would suggest that there is a growing realization of the importance of such an approach. The great need is to establish the mechanism by which it can be set in motion. The local authorities and tourism associations must be the catalysts but the private sector will inevitably be a major financial contributor as it is likely to be the greatest beneficiary in the long term.

14

Interpretive Planning for Regional Visitor Experience: A Concept whose Time has Come

Alan Capelle, John Veverka and Gary Moore

Introduction

A vital component of any directed, successful visitor services programme is the need for a detailed systems interpretive plan. However, interpretive planning in many countries today still remains largely misunderstood and ignored by many agencies responsible for interpretive services. It is often characterized by:

* a bewildering and confusing array of methodologies many of which remain outdated but utilized mainly for the purposes of tradition, rather than their effectiveness or ease of understanding;
* the following of a strict agency perspective when planning is undertaken, with little regard to neighbouring resource sites which may directly relate thematically; and
* a strong programming emphasis on the part of the managers, who either ignore or push aside planning. In many instances, it would appear that high level agency administrators are more interested in maximum site (or overall agency) programming data than in whether programme objectives are being met, or whether the programme reflects the particular site resources. In addition, because many site interpreter staff levels are relatively 'thin', planning tends, unfortunately, to be placed very low on the priority list of responsibilities.

The lack of proper attention to the need and value of interpretive planning often reflects unorganized interpretive activities which not only are 'homogeneous' in nature, but often reflect the interests of the interpreter, not the resource base or the visitor. As Cherem (1979) states, 'this piecemeal approach can result in such a jumbled and overlapping array of offerings, that it is a wonder the visitor takes away anything at all from his regional interpretive experience. As a result, key linkages between themes and subthemes are seldom made.' There is a need for better co-ordination between agencies in planning the visitor experience on a *regional* basis, rather than agencies continuing to 'do their own thing' in a somewhat isolated vacuum. Each resource area is unique and some themes are better represented in certain areas than others in a given region.

What Is the Systems Approach?

The regional, systems approach is 'simply a way of thinking about the total system and its components' (Systems Planning Group, Alberta Provincial Parks, 1977). Planners at each park or site within an agency would consider the stories, themes and facilities at other parks or sites both within and outside the administrative and geographical boundaries of that agency.

This would result in more economical resource use, more effective message presentation and would provide a more complete understanding of the central themes for visitors who may visit more than one park or site within a given region. Visitors may be encouraged to visit other parks or sites in the region to 'complete the story' they began at one park or site within the area covered by the scope of the interpretive systems plan. (Traweek et al., 1979).

Value of Regional Interpretive Planning

The value of undertaking inter-agency interpretive planning on a regional basis is substantial and well worth the effort:

The following are but a few of the potential advantages associated with the systems approach:

(1) It integrates related facilities, themes and stories within an agency or with several agencies.
(2) It facilitates the utilization of natural, physiographic, historical and cultural resources and stories which might otherwise be ignored or overlooked.
(3) It makes evaluation of interpretive plans and programs easier and more meaningful by pointing out excessive duplication and omissions within the interpretive system. (Traweek et al., 1979)

Recent Advancements

Fortunately, in the past few years, the concept of regional systems planning for interpretation has been advanced by a few agencies and individuals. The following represents a sample of some of these noteworthy achievements:

* Establishment of regional based inter-agency committees focusing on information exchange, interpretation and educational activities in the states of Minnesota, Michigan and Illinois (USA);
* Completion of a 'Biocultural Systems Plan' for the Minnesota State Parks System in the USA;

* Completion of the first systems plans for Metro Parks, Columbus and Franklin County, Ohio, USA in 1984, and the Illinois and Michigan Canal National Heritage Corridor in Joliet, Illinois, in 1988;
* Integrating interpretive activities into regional tourism plans and activities such as been done very successfully in Rochester, New York, for several years, in the state of Hawaii through the 'Interpret Hawaii Project' and now along the riverfront in Minneapolis, Minnesota;
* Such universities as Ohio State, Winona State and the University of Alberta (Canada) have developed systems-oriented interpretive field studies and planning courses.

Regional Planning and Recent USA Federal Legislation

Recent federal legislation for certain units of the national park system has not only facilitated, but mandated the necessity for inter-agency co-operation in interpretive planning efforts. A linear corridor in the state of Illinois (USA) highlights the uniqueness of this relatively new legislation.

On 24 August 1984, Public Law 98-398, the 'Illinois and Michigan Canal National Heritage Corridor Act of 1984' took effect. This legislation cited the fact that there was an abundance of sites and structures within a ninety-five-mile linear corridor stretching from Chicago to LaSalle-Peru, Illinois. The purpose of this title was to retain, enhance and interpret the cultural, historical, natural, recreational and economic resources of the corridor, where feasible, consistent with industrial and economic growth. A twenty plus member commission was established on a fixed term to carry out the duties of Public Law 98-398, and encourage *voluntary* co-operation and co-ordination between the federal government, the state, political subdivisions of the state, and non-profit organizations with respect to ongoing interpretive services in the corridor.

Impact of Legislation on Interpretive Services Planning

Since the National Park Service and the Illinois and Michigan Canal National Heritage Corridor Commission were not bestowed any land ownership responsibility in the Act, it has created a situation where this corridor and its multitude of federal, state, county, city, private and non-profit agencies/organizations must co-operate with each other in interpretive planning, site planning and development, and programming efforts. The process of utilizing a regional, inter-agency approach to planning visitor experiences in the corridor has been very successful. Each organization has an equal opportunity in decision-making, and the interpretive activities for each site best represent those themes that are representative of each individual site within the 'system'. A formal, inter-agency committee is charged with the responsibility of co-ordinating current and future interpretive developments, and appears to be working quite efficiently.

Toward a Global Approach to Interpretive Planning

The previously cited regional systems interpretive plans, in addition to evolving inter-agency advancements, clearly demonstrates the fact that in preparing ourselves for the future the regional approach to planning does work effectively and should be seriously considered by all agencies as the 'standard' approach to interpretive planning. The development of regional interpretive experiences can, and does, work successfully if agencies take the initiative and allow the process to occur in a supportive and uninhibited climate. Just as it is no longer appropriate to hire interpreters who begrudgingly communicate with visitors, no longer is it appropriate for agencies to work reluctantly with sister agencies in interpretive planning activities. The 'yoke' of the territorial imperative must be lifted off the backs of agencies by sensitive and enlightened managers who can appreciate the benefits of planning interpretive services on a regional scale, not the traditional site-only basis.

The limited but growing success in the United States and Canada in employing this concept bodes well for expansion of the regional systems approach on a global scale. Any country contemplating interpretive planning should seriously consider employing a regional, systems approach. As Cherum (1979) states, 'the need for regional organization and balance in our interpretive offerings has never been more apparent. Further, those who travel to another region will become less and less tolerant of non-coherent and overlapping interpretive experiences.' Interpretive planning for co-ordinated and balanced regional visitor experiences not only makes sense from an operational and financial accountability standpoint, but the process is truly a technique 'whose time has come'.

References

Capelle, A.D. (1985) *Interpretive Field Studies: Agent for Inter-agency Cooperation and Coordination.* First World Congress on Heritage Interpretation & Presentation, Banff, Alberta, Canada.

Capelle, A.D. (1986) *Improving Professional Productivity Through Regional Inter-agency Coordination.* Developing Human Potential in Natural Resources Conference, Tennessee Valley Authority, LBL, Golden Pond, Kentucky, USA.

Cherum, G.J. (1979) *Regional Interpretation Systems. Western Interpreters Association Journal.*

Moore, G.R. and Veverka, J.A. (1987) *An Interpretive Systems Master Plan: a Working Model Plan for Interpretive system Managers.* Association of Interpretive Naturalists/Western Interpreters Assocation National Interpreter's Workshop, St Louis, USA pp. 109–14.

Traweek, D.E. and Veverka, J.A. (1979) 'A systems approach to interpretive planning', *Journal of Interpretation*, 4, 1, 24–28, Assoc. of Interp. Nat. Derwood, Maryland, USA.

15

On-Site Real-Time Observational Techniques and Responses to Visitor Needs

Paul Risk

Observational techniques are used, usually unconsciously, on a continuous basis in everyday communication. They provide a basis of data for modification of our delivery to meet different or changing situations. The same information can be of great value in improving the effectiveness of interpretive communication.

Together with observation, it is imperative that interpreters understand their 'client' groups and the influence their previous environmental experiences have had on them. Urbanization, the industrial and technological revolutions, have largely removed the average person from relevant involvement and comprehension of their interaction with the environment. Fast food, for example, was once when someone else chopped off the chicken's head and plucked it for our grandparents. Today, for all we know, chickens may be born golden brown and crisp in a basket.

Visitor rapport is essential in interpretation and may be gained through informal conversation prior to a presentation as well as careful observation of non-verbal feedback. Non-verbal feedback accounts for about 65 per cent of any interpersonal communication. Body position, posture, facial expressions, direction of gaze, eye contact, movement and coughs together with many other indicators offer interpreters important data for interpretive enhancement. In the application phase, delivery characteristics such as pitch, rate and volume as well as overuse of technical jargon and inappropriate humour may doom a presentation. Delivery modification based upon successful observation of visitor behaviour is critical to effective interpretation. And, finally, interpreter credibility, both initial and terminal are vitally important and controlled to a large degree by verbal and nonverbal skill and the ability to accurately 'read' the audience.

The purpose of this chapter is to re-emphasize to interpreters the importance and usefulness of 'reading' their audience; their clientele. It is the author's experience that most people who must speak to the public are most sensitive to feedback from their groups when they are first employed and that this tends to lessen in direct proportion to the time on the job. It may be that initial insecurity and/or outright fear play a very important part in prompting us to closely examine audience response at the start of our career. And perhaps, as we gain confidence or as complacency sets in we tend to be less and less aware of important cues from our listeners. Whatever the case, accurately assessing feedback from audiences can be invaluable to the interpreter's ability to meet visitor needs and desires. The absence of such assessment too often results in what may be described as the 'museum guide syndrome'.

Delivered in a stale, automatic manner such presentations too often do more to anaesthetize listeners than stimulate them! Sincerity may be one of the most important characteristics projected by effective interpreters. Made up of two Greek roots, 'sin' meaning without and 'cere' from the word for wax, sincere means literally 'without wax'. It apparently originates from ancient times when unscrupulous sculptors would fill flaws such as chipped places in their work wax. The wax closely resembled the marble from which the work of art work was created. And it was only later, when a change in temperature caused the patch to fall out, that the unwitting customer learned the truth. As a result, sculptors, in an effort to indicate the quality of their product would engrave the work 'sincere' on their statuary indicating that what you saw was what you got. There were no carefully concealed flaws.

Understanding Audiences

No two audiences are alike and quite probably no individual responds in exactly the same manner when attending the same interpretive programme. But there *are* commonalities. And, knowing some of the things which are common to most people may be critical to interpretive success.

Initial and Terminal Credibility

Credibility is a measure of believability. It is a feeling on the part of the visitor of whether interpreters are accurate in what they say; whether they can be trusted. Arbitrarily, a scale from one to ten can be used to give some idea of range, with 'ten' as perfect, glows in the dark and walks on water while 'one' might be defined as rotten, can't be seen in full sunlight and sinks into solid rock! On this scale 'five' could be considered as average, acceptable or mediocre depending upon whether initial or terminal credibility was involved. Initial credibility is usually established within a very short time after the interpreter makes his or her appearance before the audience. In a discussion with an executive from the American Telephone and Telegraph Company (AT&T), the statement was made that initial credibility is critical in job selection at the personal interview state. He stated that a hire/no hire decision based on initial credibility was usually reached in between thirty seconds and a minutes and a half.

Initial credibility is based upon a series of factors which may be controllable or uncontrollable. The following are some factors which might be found in the two categories:

Controllable	*Uncontrollable*
Grooming	Height
Attitude	Sex
Posture	Race
Nervous mannerisms	Handicaps
Eye contact	Eye colour
Facial expressions	
Gestures	

Terminal credibility is that level of believability which exists at the conclusion of the interpreter's presentation. And it is controlled not only by the above factors but by many others including: verbal and non-verbal characteristics, perceived knowledgeability of the subject, interpersonal attractiveness, enthusiasm, demeanour, etc. An interpreter should normally begin *any* presentation at least at level 'five'; acceptable.

The very fact that the agency trusts the interpreter enough to permit him to give public programmes should dictate at least a position of neutrality on the scale of credibility. Then whether the rating rises or declines is a function of the interpreter's overall communication skill. Of course, it is possible to start at less than 'five' if any of the factors in the above controllable or uncontrollable lists so overwhelms the visitor. But, given a 'five' start, most interpreters should be able to end up at a higher credibility level at the end of their programme. The very worst acceptable scenario should find the rating unchanged at the conclusion.

Unfortunately, too many interpreters discount or do not consider some of the factors in the uncontrollable column and they may begin (for the sake of argument) at a 'two' level. Even if they then are able by virtue of their sterling performance to rise, let us say, three points they will only end with a final rating of 'five'. In this case, a 'five' represents mediocrity!

Visitor Biases

Several considerations influence visitor biases including place of residence, prior life experiences, familiarity or lack thereof with the topic or area, fears, preoccupation and hurry. Unfamiliarity often breeds fear while urban lifestyles may cultivate unfamiliarity. For the uninitiated, predation or toxic plants may seem unacceptable since these things are often not a noticeable part of their normal environment. Sometimes visitor (interpreter) biases may be placed into two extreme definitions. The first might be called 'Bambi,

Beauty and Bounteous Love' (BB & BL) while the second might be identified as 'Hunt, Fish, Trap, Live in a Log Cabin and Carry Heavy Loads Up Slippery Trails'. (HFTLLC & CHLUST).

The Basics of Reading Audiences

Approximately 65 per cent of communication is non-verbal and while it may involve vocalization it may *not* include wording. It has been called paralanguage, and any teenager who has responded in an inappropriate manner to a parent only to find themselves in deep trouble clearly understands the prime commandment in non-verbal communication: It isn't *what* you say; it's *how* you say it! A sign posted in a store behind the cash register stated, '*90 per cent of the friction in life is caused by someone using the wrong tone of voice!*' And, *how* you say it also has to do with a whole set of attributes including posture, body and body parts movement, gestures, facial expression, tone of voice, pitch, rate and volume.

Factors Influencing Audience Response

Uncontrollable factors include environmental and personal situations. Weather characteristics such as temperature, wind, sun (glare), humidity and seating comfort are important. Personal situations may include health considerations such as chronic or acute conditions. This may involve everything from recovering form surgery to serious disease, colds, flu and state of digestion.

Attitude is also an important personal consideration and involves desire to attend, arguments just prior to coming, and responses to other people.

Controllable factors are all those previously mentioned under credibility.

Feedback Indicators

In order for the interpreter to respond, it is essential that one knows what to look for, what the indicators may mean and be flexible enough to modify their delivery in midstream. And, it should be held in mind that static conditions are frequently less important than *changes*.

Thus, a shift in body position or a sudden tilt of the head, a flick of the eyes or a shrug may signal important evaluative information. Usually the key is the *appropriateness* of the change.

Head

Perhaps because our attention is usually directed toward the eyes, the head is often a source of important feedback information. Tipping or tilting may indicate a question or lack of comprehension. Nodding is usually a sign of accord. (But if it is a slow sag it may just be slumber!) Shaking the head, while usually a sign of *dissension* may be desirable especially if the interpreter has just told a story from which he would hope to elicit such a response. In such a case it may indicate emotional empathy or sympathy with the interpreter or the story and be a positive bit of information. This is especially true if accompanied by a sympathetic 'tsk! tsk!'

Eyes, it has been said, are the windows of the soul. Certainly we have all heard everything from war cries of 'don't shoot 'til you see the whites of their eyes!' to comments such as, 'I felt I was falling into the depths of his/her beautiful blue eyes' to 'their eyes are so *expressive* and *thoughtful!*'

Eye contact is particularly useful. A person giving rapt attention will usually focus on the interpreter's eyes and seldom break this contact. Therefore, the duration or contact and warranted or unwarranted breaking of contact with the eyes are important in the interpretive assessment. Warranted breaks usually occur when the person is hard at work thinking about something. If such a break takes place following a thought-provoking comment or question it is warranted. On the other hand, if it happens for no apparent reason it is a warning that the visitor's attention is wandering.

Eye movement such as tracking, gaze direction and rolling are also enlightening. Failure to track toward something pointed out by the interpreter is a problem sign. Tracking something and gazing towards something the interpreter is not talking about should cue the interpreter to observe what is attracting the visitor's attention. Something serendipitous may be taking place about which the interpreter ought to comment. Eye rolling may show displeasure ('You've got to be nuts!!') but also may indicate sympathy with the interpreter's stand on an issue. If you are interested in testing the power of the point of focus of the eyes try closely watching another person's front teeth while conversing with them. Quite soon they will become very uncomfortable and carry out a tooth-grooming tongue sweep of their teeth assuming they must have some of their lunch caught there! Or focus on the other person's ear lobe and notice the discomfort such a gaze causes.

Of course, the twenty-mile stare should be high on the interpreter's list of concerns. Absently gazing into the distance most often indicates that the visitor is caught up in their own thoughts. Ideally, that is because they were sent in that direction by the interpreter's comments, But even so, they are no longer 'on track'. More generally, it simply means you have lost them completely out of boredom. A composite scan of the face is also useful. Expressions are complex feedback indicators.

But generally interpreters will recognize facial feedback indicative of: confusion, questioning, resentment, anger, surprise, shock, fear, revulsion, happiness, joy, etc. Smiles and frowns seem to cross cultural barriers with little or no need for translation.

One particular part of the face is worthy of special note. That is the eyebrows. Interestingly, we tend to involve the eyebrows in communication in ways which are at once important and unconscious. Of course, a lifted eyebrow may be quite conscious and intended to display lack of belief or surprise. But research, using slow-motion moving pictures, has disclosed a uniquely useful bit of information on a phenomenon called 'the eyebrow flash'. Eyebrow flashes generally take place when people who know each other well and are comfortable in each other's presence meet, particularly if the meeting is a surprise. The flash takes place so fast that unless one is concentrating and entirely aware of what to look for it will go unnoticed. In practice, it most often occurs sandwiched into a greeting such as 'Bill! How're you doing?' (Bill, it turns out, is a brother or close friend.) It is often accompanied by a smile. The eyes seem to brighten and there is an extremely quick (subliminal to most people) upward jump of both eyebrows. Bill, unconsciously perceiving this, responds in a manner completely different than if the flash had never taken place. He is warmer, chattier and less formal. He lowers his reserve and relaxes. A kind of quick bonding takes place.

The author, in discussing this concept with a park naturalist on one occasion, found that the interpreter in question tends to 'flash' most people they meet. The result, according to their supervisor, is an overwhelmingly positive response from visitors. People tend, without comprehending the reason, to respond to this particular interpreter far more warmly and co-operatively than to others.

Eye contact and eyebrow flashing combine in an interesting manner. People walking toward one another tend to maintain what has been described as 'civil inattention' until they are close enough to determine whether they know each other or not and, if they do, on what basis. If no identification is made they drop their eyes to the ground (which sounds painful, but is not) and pass without further non-verbal or verbal interaction. What I am proposing is that interpreters practise being flashers. If this is done as described it can instantly warm up interpersonal relations in the field but will not get you arrested!

As a test of this technique, pick a stranger on the street. Next, walk toward them maintaining eye contact continuously well inside the normal distance for ordinarily breaking contact. At the last moment and just before passing them give an eyebrow flash and say 'hi' or 'hello!' But be aware that this can be terribly disconcerting. Their mental switchboard has suddenly lit up with flashing red lights which normally only come on in the presence of their children, spouse or other close friend or loved one. The result is likely to be a precipitous halt while whirling around to look more closely at you. (Be cautious about this. If it's carried out on icy sidewalks the other person may go into a critical slide and crash to the ground!) Now imagine how useful this simple eyebrow flash may be in subconsciously making a park visitor feel more welcome.

Body

Posture, position or motion of fingers, hands, arms, legs and feet can all provide clues to the effectiveness of your communication. A slouching posture may indicate boredom or might also denote a relaxed visitor. But if the visitor started out alert, upright and watchful and became more and more recumbent, you are likely to be in trouble. Arms crossed across the chest are sometimes an indication of a lack of acceptance of your message.

The arms in this position are considered a barrier display. Finger tapping, manipulating objects in an absent-minded manner are usually indications of lack of interest, and nervousness. The same may apply to rubbing or manipulating a piece of clothing or an eyebrow. Shuffling feet are also a danger sign.

Activities

Watching closely, participating, note taking are certainly all helpful in identifying the visitor who is interested and enjoying the presentation. Loss of concern with self is a definite plus. People who are hanging on every word tend not to sneeze, cough, clear their throat, squirm, yawn or *leave*. The tickle in the back of the throat which triggers sneezing and coughing tends to disappear when a person's attention is diverted. In other words, it is possible to *listen* to an audience and get some indication of their attentiveness. Quiet audiences are either listening carefully or asleep! Of course, listening quietly is not a guarantee that they approve of what they hear. They may be listening in shocked disapproval. Other feedback indicators must be observed to be sure.

Interestingly, talking to others may be appropriate. The interpreter's comments may have created just the revelation and/or provocation desired and the point is under quiet discussion. Of course, this can be carried to extremes and become distracting to others as well as interfere with continued interpretation. In order to know how to respond to intra-group conversations one must determine the subject. Irrelevant comments and communication certainly would or should trigger concern.

Dissociative behaviour may or may not be cause for alarm. Particularly in evening programmes, parents may take children out to go to the bathroom or to bed. A few early departures is not a serious concern. But if a pattern emerges the interpreter may assume that they are not holding the group's attention. Successful interpretation is a juggling act. Not only must the interpreter concentrate on what to say and how it is said. They must also constantly monitor not only themselves but also every nuance in the feedback from the audience, and be ready to respond.

Proxemics

A person may exhibit some forms of dissociative behaviour simply because the interpreter has invaded their 'personal space'. Each of us carries with us an invisible 'envelope' of sensitivity. This envelope is actually made up of layers. The layers or levels occur at different distances from us depending upon whether approach is from the front, rear or sides. Most people are more sensitive to invasion from the front.

Studies in North America indicate that this personal space may be divided into six distinct zones:

(1) Intimate = 6–18 inches
(2) Personal = 1.5–4 feet
(3) Social Close = 4–7 feet
(4) Social Far = 7–12 feet
(5) Public Close = 12–25 feet
(6) Public Far = > 25 feet

The intimate zone is usually reserved for those we have special feelings for, such a family members.

Personal is that zone into which we move when in one-to-one communication with most people. The other zones relate to the distances maintained in various forms of interpretation.

For example, public close and public far would probably by the distances involved in conducted activities and sit-down programmes in an amphitheatre.

Although generalizations are possible, distances tolerated or found desirable show strong cultural and personal differences. For example, an Arabian or Hispanic may easily back a North American or British interpreter right into a corner. In the Hispanic or Arabian culture it is very common for what a Britain or Northern American would think of as intimate distance to be only personal range. As a result, the visitor continues to advance while the interpreter retreats. The visitor wonders why the interpreter is so unfriendly and the interpreter wonders why the visitor is so friendly! It may end only when the interpreter strikes an immovable object.

Whatever the reason, interpreters must be aware of each person's unique space requirements and be sensitive enough to modify their own behaviour to accommodate them. At the same time, a visitor retreating from the advances of the interpreter may be indicating that the interpreter has a personal problem such as bad breath or body odour of which the interpreter is unaware. At the very least, the manner in which the interpreter is carrying out the communication is in some way offensive to the visitor, and changes need to be made.

Conclusion

Interpreters must therefore constantly monitor or 'read' their audiences and develop ways to modify their own behaviour in the communication situation in order to remedy difficulties.

As the professional perfects the ability to do this, their competence in meeting the needs of the visitor will grow.

Recommended Reading

Grater, R.K. (1976) *The Interpreter's Handbook*, Southwest Parks & Monuments Assn, Globe, Arizona.

Hart, R.P., Friedrich, G.W. and Brooks, W.D. (1975) *Public Communication*, Harper and Row, London.

Huseman, R.C., Lahiff, J.M. and Hatfield J.D. (1976) *Interpersonal Communication in Organizations — a Perceptual Approach*, Holbrook Press, Boston, Mass.

Knapp, M.L. (1972) *Nonverbal Communication in Human Interaction*, Holt, Rinehart & Winston, New York.

Lewis, W.J. (1980) *Interpreting for Park Visitors*, Eastern Acorn Press, Eastern National Park & Monument Ass.

Makay, J.J. and Sawyer, T.C. (1973) *Speech Communication Now!*, Charles E. Merrill, Colombus, Ohio.

Risk, P.H. (1982) 'Conducted activities', in Sharpe, G.W. (ed.), *Interpreting the Environment*, Ch. 8. John Wiley, New York.

Risk, P.H. (1982) 'The interpretive talk', in Sharpe., G.W., *Interpreting the Environment*, John Wiley, New York.

Tilden, F. (1957) *Interpreting Our Heritage*, University of North Carolina Press, Chapel Hill.

16

Evaluation in Museums:
A Short History of a
Short History

Harris Shettel

Introduction

Any serious attempt to present a comprehensive history of evaluation in informal learning settings, which include museums, historic and natural sites, botanical gardens, zoos, and so on, in the span of twenty or thirty minutes, is doomed to failure. While the history of evaluation is a relatively short one, it is not that short. So, I shall do what any self-respecting author would do under the circumstances and disclaim up front any pretence to comprehensiveness. I feel that a more comfortable and certainly safer posture to take is one that leans toward 'history as seen through the eyes of', thereby making it almost impossible to accuse me of either of the twin sins of blatant omission or erroneous commission. This approach also allows me to fend off the accusation that my 'history' has an American bias. My eyes are American, although my intention is certainly not to deliberately emphasize the role played by Americans nor to de-emphasize the role played by those in other parts of the world.

The Early Years

When I wrote that the history of evaluation in the informal learning setting is short, I meant that it spans no more than a single lifetime — seventy-two years. The first known paper that looked at the museum visitor in a systematic way was published by Gilman in 1916, on the subject of exhibition design factors as they relate to visitor fatigue. But this early paper did not usher in a wave of similar studies, and we must jump twelve years for the next published study, by Robinson (1928). In fact, Robinson and his colleague and fellow psychologist at Yale University, Melton, are generally credited with being the 'fathers' of museum visitor studies. Between 1928 and 1936 they produced a total of ten important papers (Robinson, 1928, 1930, 1931a, 1931b, 1933; Melton, 1933a, 1933b, 1935, 1936; Melton et al., 1936).

It should be noted that the primary methodology used by Melton and Robinson was the unobtrusive observation of the visitor, and their primary dependent variable was time, measured in terms of the holding power of the exhibition once the visitor was attracted to it. The educational value of the museum experience was not measured directly, but was inferred from the amount of time visitors spent at the exhibition. In other words, time was equated with attention which was equated with learning. A very shaky paradigm, but a solid beginning to the systematic study of visitor learning in the museum setting. One might have thought that these early studies, carefully carried out by two well trained psychologists and reported in the museum literature, would encourage others to apply what had been learned as well as to expand on the base of knowledge and methodology that Robinson and Melton had developed.

But, in fact, the work of these two investigators was largely ignored by the museum community, as reflected by the number of published reports on the subject, which actually declined in the 1940s and 1950s to a total of four and five respectively. The Second World War may account for some of this neglect, but I suspect that it was also a case of lack of interest in the visitor as an important part of a museum's legitimate area of concern. Perhaps it could be said for many institutions in those days that presentation was more important than interpretation; that showing what the museum had was more important than making what it showed intelligible to the visitor.

The Formative Years

However, the picture changes rather abruptly with the decade of the 1960s, when we find a total of 36 published reports, most of them (70 per cent) in the latter half of the decade. And this was not another brief interlude of interest; it was followed by two decades of ever-increasing activity, with 99 publications in the 1970s and 225 so far in the 1980s. This means that of the 384 publications that I have identified, 58 per cent were published in the period 1980 to 1988, and 94 per cent in the period from 1965 to the present.

What happened in the mid-1960s that triggered such a flurry of activity, which seems to have captured a permanent, although relatively small, place in the museum firmament?

It is said by some that history can be written as an extension of the lives of famous people. Others believe that history is the expression of important and new ideas and movements. While I suspect that the truth lies in the interplay between the two, I believe that the history of museum evaluation in the mid-1960s can be most clearly seen in the context of three rather large movements that came together in an exciting way: (1) accountability, (2) measurement, and (3) museum education.

Accountability

The 1960s saw an intense interest, in the United States at least, in making programmes and projects, especially those funded with federal dollars, accountable for whatever they were supposed to accomplish. Remember that the United States government was heavily involved in social engineering during the reign of Kennedy and Johnson, funding vast public programmes in education, job training, housing, health, basic research, the Peace Corps, and many, many others. There was both a strong moral and fiscal need to account for how the money was being spent and what was achieved in spending it. 'What kind of a bang are we getting for our buck?' was the clarion call of the day. Social scientists were heavily supported during this period in an effort to find answers to this question, doing evaluation studies on a very large scale. Accountability was 'in'.

Measurement

During this period there was also a marked increase in research activity into ways of evaluating the impact of social programmes more adequately, and much of this work was concentrated in the areas of training and education. Based on a behaviouristic/positivistic foundation, this work emphasized the definition of terms, the specification of goals and objectives and the preparation of clearly stated criteria for determining the success or failure of the activity being evaluated. This was the era of the Skinner box, the teaching machine, programmed instruction and Magerian objectives. And, I might add, the beginning of computer-based instruction, as well as the precursor of the work now being done in information mapping and so-called artificial intelligence (the latter now firmly captured in the current *zeitgeist* of 'cognitive studies').

A whole new way of thinking about assessment and evaluation was developed during this period. The normal curve was 'out'; the criterion-based test was 'in'. Trick questions and problems were 'out'; questions based directly on the previously prepared objectives (behavioural, of course), were 'in'. Motivation was 'out'; performance was 'in'.

We now have the basis for a meeting of interests and needs between the demand for accountability and the development of the 'new' evaluation methodology that could, it was said, determine to what extent programmes were meeting their intended objectives. One idea fed upon and was nourished by the other. As a young (or younger) researcher who was heavily involved in the world of training and education, and frustrated with the traditional ways of assessing their effectiveness, I, along with many others, became a convert to these powerful ideas (Shettel, 1968, 1973). I believed then, and still believe, that without a means to evaluate your progress, you cannot be certain you are making any. As Mager said at the time, 'If you don't know where you are going, any road will get you there.'

Museum Education

What does all this have to do with museums and informal learning, you may well ask. A third factor, more subtle perhaps, but an important ingredient to add to our ideational stew, was the increased recognition during this period of the educational value of museums. A survey carried out by the National Endowment for the Arts in 1974 found that 92 per cent of all museum directors in the study (N=728) said that a major purpose of their museums was 'providing educational experiences for the public'. While cynics were quick to point out that federal tax advantages were contingent upon museums being designated as 'educational institutions', there seemed little doubt then (or now) that museums truly perceived themselves as having a very definite educational role to play in our society.

We now have the three ingredients needed to account for, I think, the burst of activity in exhibition evaluation that occurred in the mid- to late 1960s. The verbal equation that combines the three ingredients went (and still goes) something like this: Museums say that they are very much in the business of educating the public, yet there is almost no objective evidence to support this assertion (and considerable evidence to question it). Museums are therefore not being accountable to their audience, the visitor, nor to those who provide the funds for their support, which are often public funds. This situation is untenable because it is possible to evaluate exhibitions and programmes so that what is effective and what is not effective can be determined, and what is not, corrected. Museums can thus become accountable to their audience and to their funding sources.

Interestingly, the people who were saying this the loudest were not, by and large, museum people but educational, training and media research people, largely coming from the behavioural tradition of the day. Also, the studies carried out during this period were supported more by universities and the federal government than by museums themselves. Of the five major studies that I carried out between 1965 and 1974, for example, four were directly supported by the US government and one was indirectly funded by the government through a museum. Screven's seminal work during this period was often supported by his university and by government grants (Screven, 1974). Even those evaluators working within museums, like Minda Borun at the Franklin Institute Science Museum in Philadelphia and Patty McNamara at the Science Museum of Virginia in Richmond, were (and still are) supported by 'soft money', that is, money obtained from government grants to the museum.

But I think it is safe to say that this period in our history was one of great excitement and creativity and expectations for the future. In fact, I felt safe during this period in predicting that within ten years at most, *all* exhibitions and educational programmes developed by and for museums would benefit from some form of evaluation. This was not, I hasten to add, a very good prediction, but it reflected the enthusiasm of the times.

Out of this ferment of studies, papers and arguments came a host of ideas, and methodological tools and approaches that are still valid today. Here are several, but by no means all of them:

- Using specific knowledge of the visitor's level of understanding of the subject matter of the planned exhibition to help in designing the exhibition and in preparing its textual material.

- Using adjunct questions that encourage visitors to read labels and view objects.

- Refining the methodology of tracking studies, leading to more useful measures of the attracting and holding power of exhibitions.

- Preparing both cognitive and non-cognitive objectives during the exhibition planning stage and later measuring both by means of interviews, questionnaires, and visitor observation.

- Testing with real visitors mock-ups of exhibitions or elements of exhibitions to see what works and what does not while changes can still be made inexpensively (now usually called formative evaluation).

- Using the technique of cued testing to provide an accurate measure of what the maximum teaching or educational potential of an exhibition is, against which the effectiveness of the exhibition with casual visitors can be compared.

- Using advanced organizers to help visitors understand the purpose and layout of the exhibition and to give the visitor a meaningful context within which they can relate to the information in the exhibition.

It should be noted that much of this early work had, quite understandably, a research emphasis. Single studies were carried out in which data were collected and reports published, but the impact of this work on the way museums prepared exhibitions was quite limited. However, there were exceptions to this, and I want to mention one outstanding example of effective adaptation to these new ideas.

The British Museum (Natural History) made a commitment in the early 1970s to do a more effective job of taking into account the needs and interests of the visitor in its exhibition planning process. Under the direction of Roger Miles, and called the 'New Exhibition Scheme', it reorganized its entire staffing pattern to accommodate this fundamental, second-order change. Curators, for example, were given roles consistent with their expertise and interests, and were no longer automatically in charge of the exhibition development process. While Miles would be first to acknowledge that the task has been formidable and not without its hazards and setbacks, his institution has come closer to building in the necessary steps to take into account the needs of the evaluation process than any other that I know of. For example, they regularly carry out studies to find out what their visitors are interested in and what they know and don't know about the subject of planned exhibitions. They carefully consider the teaching points that they want to communicate to the visitor and keep these in mind as they design the exhibition and prepare their interpretive labels. They often do formative testing of mock-up exhibits to see if the visitor is able to grasp the basic ideas and essential content of the exhibition, using the previously prepared teaching points as the basis for the questions they ask. They revise the exhibition if it is not meeting its objectives and retest it to be certain that it is. And they are not averse to evaluating a completed exhibition to see if it is still doing its job and, if it is not, tearing it down and redoing it.

Of course, one could mention other examples of the early use of the evaluation process by museums to enhance exhibition effectiveness, examples from the US, Canada (which deserves special mention for its consistent support over the years), Germany, France, and other countries as well. Formative exhibition testing has become standard practice in a number of institutions and is, perhaps, the single most important contribution made by the early work of the 1960s.

Obstacles to Acceptance

But I do not want to leave you with the impression that exhibition evaluation is now the accepted practice of museums in general. The vast majority of exhibitions are prepared without any input from the evaluation process. Why is this so? Why are major institutions whose names you would instantly recognize not using this proven approach on a regular basis, or even an irregular basis? Why was my prediction of twenty years ago so far off the mark?

I think that there are two broad classes of reasons, one I will call philosophical and the other practical. First, the philosophical. There are those who simply did not agree from our earliest studies that the museum experience can be fitted into the standard educational measurement paradigm. While many of us pointed out the need to adapt this paradigm to the unique features of the informal learning world, and have done so, the claim is still made (although less often and less loudly) that evaluation trivializes the museum experience, missing all the subtle and wonderful things that are really happening to visitors but that can't be measured.

I must say that I am quite sceptical about these arguments because I have seen them used before not as a challenge to improve one's methodology (which is a valid challenge) but as a hiding place for those who do not want to change or to face a possibly unpleasant reality. With few exceptions, museums are inherently conservation institutions and one should not be surprised to find them slow to accept basic changes in the way things are done. Evaluation does force one to look critically at one's work and to face up to the distinct possibility that it is falling short of its goals. Not doing evaluation avoids this problem just as not going to the doctor avoids ill health.

Perhaps the philosophical objections to evaluation reached their apogee in an article written by Alt (1977) entitled 'Evaluating didactic exhibits: a critical look at Shettel's work.' Using as his target the first study that I did ten years earlier called 'Strategies for determining exhibit effectiveness', Alt attacked the very foundations of not just my work but, indirectly, that of many of my colleagues who shared a common approach. Some of his points were quite good and were in the process of being implemented as we refined our approach over the years since 1967. Others seemed to me to miss the mark completely and led me to respond (Shettel, 1978) with, 'A critical look at a critical look: A response to Alt's critique of Shettel's work'. The point is, an underlying scepticism existed, and still exists among some, that it is neither possible nor desirable to use objectively arrived at indicators of visitor outcomes as a tool in improving the exhibition development process.

But there is another more practical reason for my bad prediction – implementation. This is perhaps the more compelling problem because it addresses forthrightly some of the pressing issues of the recent and current museum scene – that is, resources and competitive pressures. Ever more demands are being made for the fewer dollars, pounds, marks, etc., available to help support museums in all their myriad functions. This is forcing museums to move into the more public arena and compete for funds with other institutions that are trying to capture the leisure time of the public. A museum that charges four or five dollars for adults and one or two dollars for each child, is placing itself in direct competition with the theatre, movies, amusement parks, and a host of other 'entertainments' that charge a fee. Modern exhibitions are becoming increasingly costly, especially with the pressure to use such devices as computers and video-disc players so that visitors will be sufficiently entertained and awed. A recently opened exhibition at the Smithsonian Institution's National Museum of American History cost $1.75 million. In this heady environment, concern for the educational effectiveness of exhibitions, especially when that concern translates into increased costs of preparing exhibitions, leads directly to a problem of implementation.

I have heard it many times. 'We would like to do formative testing and front-end analysis, etc., but our board and our funding sources simply will not agree to spend the money. We have too many other more pressing needs.' My answer is equally forthright. 'But you can't compete on the grounds of entertainment – you must have interesting and effective programs and exhibits that are consistent with your mission as an educational institution. Now, more than ever, you need to stay in touch with your visitor. Evaluation is the only objective way of doing that.'

There must be, in short, a very strong and consistent commitment to the visitor at the highest levels of the institution in order to support a truly effective evaluation effort.

The Future

I am now convinced that the need to know more about our visitors, and apply what we know, is a need that will not go away. We have established a small but permanent beachhead in the museum community. The recently formed International Laboratory for Visitor Studies (or ILVS as it is known), located in Milwaukee, Wisconsin and directed by Chan Screven, is a good example of the growing level of interest that we now see in the field. ILVS has already published the second edition of a comprehensive bibliography of museum visitor studies (Screven and Gessner, 1988) and is in the process of publishing the first issue of its research journal. Steve Bitgood in Jacksonville, Alabama, has been publishing his informative quarterly newsletter, *Visitor Behaviour*, since 1986. He has several hundred subscribers from all over the world. Loomis (1987) recently wrote an excellent book, *Museum Visitor Evaluation: A New Tool for Museum Management* and Miles et al. (1988) have just put out the second edition of their fine book, *The Design of Educational Exhibits*. The American Association of Museums has a very active Evaluation and Research Committee which sponsored six panel sessions at the recent annual meeting in Pittsburgh. And I could go on to mention many other examples of growth and activity and interest in the field. So I feel safe in saying that while we still have much to learn about our work, we are continuing to develop a clearer voice and a clearer notion about our role. We are being heard in more and more places!

I firmly believe that those institutions that will become a vital force in the 1990s and beyond will do so not by cutting back on efforts to understand the visitor but by increasing those efforts. Such museums will build on what we have already learned, they will maintain their integrity as unique and effective educational institutions, and they will be accountable to their audience. And evaluation must and will play a vital role in all of these activities.

References

Alt, M.B. (1977) 'Evaluating didactic exhibits: a critical look at Shettel's work', *Curator*, 20(3), 241–58.

Gilman, B.I. (1916) 'Museum fatigue', *Science Monthly*, 12, 62–74.

Loomis, R.J. (1987) *Museum Visitor Evaluation: a New Tool for Museum Management*, American Association for State and Local History, Tennessee.

Melton, E. (1933a) 'Some behaviour characteristics of museum visitors', *Psychological Bulletin*, 30, 720–1.

Melton, A. (1933b) 'Studies of installation at the Pennsylvania Museum of Art', *Museum News*, 10(14), 5–8.

Melton, A. (1935) 'Problems of installation in museums of art', *American Association of Museums Monograph* (New Series No. 14).

Melton, A. (1936) 'Distribution of attention in galleries in a museum of science and industry', *Museum News*, 14(3), 5–8.

Melton, A., Goldberg, N. and Mason, C.W. (1936) 'Experimental studies of the education of children in a museum of science', *American Association of Museums Monograph* (New Series No. 15).

Miles, R.S., Alt, M.B., Gosling, D.C., Lewis, B.N. and Tout, A.F. (1988) *The Design of Educational Exhibits*, 2nd edition. Unwin Hyman, London.

Robinson, E.S. (1928) 'The behaviour of the museum visitor', *American Association of Museums Monograph* (New Series No. 5).

Robinson, E.S. (1930) 'Psychological problems of the science museum', *Museum News*, 8(5), 9–11.

Robinson, E.S. (1931a) 'Exit the typical visitor', *Journal of Adult Education*, 3(4), 418–23.

Robinson, E.S. (1931b) 'Psychological studies of the public museum', *School and Society*, 33(839), 121–5.

Robinson, E.S. (1933) 'Experimental education in the museum: a perspective', *Museum News*, 10(16), 6–8.

Screven, C.G. (1974) *The Measurement and Facilitation of Learning in the Museum Environment: an Experimental Analysis*, Smithsonian Press, Washington DC.

Screven, C.G. and Gessner, K. (1988) *ILVS Bibliography and Abstracts*, 2nd edition. The International Laboratory for Visitor Studies, Milwaukee, Wisconsin.

Shettel, H. (1968) 'An evaluation of existing criteria for judging the quality of science exhibits', *Curator*, 11(2), 137–53.

Shettel, H. (1973) 'Exhibits: art form or educational medium?', *Museum News*, 52, 32–41.

Shettel, H. (1978) 'A critical look at a critical look: a response to Alt's critique of Shettel's work', *Curator*, 21(4), 329–45.

17

Heritage as Media:
Some Implications for
Research

Roger Silverstone

Introduction

Two hours' drive north of Toronto, Canada, near the town of Midland, can be found the reconstruction of an early Jesuit mission among the Huron Indians. St. Marie-amongst-the-Hurons is an elegant and effective example of a contemporary heritage exhibition. Beautifully built of Canadian pine, new and still sweet smelling, and peopled by appropriately costumed students on summer vacation (who play the Jesuits and their fellow travellers) and by Ojibwe Indians (who, of course, play the Indians), it attracts large numbers of visitors who, I assume, relish the experience of travelling back through time, of getting a feel for the authentic, of being put in touch with an, actually rather tarnished, aspect of their history.

Before entering the compound proper, the visitor is encouraged to attend a tape slide presentation which recounts the history of the Jesuit mission. This ends with a full-frame image of the compound, which fills the projection screen. At the point at which the image is firmly fixed in the viewer's eye, the entire wall on which it has been projected slowly rises to reveal the identical image – only this time 'for real'. The visitor then walks through the frame, through the screen, (through the looking glass) and into the past.

I refer to this extraordinary (and extraordinarily impressive) piece of multimedia legerdemain for one reason only. It is to make the point that the heritage industry (to borrow Hewison's [1987] phrase) is in the business of mass communication and that the boundary between museums and media, and that between reality and fantasy, between myth and mimesis in both sets of institutions and practices, is becoming increasingly blurred, increasingly indistinct. Hewison (1987) himself points to a similar fuzziness when he notes the frequency with which television crews use the reconstructed village of Beamish in Northumberland (a village entirely constructed of original buildings but on a green field site) as a location for period filming. 'Heritage' informs our mass-mediated culture (especially advertising; the Hovis advertisements are wonderful examples), just as our mass-mediated culture informs the work of the heritage industry.

These perhaps rather unexceptional observations have, I want to suggest, one major implication for research. It is quite simply this. If museums, exhibitions and displays – of art, of science and technology, of culture and industry – are, as indeed they are increasingly becoming, exercises in mass communication, then an understanding of the way they work, of their effects and effectiveness ought to be informable by the procedures adopted in the study of mass communication and contemporary culture.

I would like to make a case for treating museums and heritage displays as mass media and to explore the usefulness of some of the more recent research efforts in media and cultural studies for research in this new field. I should point out right away that much of this recent work, certainly the most interesting and suggestive work, is qualitative research. It draws heavily on work in literary theory, semiology and increasingly on an ethnographic approach to data collection (for a recent review see Fiske, 1987). I shall have something to say about all of this shortly, but before I do there is one point which needs to be made.

Questions for Research

Karl Popper, the eminent philosopher of science, recounts a story in which he once instructed his Vienna students to: 'Take pencil and paper; closely observe, and write down what you have observed.' His students asked, of course, what it was that Popper wanted them to observe. Without instructions, without concepts, without theory, meaningful observation is, as they quickly realized impossible. 'Observation is always selective. It needs a chosen object, a definite task, an interest, a point of view, a problem,' (Popper, 1963, p. 46).

Any discussion of research methodology, therefore, cannot begin without reference to theory, to the ways in which the object of investigation is to be conceptualized or framed. Research is not simply a matter of observation, measurement and report. It requires a prior commitment and prior questions. Social scientific research is no different from natural science research in this respect. The questions might be – How are we going to think about this? What are the key issues? What ideas, what models, will help us frame the problems? How are we going to design a set of research strategies adequate to these problems? There is another question too, of course – What do we want this research for?

I now want to take up some of these questions, and suggest a way of thinking about museums and heritage displays as media. I will then briefly suggest a model for research which is informed by this thinking and which I would expect to have some general relevance in this new and important field.

The first question to answer, however, is the last one I posed. What is research for? Of course there are potentially many different kinds of answer, but it seems to me that research can offer two broad routes into museum practice and heritage display. The first is in its ability to address a set of questions about the work itself and to throw substantial light on the context and processes of exhibition design and creation. How do curators and designers go about their business, and can research provide something of a mirror in which they can recognize themselves, and in their recognition change or improve their practice? The second is in its ability to assess an exhibition's effectiveness and impact. This obviously involves issues of evaluation. I shall suggest, at the end of this paper, that these two dimensions of the research agenda are intimately related and cannot properly be undertaken in isolation from each other.

But there is another reason for research, and that is to provide a basis for critical understanding of the changing role of the museum and of the relatively newly established role of the heritage exhibition in contemporary culture (see Lumley, 1988). Involvement in the minutiae of the work of curators and visitors should not blind us to this equally essential task.

Museums as Media

So, what do museums, heritage displays and, for example, television, have in common? They are all mediators. They mediate between the otherwise inaccessible, the unfamiliar, and the world of everyday life. They must adopt strategies in the design and layout of their texts (the gallery, the exhibition, the reconstruction, the programme) which allow the lay visitor to come to some kind of terms with things which may not only seem to be incomprehensible or strange but may also seem threatening or wonderful, irrelevant or dull. The visitor, the viewer, the audience, is to be informed, educated and entertained. Lord Reith's famous definition of the role of the BBC in prewar Britain stands today as the measure of success for a much wider range of mediated experiences, but it also raises a whole set of further questions about what each of these activities involves. Information, education, entertainment are, none of them, unproblematic categories in the world of heritage display or the museum, any more than they are in the world of the mass media as a whole.

All these mediated experiences rely on communication technologies: the printed word, moving and still images, sounds, objects (and sometimes smells) to convey their messages. They all rely, to a greater or lesser extent, on the use of the familiar narratives of myth and folklore to fix the unfamiliar or the indigestible into a secure and familiar framework which aims to reassure the viewer and the visitor by its coherence, its plausibility and its legitimacy. They all rely, finally, on the popular and public metaphors of daily life in their persistent efforts to lock their sense into the familiar sense of the gossip, conversation and memory of the everyday. Step inside a museum or a reconstructed industrial site, a natural history museum (Haraway, 1984–5, p. 21ff.), tune into a television documentary, and you will cross a threshold into a confident representational world: a world of objects, stories and images whose overriding intention is to convince you of its authority and its authenticity, and to please you by its poetry and style. Aristotle distinguished between rhetoric and poetics in his discussions of cultural process. The mass media are both persuasive and aesthetic. An understanding of their significance and their power must take into account both dimensions (for a more elaborate version of the above analysis, see Silverstone, 1988).

They are also subject to a common set of problems, as kinds of mediation in which they engage become increasingly contentious: politically (where questions about the implications in particular of inclusion or exclusion – in relation to gender, ethnicity, progress, history – are becoming more pressing); economically (where decisions about conflicting responsibility to funder, consumer or scholar will increasingly intrude into the broad and fine detail of exhibition design, programme policy and corporate image); and finally aesthetically (where the competing demands of, for example, print- or video-based technologies and styles have to be assessed, and where the contrasting claims of the story and the argument, or of different kinds of rhetorical appeal, have to be resolved).

There is one other element that links museums, heritage displays and television programmes, and that is their competition for an audience and for a share of public and private funds. They are together firmly implicated in consumer culture (Morton, 1988). An economic and political imperative has already begun to transform the museum, and to transform it on the mass media's terms: the fragmentation of displays, the drawing on mass culture's own metaphors in gallery design, the premium being placed on interactivity, the peopling of restored sites by actors in accents and costumes, displays of television drama costumes. All these testify to the increasing dominance of televisual and arcade culture. And, once again, they provide an important point of entry for research.

What museums, exhibitions and restorations share, therefore, and what insists on their being brought into the same frame of reference as that used to understand the mass media as a whole, is their increasing appeal to the popular, and their common status as constructions. A gallery in a science museum, a television programme like *Horizon* or *Disappearing World*, a waxworks like 'The Oxford Story', or an elaborate restoration like Morwellham Quay on the banks of Tamar in Cornwall or Beamish, all share this. They are all designed and created. They are all artefacts. Their relationship to something called 'reality', to history, to the other, is a function of that work, human work, and they require the viewer or the visitor to read, to follow and to work with what they see, hear, read or walk through. In this sense all our media are texts: motivated, meaningful, relatively open or closed, ambiguous or clear, appealing or dull, effective or ineffective. They all express more or less visibly the marks of their construction and their ideological inflection.

This textual quality which both museums and television, for example, share threatens the unproblematic status of the real in exhibitions or displays. Eco (1987) has, of course, defined the museum and heritage experience as the search for 'hyper-reality'. What is implied both by his arguments and by mine is that the boundary between reality and fantasy and between the authentic and the reproduced is fundamentally challenged both within the exhibition and indeed on television (which in its documentary form also lays claim to presenting the real). Although it can be argued that visitors are drawn to museums by the 'aura' (Benjamin, 1973) of the objects to be found there, very often they will discover the same perplexing (often disguised, though always taken for granted) mixtures of presentation and representation, the real and the simulated, the fragment and the reproduction. Museums, heritage sites and television documentary together create reality as a textual phenomenon, in which objects or images (or sounds) of objects are textualized and contextualized in a comparable effort to claim authenticity.

I suggest that this essential and essentially shared textuality is a significant key to understanding the status of all our mass media, including museums and heritage collections, in contemporary society, and a significant key to a whole range of fascinating and important research questions.

What then are the consequences of framing the study of the museum and the heritage display in such terms for research? There are a number of dimensions to a possible answer. I would like to focus on two. The first is to consider the notion of the communication process. The second is to consider the claims of ethnography as a specific research method.

The Communication Process

The work of the museum and heritage industry is dynamic work, involving curators, designers, contractors, artists, specialists of all kinds, administrators, funders and visitors. It should be studied as such. It is quite impossible to get a grip on the complex process of museum or heritage communication without an understanding of the constraints and contradictions associated with each stage of its development – with each stage of the emergence of a text (the display, the gallery, the open air site) – and without an understanding of the interrelationship between, for example, the intention of the creators and the response of the visitors.

The key to unlocking the complexity of this process is the analysis of something I have referred to already a number of times: the text. Why text? At the heart of any act of communication is a discrete organization of signs – words, images, sounds, objects – that in their ordering lay claim to meaning. The work of design and production is oriented solely to the creation of a text in this sense; the work of the visitor is that of deciphering and then recreating the text for him or herself. The process of meaning construction is therefore continuous. The text is both fixed (in so far as a display remains relatively unchanged) and fluid (it is subject to the continuous and indeterminate work of the visitor). Creation – 'writing' – and reception – 'reading' – are parallel processes and one might argue that an understanding of the textuality of an exhibition, that is of its meaning for all those who are involved in it, is dependent on an ability to understand the continuous nature of this process of communication, a process which does not stop until the visitor has left all memory behind.

Research therefore needs to get inside the textuality of the museum or the heritage site if it is to have any purchase on the processes of its communication. Such research needs, in turn, to attend to a number of aspects of that process. I will identify these, provisionally, as thematics, poetics and rhetoric. They can be discussed as analytically discrete, but of course any empirical study would find it impossible unambiguously to separate them.

Thematics

The thematics of museum and heritage research consists in the study of the history and the archaeology of display. It is concerned with the genres of exhibition design; with the decision-making process associated with the selection of content. What issues are being defined as important for display and how can these be contextualized? What factors – economic, political, bureaucratic, intellectual – have led to a decision to create one kind of exhibition rather than another, and what are the implications of selection and exclusion for the particular strategies of representation that they embody? Such a thematics can hardly avoid the thorny questions of the politics of representation. Indeed such questions are central. Bennett's (1988) discussion of the Beamish site is an excellent example of what I would call thematic analysis, above all in his tracing of the construction of what he calls 'the countryside of the mind' in the buildings, objects and people on display.

Poetics

The poetics of museum and heritage research consists in the study of the aesthetic strategies embodied in museum design. Here there are concerns with the particularities of the museum as medium: with its role as story-teller, as myth maker, as imitator of reality. Such concerns bring with them the requirement to enquire into the details of exhibition design and of the processes which lead to the selection and arrangement of exhibits.

Poetics is the province of pleasure. It is also the province of narrative (though narrative is also to be included within rhetoric). The study of the narrativity of the museum or the heritage display involves a study of an exhibition's capacity to define a route (material, pedagogic, aesthetic) for the visitor, and to define thereby a particular logic of representation, a particular legitimate and plausible coherence for itself. Such a study would need to identify the conflicting pressures on museum curators of the mythic and mimetic. What kinds of stories can be and are being told, through the display of objects in various settings? What are the possible consequences for one set of, inevitably compromised, choices rather than another? A paper by Robert Bud (1988), in which he reflects on his own curatorial experiences in gallery design, is an important and relatively unusual example of what I would call a study in the poetics of the museum.

Rhetoric

The rhetoric of museum and heritage research consists in the study of the persuasive strategies of museum design and of the effectiveness of their appeal. Rhetoric: 'the art of persuasion' and rhetoric: the study of 'how people choose what to say in a given situation, how to arrange or order their thoughts, select the specific terminology to employ, and decide how precisely they are going to deliver their message' (Medhurst and Benson, 1984, p. vii) is potentially an all-encompassing discipline. As far as the museum or heritage collection is concerned what is involved is the study of the design and arrangement of the exhibitions in their specific attempts to claim and to guide and to persuade the visitor to accept their messages. The rhetoric of the museum would consist in the study of the detailed mechanisms of their efforts at engagement, of the choice and placing of objects and labels and audio-visual gadgetry in order to define both the particular and general metaphors, figures and styles of contemporary exhibition practice (see Miles, 1988).

One key rhetorical move, for example, is the use of arrows to guide the visitor along a predetermined route. Another is the particular deployment of interactive exhibits and the attempt to create a particular response in their use. Yet a third is in the drafting and placing of labels. What becomes interesting (and important) for research in these cases is the matching of curatorial intention and visitor response, and of the assessment of the visitor's own rhetorical reconstruction of the exhibition as he or she (or they) make their own sense of it from the structures and figures which are on display. The study of the rhetoric of the museum or the heritage site therefore involves attention to the detail of exhibition design, but also to its impact. It is a major route into the study of the mechanisms of an exhibition's effectiveness.

One final point needs to be made before I discuss briefly the particular research methods that seem to me appropriate to the issues as I have defined them. It is this. The framing of the study of the museum or heritage site as text should not blind us to their quality as social and historical phenomena, to their embedding in the complexities of politics, economics and culture.

Exhibitions are produced by real people for real people in contexts not necessarily of their own making and having consequences that they cannot possibly have intended. The dangers of decontextualization, to which museums themselves can fall prey, can also affect the research activity. It is absolutely essential that the social and historical specificity of the museum or heritage display, both at the macro-level of structure and the micro-level of the patterns of activity of the everyday, should be taken into account in assessing their significance and impact. This, too, is a lesson that can be drawn from mass communication and cultural studies research.

The Claims of Ethnography

To undertake an 'ethnography' is to undertake an enquiry into the specific complexities of cultural and social life. An ethnography is essentially qualitative (though not necessarily exclusively so). It presumes the presence of the researcher amongst his or her subjects as they go about their business. Through the medium of the case study the task is to understand an organization's, a group's, a society's uniqueness, and to try and represent it as a whole. Classically, of course, this was a method used by anthropologists in their work among tribal peoples, and was grounded substantially in a long period of fieldwork, of participant observation, amongst their subjects. There are an increasing number of examples, however, of ethnographies in modern society, among scientists (Latour and Woolgar, 1979), among schoolchildren (Willis, 1977), among families (Wallman, 1984), and among television producers (Silverstone, 1985). It has become a major method of enquiry into different aspects of contemporary culture, and in the analysis of the processes of mass communication (Hall et al., 1980 pp. 73–117). Increasingly ethnography is becoming the focus of sophisticated and critical attention (Marcus and Fischer, 1986). The aim of all of these ethnographies, despite their different approaches, is to represent through description and analysis 'a particular way of life as fully as possible' (Marcus and Fischer, 1986 p. 22).

The 'particular way of life' of the museum or the heritage display is not as odd a notion as it might first appear. After all, the work of the museum – the work of the producers and the receivers of exhibitions in all their refinement – is, as I have argued throughout this paper, a complex process of mutual construction and representation undertaken within a plausibly distinct social and cultural microcosm. A museum or a heritage site is a spatially defined world of material objects, social actions and meanings. No two exhibitions are the same. Yet, together, they occupy a particular corner of contemporary cultural life, sharing, as I have also argued, much with other cultural forms and competing for attention in the complex world of the everyday. All are differently embedded in space and time; all create, in turn, their own sense of space and time.

An ethnographic approach requires the researcher to treat his or her subjects as anthropologically strange, but also to recognize his or her own involvement as a human being within that research. The researcher is also a subject. The work of observation and interpretation is necessarily grounded in the multiple subjectivities of observer and observed, and the task of the researcher is to produce, through the medium of the case study, an account of a piece of the world which is descriptively and analytically adequate, though inevitably what counts as adequate will always remain to some extent a problem and will always and necessarily remain contested.

To a significant extent, however, adequacy in ethnography is a function of the quality of the data generated, its 'richness', its coherence, its completeness. An account of museum and heritage work needs to be recognizable to those who are involved in it, but at the same time it needs to challenge that work as a result of the insights derived from a critically but sympathetically distant position of observation. An ethnography should always be specific. It should always be informed by theory, but it should also provide a basis for questioning and modifying theory. It should be grounded in a detailed programme of observation and questioning, fundamentally committed to real-time study and to an understanding of the historically situated complexity of daily life and work. As I have suggested, its medium is the specific case study, but given its fundamental concern with process, and with the embedded nature of social activity, it must produce accounts which will provide a basis for comparison and, via comparison, generalization. A programme of ethnographic work in museums and heritage displays would provide, therefore, a rich source of comparative data through the accumulation of case studies, each of which would have at the same time a direct and, dare I say, a therapeutic, relationship to the museum or exhibition upon which it was based.

Conclusion

The museum and the heritage display provide a significant but fascinating challenge for research. The conceptual and practical problems of understanding their place in contemporary culture and the particular character of their work are formidable. I have argued that they share much with the other mass media and institutions. They are playing an increasingly important role in our public culture, increasingly embedded in the world of mass communications and increasingly dependent for their survival and development on their ability to master the problems posed by this changing communicative environment. The implications for an understanding of the educational role of the museum and the heritage display are of course equally profound, for not only is it the case that learning in such settings is a matter of informal rather than formal procedure, but my arguments suggest that the problem of learning from an exhibition or a museum visit is even more diffuse than many recent studies have suggested (Miles, 1987; McManus, 1988).

It is not special pleading to suggest that the kind of research I have been outlining could provide an important factor not only for the museum and heritage industry in its bid for survival and growth, but also for the wider community in assessing and understanding the changing social significance of the museum as we move into the next century. What we have so far substantially lacked is precisely what is being suggested here: an understanding of the museum and the heritage display as social and cultural forms, and an understanding of the interrelated dynamics of production and reception within them. This seems to me to be the promise of future research, and one entirely dependent on seeing museums and heritage sites as fundamentally involved in the processes of mass communication.

If the bottom line for research on heritage presentation and interpretation is evaluation, then I wish to suggest that evaluation be seen not as a matter of measurement but of understanding, and as a matter of the study not of individual visitors but of the whole communication process in which all who are involved, both as producers and consumers, are implicated.

References

Benjamin, W. (1973) *Illuminations*, Collins/Fontana, London.

Bennett, T. (1988) 'Museums and "the people"', in Lumley (1988) pp. 63–85.

Bud, R. (1988) 'The myth and the machine: seeing science through museum's eyes', in Law, J. (ed.) *Sociological Review Monographs*, 35.

Eco, U. (1987) *Travels in Hyper-reality*, Pan, London.

Fiske, J. (1987) *Television Culture*, Methuen, London.

Hall, S. et al. (eds) (1980) *Culture, Media, Language*, Hutchinson, London.

Haraway, D. (1984–5) 'Teddy bear patriarchy: taxidermy in the garden of Eden, New York City, 1908–1936', *Social Text*, 11, 20–64.

Hewison, R. (1967) *The Heritage Industry: Britain in a Climate of Decline*, Methuen, London.

Latour, B. and Woolgar, S. (1979) *Laboratory Life: the Social Construction of Scientific Facts*, Sage, London and Beverly Hills.

Lumley, R. (ed.) (1988) *The Museum Time Machine*, Comedia/Routledge, London.

Marcus, G.E. and Fischer, M.M. (1986) *Anthropology as Cultural Critique*, Chicago University Press, Chicago.

McManus, P.M. (1988) 'Good companions: more on the social determinants of learning related behaviour in a science museum', *The International Journal of Museum Management and Curatorship*, 7, 37–44.

Medhurst, M.J. and Benson, T.W. (eds) (1984) *Rhetorical Dimensions in Media: a Critical Casebook*, Kendall Hunt, Dubuque, Iowa.

Miles, R.S. (1987) 'Museums and the communication of science, in Ciba Foundation Conference, *Communicating science to the public*, John Wiley, Chichester, pp. 114–22.

Miles, R.S. (ed.) (1988) *The Design of Educational Exhibits*, 2nd edition. Allen and Unwin, London.

Morton, A. (1988) 'Tomorrow's yesterdays: science museums and the future', in

Lumley (1988) pp. 128–43.

Popper, K.R. (1963) *Conjectures and Refutations*, Routledge and Kegan Paul, London.

Silverstone, R. (1985) *Framing Science: the Making of a BBC Documentary*, British Film Institute, London.

Silverstone, R. (1988) 'Museums and the media: a theoretical and methodological exploration', *The International Journal of Museum Management and Curatorship*, 7, 231–41.

Wallman, S. (1984) *Eight London Households*, Tavistock, London.

Willis, P. (1977) *Learning to Labour: How Working-class Kids Get Working-class Jobs*, Gower, Aldershot, Hampshire.

18

The Social Helix:
Visitor Interpretation as a
Tool for Social Development

Alan Machin

Introduction

Heritage interpretation is popularly seen as an expanding activity throughout the world. In this paper I intend to take a fresh look at the broader significance of what is involved. Tourism is seen as the 'missing link' in the range of ways that people have of discovering their world./Interpretation is described as part of a dynamic process which starts with discovery and continues through understanding, decision-making and finally action as a means of social improvement. A model is suggested for this process, called *The Social Helix*.

Rejecting the Frontier

Less than a century has passed since interpretation was established as a means of visitor communication. In the United Kingdom it has blossomed in less than two decades. The Society for the Interpretation of Britain's Heritage was formed only in 1975, and the Carnegie Awards for Heritage Interpretation were first presented in 1984. The 1990s stretch ahead to the millennium of Arthur C Clarke's sentinel in space and HAL 9000 computer of the film *2001*. I suggest that in the years to come interpretation will be much more a tool used to unlock the secrets of our own worlds, our own communities, than one tied to the outward urge of space exploration.

For more than a century we have tried to escape from the consequences of industrial cities by moving out. Emigration has been an answer and, for many, a necessity, whether to new colonies or to new suburbs. With the end of the middle ages there had come the end of the largely self-contained towns and villages of Western Europe. Exploration and printing opened windows on a world which would value mobility higher than fixity, and change higher than constancy.

As a result, interpretation came to be associated with the explaining of unfamiliar worlds. Town dwellers were shown the wonders of the countryside through excursions and visits to country parks. The inhabitants of the present were shown the past through historic houses and museums. These two activities have often become compensations for the problems of modern urban life. Interpretation has come to be seen as part of a leisure industry instead of community affairs. It is thought of as a luxury instead of an essential, which seems to suggest that interpreters have an uphill struggle in getting the subject accepted in the popular mind.

Interpretation has to help foster understanding, and the world in which most people live is humdrum and often stressful. Many interpreters are now involved with the problems of city life and the challenge of change, and without a broad perspective of the changes which are occurring they are likely to fail. Part of that perspective ought to be seeing interpretation as related to the mechanisms of change and in a wider context than it has been to date: perhaps even in politics.

Rex Beddis, until his untimely death the Humanities Adviser for Avon, called the process 'experiencing, understanding and shaping place' (Beddis, 1986). In the broader context of social change we can identify four components – discovery, understanding, debate and reaction – which drive each other in turn, and which in societies create a fourfold spiral of progress – what a systems analyst might call a social helix of change (Figure 18.1).

Such a concept sounds highly theoretical, a model of abstraction. It is not. It is an idea that has been born out of practical requirements in a lively programme of community regeneration in Calderdale, a district of West Yorkshire in the United Kingdom. It has been formulated to demonstrate the relationships between how people gain their understanding of their world and what they can do to improve it. The various roles of the mass media, education and tourism in creating and changing images can be seen (Machin, 1986). The part played by democratic discussion can be related to community action of a kind which is in sharp contrast to some of the nationally imposed solutions of the present decade.

The four components of the helix need a little more explanation.

Discovery is the first stage. People discover their world first of all from other people – parents, family, friends and acquaintances: it is a *circle of contact*. This circle can be enlarged by movement – by *travel*, and therefore by tourism, the missing link of knowledge. Next comes the *mass media*, including not only printing and broadcasting but a range of media from art to theatre and even architecture; in all of these an opinion-former can make statements which are disseminated to a huge audience. Finally there is education, drawing on all the other forms of discovery, and formalized into a distinctive and highly structured activity. These can be described as four *dimensions of discovery*.

The second component of the helix, the second stage of the process, is *understanding*. This is where the part of interpretation which deals with opinion forming comes into its own – the other communication aspect is a

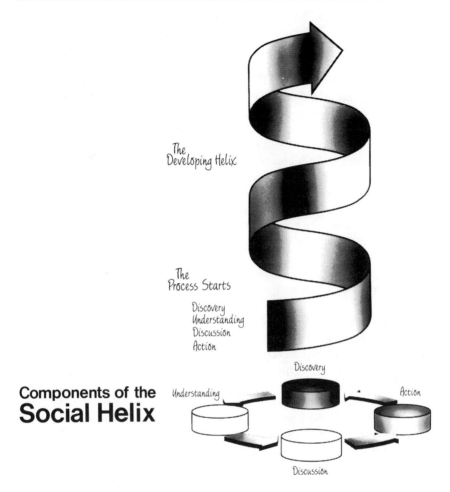

The
Developing Helix

The
Process Starts

Discovery
Understanding
Discussion
Action

Components of the
Social Helix

Discovery

Understanding

Action

Discussion

Figure 18.1   The Social Helix.

mass media activity in the discovery component. Understanding is a function of discovery, but also of individual psychology. It therefore encompasses perception, cognition, interpretation and memory.

Next comes *decision-making*, whether by *ad hoc* groups of individuals or by political and commercial processes. The decisions will be taken by individuals after personal consideration, by *ad hoc* groups, formal committees, legislatures like governments, and consultant groups of all kinds.

Finally, there is the *reaction* to discovery and discussion – taking action, through social, economic, political and cultural initiatives.

The interrelationship of these components is what forms the helix, for as they react upon each other, and action in turn spurs on further discoveries, they have a dynamic effect, driving a process of change. But since it is *change* which is generated, the circle itself moves; symbolically upward for improvement, or downward for failure. To vary the metaphor, the helix is also a spring that powers activity. It only works when the components are right and their interaction is right, which means in practical terms that communities will only be improved if the strategies adopted have the right elements related in the right way: if they are not, like any power source out of control, they will damage things around them. For ourselves, we need to remember that interpreting the world is an inescapable activity, and the question is not whether it is done at all, but how and why it is done.

The helix has been suggested before as a model for communication, notably by Dance (1967) and Noelle-Neumann (1974 and 1980) emphasizing that change is involved in communication processes. It has not, as far as I know, been used to relate discovery, interpretation, democracy and action in a theoretical form. In my own experience of Calderdale, urban renewal theorizing can seem like a substitute for action, but it is still essential to make sure we have got all the elements of our approach correct.

The Growth of Concern

Visitor interpretation has a prehistory, stretching back to the eighteenth century. Between 1780 and 1880 there were established many examples of guided visits, audio-visual centres, museums and collections of flora and fauna. In the twentieth century the interpretation of the natural world grew, especially when the need for conservation was recognized. A sense of historic change also spurred an interest in museums and monuments. To the older media of communication were added new techniques, all designed for use on-site: self-guided trails, interpretive panels, listening posts and sound guides.

Most of the new hardware has been funded as part of tourism development strategies and so a ready market has increased its use. Tourist interpretation is certainly important, but many schemes in the United Kingdom have been aimed at residents as much as visitors. The heritage centre at Faversham, for example, had a major part to play in building local awareness of the town. Warrington's nature centre at Risley Moss was formed as part of the amenities of the growing new town. Many cities have their guided walks programmes, often aimed at a local audience. In Bath the Countess of Huntingdon Centre is an important educational facility for local study of the city's architecture and history. In Barnsley, the Community Action in the Rural Environment (or CARE) project stimulates both discovery and action in the countryside around the town.

These projects are usually part of action programmes and, as such, their organizers use a wide range of media to reach their audiences, especially the mass media and education. Communications strategies are planned which may cover schools, newspapers, radio, television, street theatre, mail shots, exhibitions and public forums. To realize their full potential they are therefore adding the mass media and education to what we might regard as traditional interpretation. Several pioneering schemes are under way which are doing so for purposes of economic and urban renewal.

The Calderdale Inheritance Project provides a good example. Faced with the decline of traditional industries – textiles, carpet making, engineering and confectionery – the district has embarked on a ten-year programme to reverse the downward turn. Initiatives have included the rehabilitation of historic mill buildings for new industry and small businesses, the restoration of the Rochdale Canal for recreation and tourism, and the upgrading of fine Victorian shopping streets to encourage retail activity. 'Business in the Community', a national body representing blue-chip companies anxious to help revive declining economies, has been involved. Tourism has been developed as a means of economic growth and as a way of changing the area's image and self-image.

Leading up to the project was the re-opening in 1976 of the Halifax Piece Hall, which led not only to a reassessment of the local built environment, but to new interpretive facilities and attractions. Over the next decade, slowly at first but then accelerating, a new industrial museum, an art gallery, a countryside centre, a car museum, a few dozen guidebooks, a tourist guide service, and a countryside ranger service were added by various organizations to the local stock, which had consisted mainly of a fine folk museum and some small collections. Two factories opened their doors to visitors and began to adapt their marketing – one selling wood-and-leather clogs, the other sweets. Canal boat trips appeared on the restored Rochdale Canal, and work began on a major countryside centre at Ogden Reservoir.

Many environmental improvement projects are central to the programme, re-using old mills, restoring the Rochdale Canal and making town centres more attractive. Recently, moves have begun to broaden out the scope to work on run-down areas of housing. Much of this work followed principles suggested in a report prepared for the national Civic Trust, which encouraged the Calderdale enterprise. Michael Quinion Associates produced *Caring for the Visitor: An Interpretive Strategy for Calderdale* in November 1985.

Three major public relations exercises are under way through the 'Inheritance Project', with the historic importance of Calderdale in mind. Number one, called 'The Constant Stream', is being built up through a series of media starting with a leaflet and an audio cassette. It describes the constant efforts of local people to improve the quality of life in times of change, principally those of the industrial revolution and its aftermath. Another exercise sets out to join with several other historic areas of England in a special campaign to stress their historic importance. For Calderdale this will help place the district in the context of better known historic towns.

The third exercise aimed to take advantage of the broad interest in heritage matters. From 24–27 October 1988 a Council of Europe Conference looked at 'Heritage for Successful Town Regeneration' when it met in Calderdale. Supporting and fringe events created a kind of heritage festival, which may be repeated in future years. The Civic Trust Education Group organized a meeting on 'Education and Regeneration'. Other meetings were aimed at local people; one examined the economic future of the area, another consisted of a showing of archive films. A speaker from Cracow in Poland described the long history of conservation work there. A one-day school assessed the impact of E.P. Thompson's *The Making of the English Working Class*, a book which was partially written drawing on the wealth of archive material in and about Calderdale. There was also a heritage exhibition looking at urban renewal, tourism and educational work. Finally, a one-off publication, the *Calderdale Heritage Review*, looked at a range of schemes in northern England which relate to discovery, understanding, decision-making and action for improvement: the elements of the 'social helix' described in this paper.

The importance of all this lies in the fact that the audience for Calderdale promotion is not only that of tourists but, more importantly, local people. Other target audiences are opinion makers and potential investors, to whom the message is one of an attractive place with a store of good people and a distinctive quality of life. Deep inside the story is the heart of the matter: summed up in the 'Constant Stream' label applied both to the River Calder which carved the valley scenery, and to the unbroken tradition of enterprise which is restoring Calderdale prosperity. Heritage to these people has something to do with the past, but much more to do with the future. The blunt Yorkshire character is very down-to-earth and impatient with nostalgia. A marketing journal recently described Calderdale as: 'Regarded by professionals as one of the best attempts in the country to put the clock back' (Brown, 1986). Coverage in a national journal is praise indeed, but such an unfortunate piece of phraseology turns it into highly damaging imagery. In Calderdale, heritage as nostalgia is rejected: the legacy for the next generation is what matters.

With economic renewal and the creation of a positive image as key elements, the Calderdale Project can also act as an exemplar to overcome a major problem of the UK – the gap between the prosperous south and the declining north. Both the mass media and education tend to highlight negative images in order to illustrate differences in character. The communication strategy behind the Calderdale Project tries to replace negative images by positive ones. It is then used as a dynamic way of creating changes in attitudes and the environment. Heritage is a resource. While this is also the case in other places, the particular mix of problems, attitudes, resources and solutions occurring in Calderdale must be unique. The landscape, along with the archives and artefacts of the area, contains an unparalleled record of the effects of social change on communities. The district is large enough to show complex problems, but these difficulties are not of a scale to attract major grant aid. Consequently a network of small- to medium-scale initiatives has appeared, which has generated its own form of vitality within the community at large.

The Wider Applications

The lessons learnt in this kind of scheme can be applied on a global scale to the problems of underdeveloped countries, changing traditional opinions which were often formed in a colonial cultural ethos. With the advantage of tourism as 'seeing for yourself', and visitor interpretation providing the means to put across the message, new roles emerge for these activities. A newly independent African country, for example, could use its scenery and wildlife to attract visitors, while making available forms of historic interpretation which would avoid being propaganda but would be scripted from a local perspective. Britain has, after all, being doing that for years, and has built a massive tourism programme on it.

Interpreters will therefore need to see their role in a new context, alongside the mass media and education, influencing popular culture. The north of England gives us another good example. For a quarter of a century British attitudes to the north have been influenced by the *Coronation Street* image. In June 1988, Granada Television opened its doors to tourists in order for them to see how television works. People can now visit the famous 'Street' in its TV home. They can also find out if the north and its people are really like the media image. It is also arguable that conservationists will not win their cause unless they come to grips with an understanding of how popular images and values are formed, such as by television, and this kind of exhibition helps that.

The challenge to interpretation in the 1990s is to recognize better how it can play a part in our everyday lives as a way of solving problems, rather than being wasted as entertainment helping to escape them.

References

Beddis, R.A. (1986) *GCSE Environment Syllabus*, Southern Regional Examination Board, Southampton.

Brown, A. (1986) 'Selling Heritage' *Marketing* (23 June) 29.

Dance, F.E.X. (1967) *A Helical Model of Communication*, in *Human Communication Theory*, New York.

Machin, A. (1986) 'Changing the viewpoint', *Heritage Interpretation*, 34 (Winter), 4–5.

Machin, A. (ed.) (1988) *The Calderdale Heritage Review*, Calderdale Metropolitan Borough Council, Halifax, Yorkshire.

Michael Quinion Associates (1985) *Caring for the Visitor: An Interpretive Strategy for Calderdale*, Civic Trust, London.

Noelle-Neumann, E. (1974) 'The spiral of silence: a theory of public opinion', *Journal of Communication*, 24, 43–51.

Noelle-Neumann, E. (1980) 'Mass media and social change in developed societies', in Wilhoit, G.C. and de Bock, H. (eds) *Mass Communication Review Yearbook 1980*, pp. 657–78, Sage Publ., Beverley Hills.

19

What People Say and How They Think in a Science Museum

Paulette McManus

Introduction

In this paper I shall discuss the sort of thinking which, as evidenced by language people use in conversations, can go on moment by moment during a visit to a science museum. The thinking I will describe represents a slice across a visit to an exhibition, and the work done by groups of visitors in sorting out their experiences at a single exhibit, rather than personal assessments and conclusions about an entire exhibition. However, the events I describe would very likely have a cumulative effect on final thoughts about an exhibition, and could form the foundations of memories about a visit to a museum.

The data I present were collected during a three-year study into communications with and between visitors to the British Museum (Natural History) (hereafter referred to as BM(NH)). During the study, 1,572 visitors in 641 groups were unobtrusively observed, and 168 complete conversations recorded, as they interacted with exhibits and each other at five locations in the museum.

Talk in the Museum

The following transcripts illustrate the general tenor of conversations in the museum. Parentheses are uncertain transcriptions and empty parentheses indicate inaudible utterances. Dashes in parentheses indicate the number of untranscribable words. The parenthetical numbers are the length of pauses (in seconds) in an utterance and a micropause is indicated by (.). Extension of sound is indicated by :, and italic type indicates emphasis.

The first conversation is from a young couple (M,F) who were viewing a traditional display of twenty-four labelled models of 'Pests of Home and Store' in the Insect Gallery.

F Those are mites there (.) in the cheese (beetle) n uh: (5.0) Oh it's the house beetle (1.0) goh: Yuh: (1.0) look there's ( )

M Like what we've got under our roof

F Yeah (4.0) (heaven knows) (.) it's moths isn't it?

M No that isn't ( )

F Yuh ( ) empty (.) ( ) (4.0) that's the moth (.) brown house moth (6.0) Cheese skipper (.) er I don't like cheese (all the same) (8.0)

M (whispering) Puts you right off bacon 'n cheese (laughter)

The second conversation took place between a mother (M) and her eight-year-old son (S) who were playing the Sorting Game in the Origin of Species Gallery. At this game visitors were asked to sort ten discs, each stamped with a picture of a pond organism, into the outlines of three dishes printed on a sloping board. The aim of the game was to demonstrate that there are many ways of sorting living things depending on the criteria chosen for classification.

M Which do you have to do first (1.0) it says (2.0)

S What to do (.) start with a: clear board

M Clear board press the button below to do this (.) right (.) then it's clear (.) right (.)

S I know what to do

M Wait (.) slide the discs upwards to make three groups one group in each dish (.) so you're putting them according to which ones you think (.) put all the ones you think in this group (.) this one (.) that's right (.) this is a plant (.) this is a plant (.) right

S Here?

M Hm hm (4.0) which ones do you think are related (.) this is a (− −)

S ( ) I want to do the um: (9 seconds of inaudible speech) insects (.) what's this mummy (6.0)

M How about this one (.) this one has many (.) jointed legs too (.) you see all these have jointed legs

S What's this?

M That's just a worm a worm like creature (.) so has to be in a different group (8.0) so maybe (8.0) these two are plants these are in a different group altogether (4.0)

S those two (−)

M Maybe we put all the shells together these have shells (.) this has a shell (.) Eh:? Let's have a shell? (.) This doesn't have a shell (.) this doesn't have a shell (.) this doesn't have a shell (.) this doesn't have a shell (3.0)

S Do *this*

M Leave it alone

S No (− −)

M Well clear the board by pressing the knob

S Oh

M See [*the discs move automatically to the bottom*]

S There it's clear (2.0) in there frog (2.0) plants

M Do you know what is that? (.) I've never come across them

S Shells where

M Make another division here are the divisions I mean [*sounds of play*]

The third conversation is from two sixteen-year-old boys (*B1*, *B2*). They were at an exhibit in the 'Man's Place in Evolution' exhibition where visitors were given primate characteristics and asked to select the single primate from among six animals displayed in a case and also pictured above the push buttons on a console.

B1 OK (.) my go (1.0) which one is the primate (1.0) (– – –) I think (.) is that one a (mink)
B2 I'm not too sure actually (.) Oh stop looking at the picture
B1 (Laughter) What are they?
B2 ( ) (its mouth) ( )
B1 Ok (.) Ok now I reckon it's (small ape) it's going to be
B2 It's not the Malaysian fruit bat (laughter)
B1 This one this one (3.0) no
B2 Yes: ! The diana monkey
B1 The diana monkey?

The final conversation is from a three-generation family group of grand-mother (G), mother (M) and a six-year-old boy (B). They were visiting a traditional display of an *Iguanadon* (dinosaur) skeleton in a bay of the Central Hall.

G Who's that?
B ( )
G Not dipsi love (.) hipsi (8.0)
B ( )
G He's not tyrannosaurus love (.) not quite ( )
B What's this (.) who are they
[*The family then moved away but soon returned*]
B Don't go that way
M ( ) show Grannie ( )
G I'm just *comparing* the size of this(.) iguanadon (with diplodoccus) you see there ( ) so those models he's got (.) they're not to scale ( )
M No
G Because the (basics) are nearly as big as iguanadon
M It's not really (right)
G I mean ( ) I thought
B ( ) go round this way

The first feature of these conversations to note is their low-key everyday style. Although museums are generally seen, especially by those who work in them, as authoritative, there is no sign of a corresponding earnestness or high-mindedness in these visitors' attitudes. They attend closely to the communications presented to them – they even read out parts of labels to each other – but they are not spending time 'swotting' at exhibits, nor are they self-consciously engaged in 'learning activities'. These visitors are engaged on a walking and talking visit and a curatorial 'tell them all I know' approach or a book-on-the-wall exhibition would mismatch their intentions.

A second feature to note is the amiable, sociable nature of the interactions between visitors. The first couple share a mild joke, the mother and son in the second conversation share their sorting game harmoniously, the boys in the third conversation have been taking turns to try exhibit games and, in the last conversation, the grandmother fondly teaches her grandson the Latin names of dinosaurs. Clearly, talk in the museum is just as much for keeping the social group in touch as it is for dealing with exhibit content (see McManus, 1987, 1988, for a discussion of the effect of the social context of visits on learning-related behaviour in the museum).

The last feature to note is the evidence of engagement, and thinking about the subject of the communication, at each exhibit. The first couple sift through the twenty-four household pests and identify the one 'like what we've got under our roof'. The conversation between the mother and young son at the sorting game shows the mother working to define several sets of classification criteria, and her son, following her example, working out one for himself. The sixteen-year-old boys at the 'What is a Primate?' game resisted the temptation to get an easy answer by using the exhibit as a guessing game and the first boy was obviously dismayed when his assessment was shown to be incorrect. At the *Iguanadon* skeleton an elderly visitor made observations about the scale of dinosaur models, took care to check them, evaluated her observations and the communication presented to her and, finally, asked for a check on her evaluation. In another context this could be called scientific behaviour.

Talking and Thinking in the Museum

The above observations are drawn from a close examination of the conversations recorded in the BM(NH). We need a finer form of analysis than an examination of the surface features of visitors' conversations if we wish to have a more focused idea of the thinking activities which can be set up by an exhibit communication. A form of discourse analysis, based on that used to describe classroom interactions (Sinclair & Coulthard, 1975), was therefore developed to analyse the body of conversations recorded in the BM(NH).

Discourse Acts

I shall discuss the first stage of the analysis where all of the language used and responded to in the communicative situation is broken down into discourse acts. When we talk we link discourse acts together to express ideas and to control and structure the social aspects of conversational exchange. Some forms of writing can also be broken down into interactive discourse acts. In the museum, visitors respond interactively to the words in label texts and also introduce the phrases of exhibition teams into their conversation.

As a result, parts of exhibit texts were included in the analyses as the exhibition team's language contribution to communication.

Discourse acts are short stretches of words which, when spoken, are delivered with a single intonation contour. They are sometimes referred to as the tone group and are then seen as the unit of neurological planning of speech (Aitcheson, 1983). The unit of planning is the size of the chunk of speech we prepare in advance in readiness for utterance. Such planning is done in two stages. Outline planning, involving key words, syntax and intonation pattern begins prior to utterance or while the previous group of words is being uttered. The speaker then begins on the partly planned clause and does detailed planning, fitting in stressed and unstressed words, while near the beginning of the production of the utterance. A noticeable pause in a tone group indicates difficulty in achieving detailed planning satisfactorily and, fortunately for my purposes, slows the process down so that we can examine it. For example, here we have a visitor to the BM(NH) having difficulty in describing an anteater's muzzle: 'See his long: (2.0) nose (.)'. Clearly, she has difficulty in finding a noun for her purpose. She fills in time with: 'it's nice isn't it (.)'. And tries again: 'See his nose (.) think of him scooping up the ants'. She appears not to be satisfied with 'nose' and fifteen seconds later tries again: 'See the anteater's long: um: mouth (.) it's for snuffing up ants'.

The extensions of sound and the hesitation pause in this last utterance indicate that the visitor is still searching for a word which will name the muzzle of the animal and link form to function.

A second example of difficulty in achieving detailed planning shows a visitor deciding on the degree of force with which he will express his intention to do a social action. The first tone group is produced smoothly and he hesitates at the beginning of the next at his point of decision: 'Which one is a primate (.) shall I (.) I'll tell you which one's a primate'.

Utterances such as these bring the thinking of the museum visitors up to the surface of their language. We cannot get inside visitors' heads to look for psychological acts but it is reasonable to consider tone group utterances, discourse acts, as units which provide some evidence of thinking in progress. Twenty-six categories of acts were used to describe the communicative activities I recorded in the BM(NH). They were given self-explanatory names which describe their function in the stream of conversation.

Comparison of Exhibits Using Discourse Act Frequency

Comparison of the occurrence and frequency of acts at different exhibits gives insight into the events set in train in the visitor's mind by an exhibition team when an exhibit communication is presented in the museum.

The conversations of thirteen groups (containing thirty-nine individuals) were analysed from the 'Household Pests' exhibit from which the first

Table 19.1 Ranking of Acts, traditional display, 'Household Pests' exhibit

Rank	Act	N	%	Cum. %
1	Informative 1	59	18.8	
2	Non-verbal accept.	42	13.4	32.2
3	Text-echo	37	11.8	44.0
3	Text-inform	37	11.8	55.8
5	Elicitation 1	20	6.4	62.2
6	Accept	17	5.4	67.6
7	Attender	14	4.5	72.1
8	Marker	13	4.1	76.2
9	Informative 2	9	2.9	79.1
10	Summons	7	2.2	81.3
10	Comment 1	7	2.2	83.5
10	Comment 2	7	2.2	85.7
10	Elicitation 3	7	2.2	87.9
14	Metastatement	6	1.9	89.8
14	Informative 3	6	1.9	91.7
16	Directive	5	1.6	93.3
16	Acknowledge	5	1.6	94.9
18	Jocular directive	4	1.3	96.2
19	Comment 3		1.0	97.2
19	Evaluation	3	1.0	98.2
21	Elicitation 2		0.6	98.8
21	Reply	2	0.6	99.4
23	Loop	1	0.3	99.7
23	Clue	1	0.3	100.0
	Conclusion	–		
	Check	–		
		314	100.0	

Notes: Elicitations, informatives and comments coded 1 are concerned with objective information. Those coded 2 are concerned with subjective feeling states. Elicitations and informatives coded 3 are concerned with polarity information (yes/no). Comments coded 3 are concerned with reminiscences.

conversation reported here was recorded. This was traditional, static, 'show-and-tell' museum display with twenty-four models, each with a label underneath, arranged in four rows and enclosed in a pair of glass cases angled together. The labels named each insect model and gave a description of the damage the insect caused to home or stores.

The conversations of sixteen groups (containing forty-three individuals) were analysed at the Sorting Game, in the Origin of Species gallery, from which the second conversation reported here was recorded. This was an interactive exhibit which used instructions to set a problem game for the visitor in such a way that he was given enough room to find for himself the point of the concept the exhibit team wished to explain; that is, ways of

Table 19.2   Ranking of Acts, interactive problem, 'Sorting Game' exhibit

Rank	Act	N	%	Cum. %
1	Informative 1	183	21.6	
2	Non-verbal accept.	139	16.4	38.0
3	Comment 1	76	9.0	47.0
4	Elicitation 1	58	6.8	53.8
5	Marker	47	5.5	59.3
6	Evaluation	42	5.0	64.3
7	Acknowledge	33	3.9	68.2
7	Comment 2	33	3.9	72.1
9	Text-inform	28	3.3	75.4
9	Text-echo	28	3.3	78.7
11	Elicitation 3	27	3.2	81.9
12	Accept	25	3.0	84.9
13	Informative 2	23	2.7	87.6
14	Metastatement	21	2.5	90.1
14	Directive	21	2.5	92.6
16	Informative 3	19	2.2	94.8
17	Attender	16	1.9	96.7
18	Conclusion	10	1.2	97.9
18	Check	10	1.2	99.1
20	Elicitation 2	4	0.5	99.6
21	Clue	2	0.2	99.8
22	Reply	1	0.1	99.9
22	Summons	1	0.1	100.0
	Jocular directive	–		
	Comment 3	–		
	Loop	–		
		847	100.0	

Notes: Elicitations, informatives and comments coded 1 are concerned with objective information. Those coded 2 are concerned with subjective feeling states. Elicitations and informatives coded 3 are concerned with polarity information (yes/no). Comments coded 3 are concerned with reminiscences.

sorting depend on classification criteria. This independent discovery left the visitor in a position where he could teach or explain the point to others.

The two sets of visitors were comparable in composition, with family groups, couples and both adult and child peer groups represented. At the Sorting Game, 270 per cent more acts were recorded (Table 19.2) than at the 'Household Pests' (Table 19.1) exhibit because visitors talked more at the problem game. Figure 19.1 provides a key to aid reading and comparison of the two tables.

At both exhibits informative acts, related to stating objective information, and non-verbal acceptance acts, which allow any statement to pass unchallenged into discourse, were ranked in the first two positions, with a

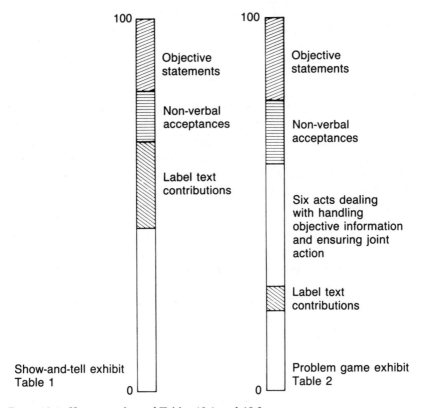

Figure 19.1 Key to reading of Tables 19.1 and 19.2.

higher percentage occurring at the problem game. The key difference in the two analyses is related to the ranking and frequency of text-inform and text-echo acts which mark the contribution of the exhibition team to communications. Their ranking at three, with a combined frequency of 23.6 per cent, at the traditional, show-and-tell exhibit (Table 19.1) and at nine, with a combined frequency of 6.6 per cent, at the interactive, problem game exhibit (Table 19.2) illustrates the differing degrees of independent mental action elicited by the two forms of exhibit communication. Comparison of the tables shows that visitors at the show-and-tell exhibit (Table 19.1) had most recourse to text, with 32.2 per cent of acts related to stating objective information and allowing contributions to discourse to pass unchallenged into conversations, occurring at greater frequency than contributions from the exhibit team. In contrast, visitors at the problem game (Table 19.2) were independent of text *once assimilated* since 72.1 per cent of acts, all related to collecting, evaluating and agreeing on objective information, occurred at greater frequency than contributions to communications from the exhibit team. Clearly, visitors at the sorting game (Table 19.2) were actively engaged in structuring their *own* ideas after having been set on a path by the exhibit team.

The ranking of the act 'Evaluation' at the show-and-tell exhibit (Table 19.1 rank 19) illustrates a passive, accepting reception of the message at the 'Household Pests' exhibit. In contrast, at the problem game (Table 19.2) this act was ranked six because the sorting game exhibit required visitors to monitor their thinking as revealed to them by their physical actions upon the game.

The rankings of acts also indicate the physical processing requirements of the differing forms of exhibit. Visitors to the show-and-tell 'Household Pests' display (Table 19.1) showed a high frequency of 'Attender' acts (rank 7) since they had to work to ensure the focusing of joint attention on items in the display which contained a large number of models. This act was ranked seventeen at the sorting game (Table 19.2).

It is interesting to examine the acts not employed at each site. The descriptive, show-and-tell 'Household Pests' exhibit contained a great deal of information, so offering varied entry points into the exhibit message. It is notable that the exhibit form did not elicit 'Check' and 'Conclusion' acts from visitors since these acts ensure joint understanding and consolidation of experience. These two acts ranked eighteen at the explanatory, problem sorting game (Table 19.2). This exhibit, which encouraged groups to work together, did not elicit the joking instructions to attend to items, reminiscences about past experiences or requests for repetition found at the 'Household Pests' exhibit where visitors could attend to the exhibit independently.

Conclusion

The conversations recorded in the BM(NH) demonstrate that visitors in groups attend to museum communications as a social unit (87 per cent of the 1,572 individuals observed in this study visited in a social group). The social unit focuses on the topic of an exhibit, and individually made observations and selectively 'activated' contributions of text from the exhibit team contribute to, and help to build, the conversations that occur. The conversations can be thought of as small learning-group discussions in which exhibit team members have a part to play. Consequently, the presentation of exhibit content, in particular exhibit labels, should be made so that such conversations are facilitated. A 'text book' style, and attempts to 'hog' the communicative situation with large segments of text, are not appropriate to the style of interaction brought to the museum by visitors.

Modern museum practice admits many ways of presenting information via exhibits. The analysis of the discourse acts occurring in the conversations recorded at two disparate exhibits demonstrates that choices made in this regard should not be made purely from a 'changing the pace of the exhibition' point of view. The style of an exhibit presentation is clearly a communicative choice which deeply affects the thinking of visitors. An object-based display would appear to give an exhibit team such loose communicative control over the thoughts of visitors that one cannot be sure that any intended points are being made. On the other hand, the effort involved in devising an exhibit which will give visitors the freedom to work independently towards forming a concept the team wishes to share will, paradoxically, give the team firm control over the communicative situation.

There is no doubt that it is desirable to employ a continuum from loose to firm control when preparing communicative situations in the museum. Both exhibition teams and visitors are helped to understand each other if this work is done self-consciously from within the museum.

Acknowledgements

My work at the British Museum (Natural History) was undertaken under a Collaborative Award in Social Sciences from the Economic and Social Research Council to the British Museum (Natural History) and the Centre for Educational Studies, King's College, London. I would like to thank Dr R.S. Miles and Professor A.M. Lucas for their consistent support and interest throughout the project.

References

Aitcheson, J. (1983) *The Articulate Mammal*, Hutchinson, London

McManus, P.M. (1987) 'It's the company you keep . . . . The social determination of learning-related behaviour in a science museum', *International Journal of Museum Management and Curatorship*, 5, 213–26.

McManus, P.M. (1988) 'Good companions . . . . More on the social determination of learning-related behaviour in a science museum', *International Journal of Museum Management and Curatorship*, 7, 37–44.

Sinclair, J.McH. and Coulthard, M. (1975) *Towards an Analysis of Discourse*, Oxford University Press, London.

20

Outdoor Education for Rural Fifth-Graders: Analysis of Attitude, Expectations, Knowledge and Perceptions

Robert C. Wendling

Introduction

This study focuses on a rural school population. As used here, the term 'rural' refers to that setting or environment in which the majority of the local economy is agriculturally based and the terms 'urban' or 'suburban' clearly do not apply. Because the term 'rural' is often used synonymously with words like agriculture, natural or undeveloped, it may be assumed that rural schoolchildren are more knowledgeable about, and have a more favourable attitude towards, the natural environment than do their urban or suburban counterparts. Research has supported these assertions, though such research is limited (Kellert and Westerveldt, 1983; Pomerantz, 1977).

While a considerable amount of research exists on children's environmental attitude, most has focused on children residing in urban settings (Crompton and Sellar, 1981; Kellert and Westerveldt, 1983). Such studies have not only revealed that urban children are characterized by lower cognitive and attitude scores about the environment (Kostka, 1976; Leftridge and James, 1980), but that significant differences exist among ethnic groups (Kellert, 1984; Metro et al., 1980).

Furthermore, and regardless of whether the child resides in an urban, suburban or rural environment, several questions deserve the attention of outdoor educators who are committed to providing meaningful educational experiences for children visiting environmental education centres (Crompton and Sellar, 1981; Ford, 1981; Gebler, 1982; Kostka, 1976; McCoy et al., 1978; Van Koevering and Prell, 1980; Wallin, 1982). These include such questions as:

(1) What do children expect to get from a field trip to an environmental education centre?
(2) What do they actually go away with?
(3) Are knowledge and attitude improved through such trips? and
(4) How can the quality of their outdoor learning experiences be improved?

Answers to these questions would be valuable to all environmental educators. They would be extremely timely in the United States, where the recent report of the President's Commission on Americans Outdoors (President's Commission, 1987) strongly advocated increased environmental education of America's schoolchildren.

The objectives of this study were to:

(1) evaluate rural students' attitude, expectations, perceptions, and knowledge prior to and after an experiential education programme on ecology;

(2) identify sub-groups within the rural student sample and compare the environmental attitude and knowledge of those sub-groups; and

(3) measure the effects of experiential education programmes on environmental attitude and knowledge.

Methods and Measures

Data for this study were collected from a rural-based county school system located in eastern North Carolina; five fifth-grade classes (134 students) were randomly selected from thirty-three classes within that system. Students in each of the five classes were heterogeneously grouped in terms of educational stratum, ethnicity, gender and socioeconomic background. The on-site environmental education programme was conducted at the 359-acre River Park North Nature Science Center located in Greenville, North Carolina.

Prior to developing the outdoor education programme the subject 'ecology' and evaluative criteria were selected from the North Carolina Department of Public Instruction's (1979, p. 188) *Competency Goals and Performance Indicators K-12*. A curriculum guide was subsequently prepared containing concept definitions, vocabulary, behavioural objectives, pre- and post-tests, pre- and post-trip classroom activities, and field trip exercises. The latter included studies of pond and grassland communities, construction of mini-terrariums, and casting of animal tracks.

Classroom teachers administered the pre- and post-tests at the beginning and end of the unit. The teachers also directed pre-trip activities which began two weeks prior to the field trip and post-trip activities which involved a one-day summary of the unit. The field trip exercises were directed by eight university students enrolled in an environmental and cultural interpretation course at a nearby university.

Objective One: Evaluation

Pre-trip Expectations

As shown in Table 20.1, virtually all children who participated in this study

Table 20.1 Pre-trip expectations of fifth-graders

| | Responses | | |
Questions	Yes	No	No response
1. Are you happy to be going to the Nature Science Centre?	99%	1%	0%
2. Do you feel that you can learn more about ecology (or nature) by taking a field trip to the Nature Science Center than by studying ecology (or nature) indoors?	98%	2%	0%
3. Have you ever taken hikes in the country or in the woods?	52%	48%	0%
4. Are you worried about any part of your field trip?	91%	9%	0%
5. When visiting the woods (or forest) do you expect to find any plants or animals that might be dangerous, harmful, or unsafe?	71%	27%	2%

were looking forward to their visit to the Nature Science Center. Ninety-nine per cent felt that they were happy to be going (Q.1), and 98 per cent felt that they could learn more about ecology through a field trip than by classroom study alone (Q.2).

Participants were from rural county schools. Surprisingly, however, nearly half (48 per cent) indicated that they had never taken hikes in the country or in the woods (Q. 3). This large number may have contributed to the high expectations which the children placed on the field trip.

Question 3, dealing with previous hikes in the country or woods, is of additional interest when comparing rural and urban schoolchildren. In a study of 324 urban children from Philadelphia and New York City, 10–16 years of age, 99 per cent reported that they had taken hikes in the country or woods prior to their school field trip (McCoy et al., 1978). This is in sharp contrasts to the 52 per cent reported in this study (see Table 20.1, Q. 3) and may suggest that rural children (1) are not more knowledgeable about the natural world than urban children; (2) do not feel the need to 'get away from it all' since they live in the country; and/or (3) their parents do not have the same amount of leisure time (8 a.m. – 5 p.m. jobs and weekends off) as their urban counterparts.

Previous studies have reported that many children seem to have some fear of the natural environment (Devlin, 1973; Kaplan, 1976; Metro et al., 1980). Consequently, children participating in this study were asked to respond to questions concerning their fears. As shown in Table 20.1, 91 per cent reported that they were worried about some part of the field trip (Q. 4), and 71 per cent reported that they expected to find plants or animals that might be dangerous, harmful or unsafe (Q. 5).

To assess the fear problem more accurately, students were asked on both

Table 20.2 Forest dangers most often identified by fifth-graders by pre- and post-test responses[1]

Type of danger	Pre-test	(frequency)	Post-test
ANIMALS	136		144
(Snakes)		(70)	(64)
(Rats)		(6)	(2)
(Dogs and Cats)		(7)	(4)
(Other)[2]		(53)	(44)
PLANTS	63		60
NOTHING	33		36
INSPECTS AND SPIDERS	16		22
TOTAL	248		232

[1] Includes multiple responses.
[2] Other animals included alligator, bear, crayfish, deer, duck, fox, lion, lizard, owl, porcupine, skunk, snapping turtle, squirrel, tiger, wolf.

the pre- and post-test to identify plants or animals found in the woods that might be dangerous, harmful or unsafe. As shown in Table 20.2 animals, especially snakes, were most frequently identified, followed by plants (e.g., poison ivy and oak, briars). It should also be noted that some of the animals identified were not indigenous to the area (e.g., alligator, lion, porcupine, tiger, wolf). Pre- and post-test comparisons revealed virtually no differences before and after the trip.

Post-trip Perceptions

As revealed in Table 20.3, a majority of the children perceived their experience at the Nature Science Center in a positive manner. Seventy per cent felt that the field trip turned out as expected (Q. 1), 63 per cent felt that it was better than spending the same amount of time in the classroom (Q. 2a), and 60 per cent felt that the field trip was better than visiting relatives out of town (Q. 2b). A relatively small amount of dissatisfaction with the field trip was identified; 6 per cent of the children felt that the groups they worked with, ranging in size from six to eight students, were too large (Q. 3), while 2 per cent felt that the trip should be shorter (Q. 4).

The children unanimously agreed that they learned 'a lot' at the Nature Science Center (Q. 5). Of all the activities engaged in during the field trip, educational activities (Q. 6a, b, c) were the most frequently enjoyed. However, 'meeting new teachers' and 'getting to know your classmates better' were quite popular; 'playing a game' was least popular, through 77 per cent of the children still identified it as enjoyable. These findings indicated that

Table 20.3 Post-trip perceptions of fifth-graders

Questions	Yes	No	No response
1. Did the field trip to the Nature Science Center turn out as you had expected?	70%	30%	0%
2. Do you feel that the field trip to the Nature Science Center was better than:			
(a) spending the same amount of time in the classroom?	63%	22%	15%
(b) Visting your relatives out of town?	60%	35%	5%
3. Do you feel that the size of the group that you worked with at the Nature Science Center was too large?	5%	95%	0%
4. Do you feel that the field trip should be shorter?	2%	98%	0%
5. Do you think that you learned a lot at the Nature Science Center?	100%	0%	0%
6. What things did you enjoy doing at the Nature Science Center?			
(a) Casting animals' tracks?	93%	1%	6%
(b) Studying the food web of the pond?	90%	6%	4%
(c) Building a terrarium?	88%	5%	7%
(d) Meeting new teachers?	88%	5%	7%
(e) Studying the food web of the grassland?	84%	6%	7%
(f) Playing a game?	77%	16%	7%
(g) Getting to know your classmates better?	76%	14%	10%

learning and socialization which occurred during the field trip were enjoyable and important processes.

Environmental Knowledge and Attitude

The effects of utilizing (a) traditional classroom lectures, (b) hands-on classroom activities, and (c) a field trip were evaluated by a one-way ANOVA on data collected from five groups of students. The five groups included students who participated in (1) only traditional classroom lectures (representing the control group), (2) only hands-on classroom activities), (3) both traditional classroom lectures and a field trip, (4) both hands-on activities and a field trip, and (5) hands-on activities, field trip, and a post-trip summary.

Knowledge: The effect of the field trip on learning about the natural environment was measured using fifteen multiple choice questions on ecology. Initial construction resulted in twenty questions; their selection was based on a review of related research (McCoy et al., 1978), the behavioural

Table 20.4 Mean ecology exam scores by Group[1]

Groups	1	2	3	4	5
Pre-test	9.12	8.36	8.75	8.54	9.31
Post-test	7.80	9.64	8.86	10.62	9.93

[1] Groups:
1. Control (traditional classroom lectures only).
2. Hands-on classroom activities only.
3. Traditional classroom activities and field trip.
4. Hands-on classroom activities, field trip, and post-trip summary.

objectives identified in the curriculum guide, and input from fifth-grade teachers. Subsequently, the twenty questions were reviewed and edited by fifth-grade teachers. The editing process retained fifteen questions which were pre-tested on sixty fifth-graders. After minor editing changes, the fifteen multiple choice questions were finalized. (Interested readers may contact the author for a copy of the finalized list of questions.)

Table 20.4 shows that the ecology exam scores changed more in some groups than in others. Statistical analysis (an analysis of variance on pre-post change scores) showed that the group differences were not due to chance [$F(4, 129) = 5.39$, $p = .0005$]. Students who participated in hands-on classroom activities (Groups 2, 4 and 5) learned more than those who did not (Groups 1 and 3) [$F(1, 129) = 15.67$, $p < .0001$], and those who participated in the field trip (Groups 3, 4 and 50 learned more than those who did not (Groups 1 and 2) [$F(1, 129) = 3.80$, $p = .05$].

Additional analysis showed that the increase in exam scores was not due to chance for students who did have hands-on classroom activities [$t(78) = 4.55$, $p < .001$] or did participate in the field trip [$t(78) = 2.98$, $p = .004$], but that there was no statistically significant amount of learning in the students who did not have hands-on classroom activities [$t952) = -1.30$, $p = .20$] or did not participate in the field [$t(52) = 0.12$, $p = .90$]. That is, both hands-on classroom activities and participating in the field trip produced superior learning as measured by the ecology exam scores.

Attitude: Students' attitude toward the natural environment was measured using a Likert scale consisting of the following five items:
(1) the woods (or forest) are unsafe;
(2) the woods are full of life;
(3) the woods are of no interest to me;
(4) the woods would be a fun place to study ecology (or science);
(5) I can have more fun on the school playground than studying ecology in the woods.

Initial assembly identified ten statements as was based on a review of related research (Burch, 1977; McCoy et al., 1978; and Metro et al., 1980) and discussions with fifth-graders about the natural environment. Subsequently, the ten statements were edited for brevity; eliminated were those that contained more than one central idea and those that did not specifically pertain to the natural environment.

The editing process retained the indicated five statements which were pre-tested on sixty fifth-graders. Minor editing changes were required, resulting in the final five-item scale. To minimize response sets, the five statements containing both favourable, and unfavourable, statements were randomly mixed. Consideration for constructing a scale with face validity was reflected in the extensive amount of planning and pre-testing, the high response rate (i.e., 100 per cent returned and completed questionnaires), and the willingness of respondents to complete the questionnaire.

The attitude data were subjected to the same statistical analyses used on the ecology exam data, but no statistically significant differences among groups were found (P > .20 for each comparison). However, a statistically reliable improvement in attitude across groups was found (pre-mean = 12.48; post-mean = 13.25; most favourable score possible = 15; t(133) = 4.07, p < .0001). That is, student attitude toward the natural environment improved regardless of teaching method. This finding contradicts previous research by Kostka (1976) which found that environmental education methods (that is, involving one nature centre visit per year and related school activities) made little impact on the environmental attitude of sixth-graders from inner-city and suburban populations.

Objective Two: Identifying Subgroups

As reported under objective one, treatment effects on attitude were not significant at the 0.05 level. Race was not considered in that analysis and accordingly all variance due to race was considered error variance. Using race as a factor in the analysis of objective two's data allowed not only detection of racial effects, but also a more powerful analysis of effects of the three educational treatments. It should also be noted here that though black/white differences in attitude toward the environment were identified by treatments, such differences in knowledge about the environment were not.

Pre-test Scores

An analysis of the pre-test scores revealed a significant racial difference in attitude toward the environment (t(132) = 3.823, p < .001), with whites characterized by a more positive attitude (mean = 13.27) than non-whites (mean = 11.92). These findings support attitude research on urban children conducted by Kellert (1984) and Metro et al. (1980).

Objective Three: Effects on Attitude

Attitude change scores were computed for each subject by subtracting the pre-treatment score from the post-treatment score. A two-way ANOVA indicated a significant interaction between the treatment and race $(F(1,130)=8.26, p=.005)$ (See Table 20.5).

Table 20.5 Mean attitude change

Race	Hands-on	
	No	Yes
White	1.18	0.21
Non-white	0.16	1.39

Table 20.6 Mean post-test attitude scores from hands-on classroom activities

Race	Hands-on Classroom activities	
	No	Yes
White	14.09	13.71
Non-white	11.93	13.40

Hands-On Classroom Activities: The significant interaction was further investigated by t-test analyses of simple main effects. Hands-on classroom activities did not significantly affect attitude change in white students $(t(54)=1.971, p>.05)$, but it did in non-white students $(t(76)=2.259, p=.03)$. The racial difference in amount of attitude change was not significant for control subjects $(t(51)=1.454, p>.05)$ but was for subjects who received hands-on experience $(t(79)=2.835, p=.006)$. Hands-on classroom activities produced a more positive attitude change in non-whites than in whites.

A two-way ANOVA on post-test attitude scores indicated a significant interaction between the treatment and race $(F(1,130)=7.73, p=.006)$ and a significant main effect of race $(F(1,130)=13.58, p<.001)$ (see Table 20.6). Simple main effects analyses revealed that among whites the hands-on classroom activities were not significantly associated with attitude scores $(t(54)=1.040, p>,05)$, but among non-whites attitude was significantly more positive for those that participated in hands-on classroom activities than for those who did not $(t(76)=2.953, p=.004)$. Among students who had not participated in hands-on classroom activities there was a significant racial difference $(t(51)=3.211, p=.002)$, with whites having a more positive attitude towards the environment than non-whites. Among students who did

Table 20.7   Mean post-test attitude scores
from field trip

| Race | Field trip | |
	No	Yes
White	13.57	14.03
Non-white	12.16	13.28

participate in hands-on classroom activities, there was no significant racial difference (t(79)=0.958, p>.05). These results have indicated that when hands-on classroom activities are combined with the traditional classroom lecture, significant pre-treatment racial differences in attitude scores are eliminated.

Field Trip: A two-way ANOVA on attitude change scores revealed no significant effects of the field trip, of race, or of race by field trip interaction. Whites did have a significantly more positive attitude on the pre-test than did non-whites. A two-way ANOVA on post-test scores showed significant main effects of race (F(1,130)=10.09, p=.002) and of the field trip (F(1,130)=5.42, p=.02) but no significant race by field trip interaction (See Table 20.7). That is, in both races the post-test attitude scores were significantly more positive for those who had participated in the field trip than for those who had not, but the racial difference was not greatly attenuated; whites were still characterized by a more positive attitude towards the natural environment than non-whites, regardless of whether they participated in the field trip or not.

Summary

This study identified both similarities and differences between urban and rural schoolchildren; furthermore, it presented a comparison of black and white schoolchildren from a rural setting. Results of the data analyses included the following:

(1) Fifth-graders who visited the Nature Science Center received an excellent outdoor learning experience as reflected in their positive responses to the education activities engaged in during the visit and their improved scores on the ecology exam.

(2) Socialization, which is also a learning activity, was regarded very highly by the students and contributed to the positive experience.

(3) Somewhat surprisingly, a relatively large number of children (22 per cent) reported after the trip that they would rather spend the same time in the classroom. This may be a reasonable expectation since a field trip could be considered stressful to some children; remember they are being removed from a 'safe' and comfortable classroom and their usual daily routine. As

reported in this study, over 90 per cent of the children did, in fact, indicate concern about some part of the trip, and many perceived the woods as a home for harmful plants and animals. Thus, it is not surprising that some would prefer to stay in a 'safe' classroom; they would probably also rather watch cartoons on Saturday morning than go for a walk in the woods.

(4) Prior to making black/white comparisons of the sample, results indicated that learning was improved by hands-on classroom activities and the field trip; however, attitude toward the natural environment was not significantly changed by the field trip beyond the change produced by in-class learning activities. The students in this rural sample exhibited a positive attitude before and after beginning their study on ecology. To be more specific, initial results indicated that learning was promoted by both the field trip and hands-on experiences while attitude was improved by all educational methods studied.

(5) Further analysis of black/white differences indicated that (a) while the field trip improved the environmental attitude of both whites and non-whites, it did not eliminate racial differences afterwards; and (b) hands-on classroom activities did effectively eliminate pre-test differences between races by improving the attitude scores of non-white. Previous research, which focused on urban populations, has demonstrated that non-whites are characterized by a less favourable environmental attitude; these findings support earlier research by Shepard and Speelman (1985 – 6) and suggest that rural non-white populations are similar to their urban counterparts.

Recommendations

The above findings support the view that outdoor education should recognize logistical, social and attitudinal considerations which may affect their school group visitors. These include the following points:

(1) Effective time use and small group size are important in planning and delivering outdoor education programmes. In this study, students were divided into groups of six to eight students and each group participated in five 45-minute programmes over a five-hour period.

(2) Children perceive the existence of dangers in the outdoors especially those relating to animals. Outdoor educators should help students resolve those fears as well as correct falsehoods about what animals are indigenous, or not indigenous, to the local area. This would be accomplished most effectively both prior to and during the trip.

(3) The question of 'why hands-on classroom activities were more effective than the field trip' is obviously important to outdoor educators. As this study has shown, non-white rural schoolchildren were characterized by a less favourable environmental attitude score than their white counterparts; it may be inferred that they have negative feelings about or feel reluctant to participate in field trips. These feelings or reluctance may consequently

influence the effectiveness of the field trip. Outdoor educators must recognize this possibility.

A significant amount of research has suggested that ethnicity (i.e., racial background) plays an important role in shaping attitude and behaviour (Cheek et al., 1976; Kornegay and Warren, 1969; Peterson, 1977; Taylor, 1979; Washburn, 1978; Wendling, 1980). As Pettus (1976, p. 51) stated: 'Cultural and subcultural beliefs and background play a large part in developing environmental attitudes.' If this does occur, outdoor educators need to be aware of those differences and develop outdoor education programmes that non-whites can relate to, such as that conducted by Lewis (1979).

(4) Racial differences in environmental attitude may be significantly changed through the use of hands-on classroom learning experiences. The effectiveness of field trips on non-whites might also be improved by hands-on classroom activities prior to the field trip; this would provide a means of acclimatizing those students to education experiences outdoors.

(5) Though this research has documented the value of hands-on learning, and field trips are certainly a way of providing hands-on experience, the future of this teaching methodology in the United States is uncertain, as documented in a recent study of American public schools. In that study, Weiss (1987) reported a significant decrease over the last decade in the amount of hands-on learning opportunities available to schoolchildren. Obviously this situation demands the immediate attention of outdoor educators.

Acknowledgements

This research was funded by a (1) 1982 East Carolina University Teaching Effectiveness Grant awarded to Dr Robert C. Wendling, Associate Professor of Leisure Studies and to the late Mr Tim R. Brinn, Former Director of the Regional Development Institute, East Carolina University, Greenville, NC 27834, and (2) National Science Foundation Grant (NO. SED72-05823) awarded to Dr Charles R. Coble, Dean, School of Education, East Carolina University, Greenville, NC 27834. The author also wishes to thank Dr Karl Wuensch, Ms Bambra Christiano, Assistant Professor in the Department of Psychology and Graduate Student in Leisure Studies, East Carolina University, respectively, for their assistance in this study.

References

Burch, W.R. Jr. (1977) 'Urban children and nature: a summary of research on camping and outdoor education', *Children, Nature and the Urban Environment: Proceedings of a Symposium Fair*, USDA Forest Service General Technical Report NE-30, Northeastern Forest Experiment Station, Broomall, Pennsylvania.

Cheek, N.H. Jr., Field, D.R. and Burdge, R.J. (1976) *Leisure and Recreation Places*, Ann Arbor Sciences, Ann Arbor, Michigan.

Crompton, J.L. and Sellar, C. (1981) 'Do outdoor education experiences contribute to positive development in the affective domain?', *Journal of Environmental Education*, 12 (4), 21–9.

Devlin, A.S. (1973) 'Some factors in enhancing knowledge of a nature area', in W.F.E. Preiser (ed.), *Environmental Design Research: Volume Two, Symposia and Workshops*, pp. 200–6. Dowden, Hutchison and Ross, Stroudsburg, Pennsylvania.

Ford, P.M. (1981) *Principles and Practices of Outdoor/Environmental Education*, John Wiley, New York.

Gebler, C.J. (1982) 'Off-season, off-site interpretation', in G.W. Sharpe (ed.), *Interpreting the environment*, pp. 366–91. John Wiley, New York.

Kaplan, R. (1976) 'Way-finding in the natural environment', in G.T. Moore and R.G. Colledge (eds), *Environmental Knowing Theories, Research, and Methods*, pp. 46–57. Dowden, Hutchison and Ross, Stroudsburg, Pennsylvania.

Kellert, S.R. (1984) 'Urban American perceptions of animals and the natural environment', *Urban Ecology*, 8, 209–28.

Kellert, S.R. and Westerveldt, M.O. (1983) *Children's Attitude, Knowledge, and Behaviour Toward Animals*, Government Printing Office, Report No. 024-010-00641-2, Washington, DC.

Kornegay, F.A. and Warren, D.I. (1969) *A Comparative Study of Life Styles and Social Attitudes of Middle-Income Status Whites and Negroes in Detroit*, Detroit Urban League, Detroit, Michigan.

Kostka, M.D. (1976) 'Nature center program impact', *Journal of Environmental Education*, 8(1), 52–64.

Leftridge, A. and James, R.K. (1980) 'A study of the perceptions of environmental issues of urban and rural high school students', *Journal of Environmental Education*, 12(1), 3–7.

Lewis, C.A. (1979) 'Nature city: translating the natural environment into urban language', *Journal of Interpretation*, 4(2), 13–15.

McCoy, R.E., Ganser, D.A. and Padalino, J.J. (1978) 'Measuring attitudes and awareness of environmental education camp users', USDA Forest Service Research Paper NE-426. Northeastern Forest Experiment Station, Broomall, Pennsylvania.

Metro, J.J., Dwyer, J.F. and Dreschler, E.S. (1980) 'Forest experiences of fifth-grade Chicago public school students', USDA Forest Service Research Paper NC-216, North Central Forest Experiment Station, Chicago, Illinois.

North Carolina Department of Public Instruction (1979) *Competency Goals and Performance Indicators, K-12*, North Carolina Dept. of Public Instruction, Instructional Services, Raleigh, NC.

Peterson, G.L. (1977) 'Recreational preferences of urban teenagers: the influence of cultural and environmental attributes', *Children, Nature, and the Urban Environment: Proceedings of a Symposium Fair*, USDA Forest Service General Technical Report NE-30, Northeastern Forest Experiment Station, Broomall, Pennsylvania.

Pettus, A.M. (1976) 'Environmental education and environmental attitudes', *Journal of Environmental Education*, 8(1), 48–51.

Pomerantz, G.A. (1977) *Young People's Attitudes Toward Wildlife*, Wildlife Division Report No. 2781, Michigan Dep of Natural Resources, East Lansing, Michigan.

President's Commission (1987) *The Report of the President's Commission, Americans Outdoors: the Legacy, the Challenge*, Island Press, Washington DC.

Shepard, C.L. and Speelman, L.R. (1985–86) 'Affecting environmental attitudes through outdoor education', *Journal of Environmental Education*, 17(2), 20–3.

Taylor, R.L. (1979) 'Black ethnicity and the persistence of ethnogenesis', *American Journal of Sociology*, 84(6), 1401–23.

Van Koevering, T.E. and Prell, R. (1980) 'Some distinguishing characteristics of successful and unsuccessful teacher-directed outdoor education experiences', *Journal of Interpretation*, 5(2), 9–10.

Wallin, H.E. (1982) 'Urban interpretation', in G.W. Sharpe (ed.) *Interpreting the environment*, pp. 392–412. John Wiley, New York.

Washburn, R.F. (1978) 'Black under-participation in wildland recreation: alternative explanations', *Leisure Sciences*, 1(2), 175–89.

Weiss, I. (1987) *The 1985/86 National Survey of Science and Mathematics Education*, Research Triangle Inst., Research Triangle Park, North Carolina.

Wendling, R.C. (1980) 'Black-white differences in outdoor recreation behavior: state-of-the art and recommendations for management and research', *Proceedings of the Conference on Social Research in National Parks and Wildland Areas*, Great Smoky Mountains National Parks, Gatlinburg, Tennessee.

Wendling, R.C. and Wuensch, K.L. (1985) 'A fifth-grade outdoor education program: expectations and effects', *Journal of Interpretation*, 10(1), 11–20.

21

Time-Lapse Photography: Advantages and Disadvantages of its Application as a Research and Visitor Behaviour Monitoring Tool

Gail Vander Stoep

Introduction

To the theoretical or pure scientist, laboratory settings provide optimal opportunities for conducting experimental research. Research designs can be carefully structured, variables of interest can be selectively introduced and monitored, and the threat of influence from external variables can be minimized.

Practitioners, however, often challenge the applied value of such research. The slow building of theory does not provide ready answers to the problems or management challenges facing them daily. Laboratory research is often done with undergraduate university students, hardly a group representative of the general population. Laboratory research usually has low 'external validity'. In other words, the results of such studies often cannot be generalized directly to real life settings, to other groups of people, or to other times (Cook and Campbell, 1979).

These constraints are particularly highlighted in deviance or depreciative behaviour research, which has its own set of special challenges. Even carefully designed laboratory experiments involve risks of subjects behaving in ways to please the researcher (termed 'respondent reactance'), or acting out a specific role they select for themselves (Webb et al., 1966). Spotlighting deviance in a laboratory can change its nature and occurrence. Additionally, most deviant behaviour is committed when the threat of recognition or of getting caught is low. When questioned about previously exhibited deviant behaviour, people tend to rationalize or justify their behaviour. This is a type of responsibility denial (Schwartz, 1977).

An alternative is to use field research. Despite its difficulties, Deaux and Wrightsman (1983) contend that without some type of experimental field research it will be impossible to understand and change deviant or non-normative behaviour. Because all extraneous variables in field settings can rarely be controlled completely, because pre/post testing is generally imprac-tical, and because subjects usually cannot be allocated randomly to experimental treatment groups, quasi-experimental designs are often used in field research. Although validity threats exist for quasi-experimental research, advantages include the capability to move beyond descriptive studies and to explore causal relationships within real world contexts (Cook and Campbell, 1979).

A Field Research Challenge

The following scenario describes a specific field research setting and management problem involving depreciative behaviour at a cultural resource site. After the research question was identified, the hypotheses clarified, and experimental treatments developed, a method for observing and recording data on the behaviour of park users had to be selected.

The setting is a national military park in the United States, a park honouring the men who fought and died there for their respective causes during the American Civil War. The 3,700-acre park protects approximately 400 statues, cannon, and monuments as well as a few historic buildings and burial grounds. Each year the park is visited by 8,000 to 10,000 youth who hike through the park following one of several 12 to 16 mile themed hiking routes. Hikers answer a variety of theme-specific, battle related questions based on their observations of the cultural features, monument inscriptions and plaques along the routes.

Although the cultural resources are exposed to natural weathering and damage to non-hikers, park managers attribute much of the human-caused damage to the hiking groups. Some malicious damage, such as graffiti and name carving, is evident, but much of the damage appears to be cumulative, becoming visible only after multiple occurrences of inappropriate behaviour. Such behaviour includes, sitting, rubbing, hitting, and climbing on the cannon and monuments. Based on depreciative behaviour and behaviour modification theory, as well as careful analysis of the characteristics of youth group hikers, three treatment messages to reduce depreciative behaviour were designed. The three treatments and a control condition were assigned randomly to twelve study weekends. Groups hiking during these weekends were greeted at the trailhead by a uniformed research assistant and given the assigned treatment message.

What data collection method would be most appropriate for this field research situation?

Selecting an Effective Field Observation Strategy to Monitor Behaviour

Once a decision has been made to conduct field research, the researcher must determine the most appropriate observation strategy to use in that specific situation. Due to the special challenges of deviance research, it is important to minimize or completely avoid any obtrusive interactions with the subjects that might alter or bias their behaviour. Therefore a variety of unobtrusive measures should be considered. Advantages and disadvantages of each type must be assessed carefully. Selection criteria include validity of resulting data, ease and reliability of data analysis, managerial constraints, cost and logistical constraints of data collection.

Three primary unobtrusive strategies can be used to gather data about depreciative behaviour: analysis of physical behaviour traces, personal observation, and mechanical observation.

Analysis of Physical Behaviour Traces

Physical traces are those physical, observable pieces of evidence remaining at a site as a result of past behaviour (Webb et al., 1966). Erosion is the slow wearing away of some material after extended use or interaction. An example would be the wearing of wooden or granite steps of a frequently visited historic building. Another is the wearing away of bronze on a statue that is continually rubbed.

A second type of physical trace is accretion, the build-up of materials deposited at a site. This could be the deposit of litter in heavily used picnic areas, or the casting away of worn out tools or equipment, such as snagged fishing line or torn nets.

A third type of physical trace is the breakage or other damage to objects or resources resulting from one-off acts rather than from the cumulative effects of constant use. This includes window breaking, graffiti, scratching and carving, breakage and removal of pieces of statuary.

Physical trace measures are insufficient for completely understanding depreciative behaviour and the effects of behaviour change strategies because they show merely the results of behaviour, not the behaviour itself nor the contexts of the behaviour. Additionally, physical trace measures can be impractical to monitor when behaviour is cumulatively damaging only over the long term, making erosion the only observable behaviour trace. Physical traces, however, can be useful when used in conjunction with other data collection strategies.

Personal Observation

Personal observation includes the variety of ways a person can observe, then record, the behaviour of others. Such observers can be visible, visible but unobtrusive, or hidden. Just as in laboratory research, visible observers can cause problems of reactance, role selection, and respondent/observer interaction. So this is an inappropriate strategy for depreciative behaviour research.

Participant observation is a technique whereby the observer is completely integrated into the setting and group(s) to be observed. The observer essentially becomes a group member, interacting with the group, constantly observing, then recording the observations out of sight of the group, usually at a later time. This is most appropriate for ethnographic or case studies in which the observer has plenty of time to get to know the group(s), to become integrated and trusted. In many leisure settings where users are constantly changing, this opportunity does not exist, making participant observation inappropriate. Other potential sources of error in participant observation are 'control effect' (occurring when the observation itself causes subject behaviour changes) and 'biased viewpoint effect' (occurring when the observer selectively observes, perceives and records data) (Webb et al., 1966).

Use of a hidden person to observe behaviour is probably the most appropriate personal observation strategy for deviance research. It avoids error caused by interaction effects, respondents' role selection, and observers' self-selective exposure to subject behaviour. In fact, this strategy was considered seriously as the means of data collection for the scenario described above. Nevertheless, there are a host of other considerations and sources of error in using this technique.

Managerial Constraints: The logistical needs and costs of using hidden observers in this type of research could be prohibitive. Wages and other costs for supporting a large research staff would be high. In addition to a research assistant stationed at the trailhead to contact hikers, at least one observer would need to be stationed at each of the four observation sites for a six- to seven-hour period each day. Due to fatigue factors and other observation/data recording challenges (noted below), it would be advisable to rotate two sets of two observers at each site. Problems additional to increased costs include: deployment of new observers without raising visitor suspicion; error due to observation/recording inconsistencies between observers (even if carefully trained); and increased difficulty in keeping observers hidden, quiet and inconspicuous. Also, while on duty, an observer would be unable to take restroom or other breaks without potentially missing critical observations.

Validity and Reliability: Personal observation strategies have the potential to create serious threats to both the validity and reliability of the data. Observers must make on-the-spot judgements about specific and often fleeting behaviours. Behaviour cannot be frozen in time for careful assessment, nor can it be replayed to confirm a judgement. If a large group of hikers interacts with a monument at a given time, a single person would be unable to make multiple independent judgements about concurrent forms of behaviour, and unable to record them all accurately while simultaneously observing subsequent behaviour. With multiple observers at the different sites, consistency of observations would be extremely difficult, and determination of the extent of consistency would be impossible. Additionally, consistency of observations for the same observer would be threatened by numerous external variables that could affect attentiveness and judgement (e.g., weather, fatigue, activities the night before, etc.).

Lack of Telephoto Vision: The human eye does not have telephoto or zoom capabilities. This would mean placing the observer close to the monuments (sometimes impossible; always increasing the risk of detection by hikers) or well hidden but further away, which would decrease the acuity of vision.

Missing Data/Lack of Detail: Distant observation and the need to observe numerous group members simultaneously would make it almost impossible (even with two observers on site at one time) to make judgements or record observations about details and extent of specific types of damaging behaviour. Only a general rating of overall security and time the group spent in physical contact with the monument would be possible. Even if such assessments were consistent across observers and days, loss of detail would limit analysis and understanding of the behaviour involved. Additionally, it would be possible to miss entirely a set of behaviours occurring while observations were being recorded. Use of a tape recorder might help solve this problem, but the voice would probably alert hikers to hidden observers, thus altering their behaviour and raising suspicion. Whatever method is used, the behaviour cannot be re-observed for clarification.

Discomfort in the Field: In a field setting such as this, where most of the observation sites are distant from water sources, restrooms and other civilized comforts, observers would be exposed to discomforts of weather (heat, humidity, rain, cold, wind) without opportunity for relief. Invariably, observations and data recording would be affected adversely.

Fatigue: In addition sleepiness in observers starting their watches, and field fatigue resulting from constant observation in cramped quarters could affect judgement and detail in written records. Attention span and level of attention are both affected negatively by fatigue.

Interaction Effects: Should hikers spot the observers, it is likely that their behaviour would change.

Mechanical Observation

The final alternative is the use of some type of mechanical observation. This could be video, continuous or time-lapse filming, or use of beam-breaking sensors. Many of the problems associated with personal observation can be eliminated. Logistical problems and salary costs are minimized, interaction effects are non-existent, and physical human limitations do not come into play. Mechanical observation, however, does have its own set of challenges that potentially can affect data quality.

Missing Data: Even though a camera has a zoom telephoto lens and can be placed away from the site, once the field of view has been selected, it remains constant (Figure 21.1). If the setting is selected to enlarge details of visitor behaviour, the field of view is restricted. Contextual conditions influencing group behaviour outside the field of view are unaccounted. On the

Figure 21.1 Selection of the camera len's field of view dictates the type and quality of observational data.

other hand, if a wide angle of view is chosen, details of behaviour may be lost. Additionally, a camera can view from only one side. Behaviour occurring on the far (hidden) side of the observed object would be blocked. If time-lapse photography is used, it is possible to miss behaviour that might occur rapidly during the interval between exposed frames.

Equipment Concerns: Any electrical or mechanical equipment is subject to failure. A protected site with a clear field of vision, yet within range of the observation site, must be selected (and modified if necessary). The equipment must be well hidden and protected from theft, vandalism and weather effects (Figure 21.2). Finally, the equipment must be tested and synchronized.

Proper maintenance can minimize, though not eliminate, electrical and mechanical failure. Even when enclosed in protective boxes, cameras can malfunction as a result of condensation or dust. Batteries, even when replaced frequently, can short out due to moisture or other equipment malfunctions. Condensation can fog the lens. A tiny speck of dust trapped in the diaphragm mechanism can cause the lens to remain open constantly, overexposing en entire roll of film. The result is missing data.

Spare parts, spare cameras, electrical test equipment, and continual troubleshooting tests are mandatory. In the event of malfunction, the services of a backup camera repairman who understands the critical need of rapid repair should be engaged.

If a wooden trap door (raised to let in light to activate the solar cell operating the camera) is used, as was the case in this study, the shrink/swell cycles of the wood resulting from changes in humidity can cause the door to close prematurely, shutting off the camera. Again, the result is missing data. In this case, a piece of velcro was added to the trap door to hold it in an open position (Figure 21.3).

Identifying Treated Groups: In almost any field setting, a researcher will need to differentiate between 'treated' subjects and other visitors. In deviance research, informing subjects of their participation can drastically alter behaviour. Not informing them raises ethical issues of manipulating visitors against their will. The concern is particularly serious when minors are involved and when their actions are recorded on film. The Human Subjects Committee reviewing this study waived their blockage of the experiment when researchers agreed not to identify the groups or individuals (as initially planned), and to destroy all the film within a reasonable time after the study's completion.

The problem of identifying treated groups without their knowledge was solved by using a modified 'tag and release' technique, more typically used for wildlife studies, and in at least one study to track and recontact skiers (Mills et al., 1981). A bright orange sticker (proclaiming the wearer as a '25th Anniversary Trail Hiker') was given to each treated subject (Figure 21.4). Stickers could be seen easily on the film. Lost stickers were replaced at the visitor centre located midway along the hiking routes.

As a backup for identifying groups, the research assistant meeting groups

Figure 21.2 Camera equipment must be protected from weather, theft and vandalism. In this case, the protective box was disguised as a birdhouse.

Protective Camera Box

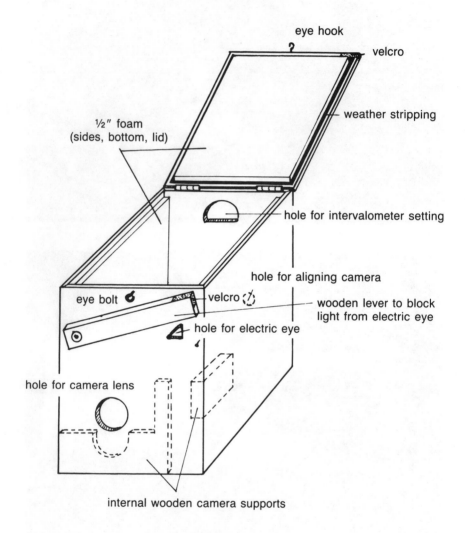

Figure 21.3 A piece of velcro was used to hold open the trap door to allow sunlight to activate the photo cell and camera.

at the trailhead recorded information on group size and make-up identifiable clothing and other distinguishing objects. (Additionally, information on weather, hikers' place of residence, and whether or not hikers had been there before were recorded to be used as covariates during statistical analysis.)

Figure 21.4 Bright orange stickers, observable on film, were used to tag treated visitors.

Data Analysis: Frame-by-frame analysis of time-lapse film is extremely tedious work. To avoid validity and reliability problems, several suggestions are given.

(1) At least two independent film judges, both blind to the experimental treatments, should be used. After careful training and analysis practice on trial rolls of film, inter-judge reliability should be calculated. If unacceptable, additional practice and consulting sessions to clarify judgements should be undertaken until inter-judge reliability is acceptable. (In this case, overall reliability for behaviour analysis at each monument was greater than $r = 0.93$.)

(2) Even with high inter-judge reliability, an average of the two judges' scores should be used because averages tend to attenuate to the norm, and thus indicate a more representative and reliable score.

(3) Observational data should be as detailed as possible within the constraints of the image on film. Data can always be collapsed for later analysis, but it cannot be separated more finely than the original recording.

Conclusion

Despite the challenges posed by both field research and use of time-lapse photography to observe visitor behaviour, there is a need for such studies. Results provide field setting applications and support for more controlled laboratory research. They add support (or pose challenges) to theory building. Finally, they provide managers with information about 'real world' effects of potential management strategies.

Weighing all the advantages and disadvantages of both personal and mechanical observation, it was determined in this situation that, despite reliability and validity threats, potential sources of error could be more easily controlled, identified and accounted for using time-lapse photography. Due to its success in this study, time-lapse photography as a tool to study human behaviour other than patterns of visitor movement is offered as an alternative field research technique.

References

Cook, T.D. and Campbell, D. (1979) *Quasi-experimentation: Design and Analysis Issues for Field Settings*, Houghton Mifflin, Boston, MASS.

Deaux, K. and Wrightsman, L.S. (1983) *Social Psychology in the Eighties*, Brooks-Cole, New York.

Mills, A.A., Hodgson, R., McNeely, J. Jr. and Masse, R. (1981) 'An improved visitor sampling method for ski resorts and similar settings', *Journal of Leisure Research*, 13 (3), 219–31.

Schwartz, S.H. (1977) 'Normative influences on altruism', in L. Berkowitz (ed.), *Advances in Experimental Social Psychology*, Vol. 10, pp. 221–79. Academic Press, New York.

Webb, E.J., Campbell, D., Schwartz, R. and Sechrest, L. (1966) *Unobtrusive Measures: Non-reactive Research in the Social Sciences*, Rand McNally, Chicago, Illinois.

Whyte, W.H. (1980) 'Appendix A: time lapse filming', in *The Social Life of Small Urban Spaces*, pp. 102–11. Conservation Foundation, Washington, DC.

22

The Formative Evaluation of Interactive Science and Technology Centres: Some Lessons Learned

Terry Russell

The Context

There is increasing evidence of a concern to make science and technology more accessible to the general public. Interactive science and technology centres are one manifestation of the general stirring of awareness. (Danilov, 1982; Pizzey, 1987).

Several interest groups can be identified as having a commitment to making science and technology more visible and comprehensible. Various affiliations with particular environmental interests have been active in bringing to public attention issues of, for example, endangered species, diminishing habitats, 'clean' energy. Public concern has also been aroused by incidents of environmental and human damage on such frightening scales as occurred at Bhopal and Chernobyl. On a more global scale – the suspected depletion of the ozone layer by CFCs – links between the health of the planet and everyday behaviour have been brought to attention through the use of CFCs in, for example, anti-perspirant propellants. There are also economic and political interests in increased scientific literacy to support industrial and commercial revival. Also committed to the movement are those professional scientists and technologists, educationalists and museum personnel, historians and sociologists who simply believe that science is intrinsically interesting and valuable as a human activity. Finally, but a significant force, there are the entrepreneurs of the communications and leisure industries who have seen and promoted the potential of science and technology to engage people as an entertainment or leisure activity. A range of motives, interests and values drives the proponents and a unanimity of purpose need not be assumed to underpin centres which on the surface might appear to have a great deal in common.

It is the intention in this paper to present some of the issues which have emerged during the evaluation of three interactive centres: 'Technology Testbed' in Liverpool, (Harlen et al., 1986); the Visitors' Centre at Jodrell Bank (Russell et al., 1987); and 'Techniquest', based in Cardiff (Russell et al.,

1988). The evaluation has been formative in the sense of attempting to provide feedback which could be used by developers to make adjustments to exhibits or exhibitions. The lessons learned through this involvement relate not only to the nature of the centres themselves but also to the nature of the evaluation instruments and procedures developed in order to carry out the evaluation.

Coupled with a particular focus of interest in science and technology is a particular mode of delivery to the public. This is often described as 'hands-on'; it implies an immediacy of experience, a physical involvement with exhibits, a message communicated directly and intuitively to visitors. The traditional museum display case is scarcely in evidence at these interactive centres, because the raw material of exhibits tends not to be unique or precious in the material sense, as is often the case in traditional museum settings. Interactive science centres are more concerned with ideas than with unique objects. It is administratively far more convenient if exhibits are robust rather than fragile, but the main purpose of an exhibit is to promote an affective, attitudinal and cognitive response in visitors.

The particular context of an exhibition determines the issues or ideas with which exhibition developers will wish to engage visitors. In this view, the interactive medium is an effective means to an end, not an end in itself. The three centres under consideration provide three different contexts. At Jodrell Bank, the visitors' centre stands within the shadow of the enormous dish of the radio telescope. Radio astronomy is the major research activity on the site, but is abstract in nature. The developers have provided a number of exhibits which explore the characteristics of parabolic reflectors and other phenomena relevant to astronomy. The interactive centre is designed to enhance public understanding of the finely focused scientific activities being conducted on the site of which it is a part. At Technology Testbed in Liverpool, the boundary is drawn more widely. The interactive exhibits are in the midst of the National Museums and Galleries on Merseyside 'Large Object Collection' of machines, vehicles, computers, telescopes and so on. The interactive exhibits attempt to illustrate in a simplified and accessible manner some of the operating principles of the surrounding machinery. 'Techniquest' in Cardiff, in its original city centre showroom premises, had to create its own context. The boundary of what might be considered relevant activities of a scientific or technological nature was practically limitless. Exhibits included closed circuit television, examples of perceptual illusions, problem-solving activities, demonstrations of scientific principles (e.g. Bernouilli effect) and so on.

The broad classification offered above seems to have wider applicability. The Discovery Dome and the Exploratory, for example, like Techniquest, create their own contexts. Since the context of an exhibition is very relevant to the definition of its objectives, this is important for the process of evaluation. It is also important simply to recognize the heterogeneity of contexts and purposes as more centres emerge and evolve, so that the frustration of being cast in a common mould of expectations is avoided.

Objectives and Evaluation

The developers of interactive centres commonly express a desire to make the public's participation a matter of pleasure and enjoyment and to shift attitudes towards a more positive view of science and technology. It is a simple enough matter to discover whether or not visitors enjoy the experience of the visit; they can be asked, or they can vote with their feet. (Whether longer-term attitudes are modified is a much less accessible question.)

A matter of greater controversy is the specification of learning objectives. It can be argued that making science accessible and demystifying it implies that it must be made more comprehensible; that a sense of control is only possible with understanding. Where an exhibition has a clear context, the specification of learning objectives is unproblematic. At Jodrell Bank, visitors would be expected to leave with a better understanding of, for example, the principles of parabolic reflectors. The objectives associated with all exhibits were made absolutely explicit by the developers. Where the objectives are more diffuse, there may be a greater reluctance to specify the anticipated outcomes.

The evaluators took the constructivist view, that all centres were providing learning opportunities even where learning objectives were not explicitly stated. This distinction shifts the emphasis towards the provision of valid and effective learning experiences for those who may learn incidentally in a recreational context, or those visitors who are more explicitly motivated to learn something from their visits.

The focus of the evaluation was neither the intrinsic merit of exhibits nor the quantity of learning that took place (Figure 22.1). Rather, the concern was the quality of the interaction between people and exhibits, both in terms of what people do, and what sense they made of their interaction.

It is unrealistic to expect exhibition developers to ensure that visitors learn things during their visits; it is realistic to expect that the experiences provided take cognizance of how visitors behave in exhibitions, how they are likely to achieve understanding, and what they actually do while interacting with exhibits. Equally, in attempting to facilitate an optimal interaction between visitors and exhibits, there is an obligation to steer visitors away from pitfalls of misunderstanding. It might also be reasonable to expect that visitors should not be 'blinded with science' by the presentation of exhibits which dazzle them with scientific virtuosity. Such exhibits may be good entertainment, but do not make science and technology any more comprehensible by being presented as magic.

Research into science learning in formal educational settings indicates unequivocally that young people construct their own understanding, very often on insufficient or wrongly interpreted evidence (Osborne and Freyberg, 1985). This constructivist view argues that individuals actively attempt to make sense of the world and in this endeavour frequently generate

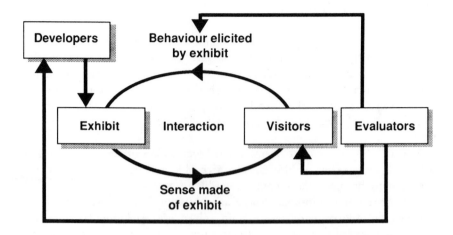

Figure 22.1 Focus of evaluation.

misconceptions. This view of learning was explicitly adopted by the evaluation team.

Interactive centres are still something of a novelty in the UK. Expressions of apprehension are sometimes voiced lest a delicate creative enterprise be damaged by the process of evaluation. These fears can be alleviated when evaluation is shown to be subtle and in harmony with the spirit of the centres (Miles, 1988). Most important, it has to be acknowledged that evaluation cannot be value-free. Where objectives are explicit, evaluation can be tailored to those objectives. Where this is not the case, it is for the evaluators to make explicit the criteria that they have chosen to adopt.

A variety of evaluation techniques have been explored including discussions prompted by still photographs, use of computerized self-report database, audio and video recording, structured and semi-structured interviews and observations of interactions using behavioural checklists. Two techniques will be described below, accompanied by some results which give an indication of the kind of information it is possible to collect with each. The first technique, 'tracking', involves the use of a checklist of visitor behaviour in relation to exhibits. The second technique describes how some understanding of the sense visitors make of their experiences is achieved through 'interviews about exhibits'.

Tracking

The technique of tracking a random sample of visitors throughout their entire visit, using behavioural checklists to record the incidence of relevant interactions, was pioneered at Technology Testbed. Visitors were randomly selected as they crossed a predetermined point near the entrance and

Date	Time	Target visitor Number	Male or Female	Age or over 30 40 50 60	Collector's Name

TIME TAKEN																				
EXHIBIT NUMBER/NAME																				
Observed Actions	**Tick Appropriate Column**																			
Helper present/in view																				
Interacted after encouragement																				
Engages with label																				
Touches apparatus																				
Moves any part of apparatus																				
Works alone																				
Collaborates with other(s)																				
Talks with other(s)																				
Watches effects of others' actions																				
Asks question(s) of helper																				
Asks question(s) of other adult																				
Repeats actions																				
Has to queue/wait for turn																				

Figure 22.2 Checklist of interactions.

observed until they left the exhibition. The random sample was intended to match the broad demographic characteristics of the visitor population as a whole. A checklist of the observed actions at each exhibit, together with the time spent, was completed for each visitor contact with an exhibit. A contact was defined as a deliberate move towards engaging with an exhibit and a notional one second was the minimum recorded in instances where only a fleeting contact occurred. The tracking record sheet is reproduced as Figure 22.2.

Tracking is a viable technique only when exhibitions have a clear boundary, when data collectors can observe unobtrusively and when the overall duration of visits is within limits which make data collection economically feasible. Tracking was not possible at Jodrell Bank where the visitors' centre encompasses several separate rooms plus outdoor exhibits including other attractions. (Jodrell Bank also has an arboretum; it was found that visitors might spend a whole day on the site, including a picnic on the grounds and repeat visits to the interactive exhibits.) Visitors' absorption in the exhibitions usually ensured that data collectors could remain unnoticed; where appropriate, teachers or parents were discreetly alerted as to the nature of the evaluation exercise. At the end of the tracking, the visitor was approached and invited to answer a few questions.

When the tracking technique was used at Techniquest, the hypothesis that visitor behaviour might vary by age was built into the evaluation procedure. The random sampling procedure was modified to produce a sample which was not demographically representative, but which enabled the behaviours of

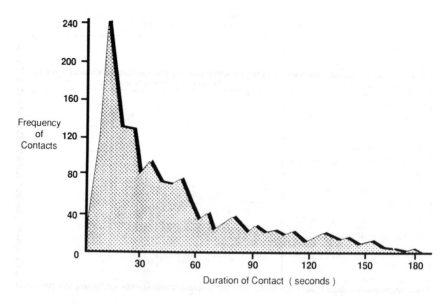

Figure 22.3   Frequency distribtion of duration of contact with individual exhibits at Techniquest (6,899 contacts with 46 exhibits by 144 visitors).

four age groups to be compared: 5–10 years, 11–13 years, 14–15 years and 17+.

At Testbed, the behaviour associated with 3,523 contacts with eighteen exhibits by 201 visitors was recorded; at Techniquest, the equivalent figures were 6,899 contacts with 46 exhibits by 144 visitors. (The number of exhibits at Testbed has greatly increased since the time the evaluation was conducted, and Techniquest has changed its site.)

From the tracking data, the overall mean duration of contact with each exhibit was computed. At Testbed, the overall mean duration of contact was 44 seconds, with a range from the notional one second to over 15 minutes. At Techniquest, the overall mean duration of contact with an exhibit was 50 seconds. Figure 22.3 shows the distribution of contact durations at Techniquest.

That the average duration of contact with exhibits was less than one minute is perhaps surprising, but as Figure 22.3 indicates, the mode was a mere ten seconds. It has to be acknowledged that duration of contact is a fairly crude measure which will be influenced by factors including the context of the visit, whether an entrance fee was paid (as at Techniquest, but not Testbed) and the specific nature of the interaction which an exhibit invites. Nevertheless, such an index is a salutary reminder to developers that exhibits must be simple and direct if they are to be effective.

It will be appreciated that the tracking technique was not essential if all that was required was duration of contact; data could have been obtained

Table 22.1 Overall Mean Incidence of Label Reading as a Proportion of Individual Contacts Made with Exhibits

	First contact with exhibits	Second contact with exhibits	Third contact with exhibits
Technology Testbed (Total contacts = 3,523)	26	14	7
Techniquest (Total contacts = 6,899)	37	24	11

exhibit by exhibit. What tracking revealed, which would not have been apparent by other means, was an unexpected phenomenon – a high rate of repeated contacts with exhibits. Visitors tended to move around the exhibition and selectively make further visits to particular exhibits. The overall rate of return visits to exhibits at Testbed, expressed as a percentage of initial contacts, was 22 per cent. Every exhibit at Testbed received some revisits; the rate ranged from 8 per cent to 26 per cent. The rate of revisiting at Techniquest was 29 per cent.

When the tracking data relating to duration of contact is examined by age band, it becomes even more interesting. The 17 plus age group had a frequency of repeat contacts of 23 per cent; the rate for the 14 – 16 age group was 34 per cent; for the 11 – 13 group, it was 37 per cent, while for the 5 – 10 age group, it was 60 per cent, or three repeat contacts for every two initial contacts. Younger visitors tended to stay longer at Techniquest, but their mean contact duration of 50 seconds was equivalent to the sample average; they simply made more contacts, perhaps because of their greater involvement or greater stamina.

Tracking using a sample stratified by age proved its worth in examining duration of contact with exhibits. It was also successful in casting some new light on the old cliché that visitors do not read labels in museums and exhibitions. The overall mean occurrence of label reading was 23 per cent at Testbed and 33 per cent at Techniquest; the incidence during first, second and third contacts with exhibits is shown in Table 22.1.

Overall mean rates of label reading are at the traditionally low rates found in museum settings, and decrease during subsequent visits. However, examining the incidence of label reading by age group is very revealing (See Table 22.2).

The incidence of label reading in the oldest group is above 60 per cent during the first contact and is maintained at higher levels during subsequent contacts. Whether this reflects a predilection for the written medium by the oldest group, or a role differentiation – adults read and subsequently explain to children – the data do not tell us. The data do suggest that it is worthwhile persisting with labels and finding out more about how they are

Table 22.2 Incidence of Engagement with Labels on First and Subsequent Contacts with Exhibits at Techniquest (Percentages by age band)

Age bands	First contact	Second contact	Third contact	Fourth contact
5 – 10 (n = 38)	20	27	7	–
11 – 13 (n = 25)	30	13	13	5
14 – 16 (n = 42)	42	20	7	8
17 + (n = 39)	62	31	20	15

used, in relation to interactive exhibits. For example, a striking iconic or diagrammatic style might be preferable to initiate engagement with the exhibit. It could be that a different style of label for reference after engaging with exhibits would be found useful to elaborate the explanation of the phenomenon that has been experienced. Perhaps adults see their role as standing back to understand the phenomena that their children experience. These questions need to be researched, together with the use of 'electronic labels' in the form of video disc and computer databases.

Interviews About Exhibits

The most effective way of finding out what sense people make of exhibits is to ask them. As they completed their interaction, visitors were approached and asked whether they were willing to answer some questions about what they thought the exhibit was about, what happened, how it worked and whether they thought it might be improved. This friendly, informal and open-ended approach was adapted to the age of the visitor. Almost invariably visitors were willing to respond, perhaps because this was in keeping with the spirit of participation around them. Feedback from visitors led to suggestions for the improvement of exhibits, as summarized in the individual evaluation reports.

One interesting outcome of talking to visitors about their understanding was the confirmation of some specific conceptual difficulties which are documented in the science education research literature. One such example occurred in an exhibit which invited visitors to touch and compare the temperature sensation from tiles made of different materials: steel, wood, polystyrene, etc. Because of the characteristic sensations which visitors sensed, for example steel feeling cold because it conducted heat from the fingertips, many visitors voiced the common misconception that the materials were at different temperatures, rather than the correct notion of them all being at ambient temperature (Erickson and Tiberghien, 1985).

Female (Age 9) 'All of them are different temperatures.' A 'correct' explanation of the phenomenon was offered by the interviewer at this point. 'They're not the same temperature, you can tell they feel different.'

Reactions of this type (and they were in the majority in relation to this exhibit) confirm that it is possible for an exhibit to reinforce misconceptions, contrary to its intentions, especially when the science involved is counter-intuitive. One of the roles of formative evaluation is to help to refine exhibits so that the logic of science and visitors' psycho-logic coincide. The example quoted is by no means unique. Anything involving electrical circuitry, for example, is likely to cause many visitors problems. Also, the direction of the causal chain of events in machinery is easily confused (Piaget, 1974). The more general issues, such as the ergonomic implications of the participation of a wide range of size and strength of visitors and the limited attention span of younger visitors who are impatient to wait for an outcome, are perhaps some of the more obvious areas about which formative evaluation can provide useful feedback.

Where it is anticipated that visitors may encounter conceptual difficulties, a useful strategy is to present a variety of exhibits each of which promotes a different facet of understanding. At Jodrell Bank, for example, four exhibits – the miniature 'Radio Telescope', 'Curved Mirror', 'Heat Reflector' and 'Whispering Gallery' (two reflectors set in the grounds which transmitted and received whispered messages between visitors) – were all concerned with properties of parabolic reflectors. Such an understanding would support an appreciation of the function and scale of operation of the massive Lovell telescope. The abstraction of the energy sources involved caused visitors some difficulties. There was some appreciation that a bowl-shaped surface could gather an invisible energy; the possibility that the parabola could also transmit effectively seemed less intuitively accessible; the notion of a bowl having a focal point seemed even more elusive. However, having identified the precise nature of the difficulties, it was possible to suggest some ways forward.

It was particularly interesting to investigate what visitors made of 'hands-on' analogies. For example, 'See to Infinity' at Jodrell Bank consisted simply of two plane mirrors facing each other. Having stood between them, the majority of visitors seemed to have experienced the exhibit as intended and an intuitive introduction to the concept of infinity was established. 'Gravity Hollow' (an exhibit seen at several different centres) presents visitors with a large black plastic conical form. Rubber balls can be rolled around the hollow to show how they accelerate towards the centre of the exhibit. The analogy to be drawn is with the speed of travel and orbits of planets in the solar system. Some visitors appreciated this fact:

Female (Age 10) 'It's flatter here, but steeper down there. It's gravity.'
Q. Why do they go faster?
A. The comet goes faster when it gets nearer the sun.

Young children in particular spent a lot of time at 'Gravity Hollow', but the affinities they perceived were more frequently with skittle alleys than with planetary motion. In this instance, it would seem that action *must* be accompanied by reflection, since the intuitive experience is not itself the direct message (as, for example, it would be in directly sensing the efficacy of a lever to shift what would otherwise be an impossible load). There are also the dangers of visitors grasping some attributes of the analogy, but not enough of them. The black cone raised associations of a Black Hole in the minds of some visitors, with the planets, presumably, spiralling into it. As with poetry, the images generated will not work for everyone. Evaluation can help to determine for whom the analogies do work, amongst the target audience.

Characteristics of Successful Exhibits

The above discussion implies that there are different kinds of interactive exhibits. It is difficult to make generalizations about the characteristics of successful exhibits in the absence of a taxonomy of interactions and anticipated outcomes. And any such taxonomy is likely to be multi-dimensional.

Whether the exhibit presents an open-ended or a closed outcome is one dimension which can be readily recognized. The construction of an arch bridge with materials provided has only one solution. Exhibits also vary in the way in which they represent ideas or objects in the real world. For example, some items are simply scale models that make a relevant principle more accessible. The Buxton Micrarium operates entirely on the principle of magnification; at Jodrell Bank are to be found a miniature radio telescope, which visitors can operate; at Testbed, a giant micrometer.

In other cases, the public simply has the opportunity to get its hands on real objects which might normally be inaccessible – a jack, a prism, a closed-circuit television system. Sometimes the 'real object' is stripped down, or opened out, so that its operating principles are revealed, as with the Ackermann steering gear at Testbed, or the periscope at Jodrell Bank. There are other attributes which seem important. For example, the degree of control that visitors may exert over particular exhibits, the degree of physical involvement, the collaborative or solitary nature of participation which an exhibit invites, and so on.

Empirically, there seems to be a fairly close correspondence between the way visitors rank exhibits as favoured and the amount of contact time exhibits receive. Tracked visitors were asked to nominate their favourite exhibit at Testbed and at Techniquest. The top three at each are shown in Table 22.3. The activities selected as favourite incorporate a wide range of content. The three favourite Testbed selections all permit (or invite) a vigorous, whole body involvement. It was interesting to note that at Techniquest six of the ten most contacted exhibits depend on visitors sensing or considering aspects of their physical presence as part of the interaction. (Twelve of the 46 exhibits were of this nature and all were among the first

Table 22.3 Tracked Visitors' Favourite Exhibits at Testbed (n = 201) and
Techniquest (n = 144)

Rank order	% Selecting	Exhibit	Description
Testbed			
1	32	Suspension Bridge	Miniature suspension bridge.
2	11	The Weights	Blocks and pulleys with 50lb. load.
3	9	Giraffe	Peristaltic pump, model drinking giraffe.
Techniquest			
1	30	On the Air	Closed circuit television, 30-second record and review.
2	9	Holograms	Static hologram images.
3	9	Bernouilli Table	Three aerofoil activities.

29 most contacted exhibits.) The outstanding favourite, 'On the Air', is an excellent example of the principle of personal involvement in the functioning of the exhibit being apparently very highly motivating. It is interesting to reflect on the favourite exhibits in Table 22.3 and speculate as to how the activities promoted match developers' intentions.

Summary

A selection of the techniques and results from involvement in the formative evaluation of interactive science and technology centres has been presented in the spirit of a constructive contribution to the debate. Some issues have been left untouched – most importantly, perhaps, the question of how social interactions mediate experiences in these centres. All the issues raised will be understood better if developers and evaluators persist in asking questions, both of themselves and of the visiting public.

References

Danilov, V.J. (1982) *Science and Technology Centres*, MIT Press, Cambridge, MASS.

Erickson, G. and Tiberghien, A. (1985) 'Heat and Temperature', in Driver, R. Guesne, E. and Tiberghien, E. (eds), *Children's Ideas in Science*, Open University Press, Milton Keynes.

Harlen, W., Van der Waal, A. and Russell, T. (1986) 'Evaluation of the pilot phase of the Liverpool Interactive Technology Centre', CRIPSAT, Dep of Education, University of Liverpool.

Miles, R.S. (ed.) (1988) *The Design of Educational Exhibits*, 2nd edition. Unwin Hyman, London.

Osborne, R. and Freyberg, P. (1985) *Learning in Science*, Heinemann, London.

Piaget, J. (1974) *Understanding Causality*, W.N. Norton, London.

Pizzey, S. (1987) *Interactive Science and Technology Centres*, Science Projects Publishing, London.

Russell, T., Van der Waal, A. and Whitelock, M. (1987) 'Developmental stage evaluation of interactive exhibits at Jodrell Bank Science Centre', CRIPSAT, Dep of Education, University of Liverpool.

Russell, T., Van der Waal, A. and Whitelock, M. (1988) 'Evaluation of the pilot phase of the Cardiff Interactive Technology Centre 'Techniquest', CRIPSAT, Dep of Education, University of Liverpool.

23

Truths and Untruths in Museum Exhibitions

Jerzy Swiecimski

Introduction

Museologists often try to define the function of museum exhibitions as (1) presenting objects of artistic or scientific documentary value, or (2) transmitting knowledge (mostly fundamental, elementary and, in every case, 'ready' knowledge) to various visitors, mostly to non-professionals. According to (1), no essential difference exists between exhibitions and, for example, museum laboratories or museum storage; or they are places where works of art are presented for contemplation, and become intentionally 'the objects of aesthetic experience' (Ingarden, 1958). According to (2), a museum exhibition is conceived as a didactic instrument, functioning in a similar way to a textbook. The role of aesthetics is subordinated to the exhibition's didacticism. The aesthetic form of the exhibition thus becomes 'the form of the exhibition content', and a means of communication (Swiecimski, 1974).

In museological papers we also find the thesis, formulated mostly as normative statements, that exhibitions, in order to fulfil either of these functions, *should* be representations of the truth. Presenting untruth is thus essentially contrary to a museum's function.

This brings us to the questions that are the subject of this paper. Can truth be achieved in a 'pure' form, or is it probably that every exhibit unavoidably transmits some untruth, which has to be 'neutralized' by the viewer in perceiving and understanding its content and meaning? And may untruth, if it is present in an exhibit's content, become under certain conditions a means of transmitting truth?

The Categories of Truth in Museum Exhibitions

The notion of truth may be interpreted in various ways in relation to the content of museum exhibitions and the following categories can be distinguished.

Group A

1. Truth connected with the entity, or with the state of being, of exhibitions.

2. Truth connected with a priori norms or definitions formulated for exhibitions, or for the objects being exhibited, whether real or conceptual. The latter occurs when objects are presented not for themselves but as symbols of general classes or types.

3. Truth connected with the content and value of assertions about particular objects or classes of objects.

4. Truth connected with the artistic concept of exhibition design, in particular with the expression of an exhibition as a whole, with its meaning.

5. Truth connected with the appearance of exhibits and their aesthetics.

Group B

1. Where the truth of an exhibition (or exhibited objects) is independent of any acts of consciousness (e.g. from the evaluation of the exhibitions content or meaning with respect to its truthfulness).

2. Where the truth of the exhibition (or exhibit) is evidently a product of acts of cognition and their expression.

Several sub-groups and variants can be distinguished within these points. And the particular cases we meet in practice often result from their combination. The discussion will be limited, however, to the main and most typical cases.

First Case

Truth connected with an exhibit's physical existence can be regarded as a quality essential to its individual identity; it thus has an ontological character. It inherently 'belongs' to the exhibit independently of any act of cognition, whether it is known to us or not. Truth of this kind may, however, be detected by analysis.

In any exhibit one can distinguish between the object's 'own' truth and the information ascribed to the object. Study may detect the object's intrinsic truth, but may be in error, for example, it does happen that objects remain undetermined despite efforts to detect their identity. Untruth, if considered analogically to this sense of the truth, can essentially never appear. Untruth may, therefore, appear in this case only in the content of the information added to the object. That 'untrue' information may be ascribed to an object is not only irrelevant for the object itself, but results from a confusion with a different interpretation of truth (see 'Second Case' below).

An individual object's truth appears whether the object is a product of a human act of creation or not. In particular, it appears in all kinds of ordinary things from our everyday surroundings (e.g. geological, zoological specimens) and in works of art. In particular, an object's individual truth may be founded in (a) its morphology, or (b) its origin. In the case of (a) the specific set of features (e.g. shape, physical substance) — even accidental defects, as often occurs among museum exhibits in palaeontology and archaeology — determines the object's identity. In the case of (b) the object's morphology becomes a factor of secondary importance. For instance, a painting received by a museum is a 'true Rembrandt' because, irrespective of the features used to recognize it as an authentic Rembrandt, it is Rembrandt who was its author, irrespective of whether we know it or not, and whether analysis confirms the object's identity or not. Another painting will 'possess' its own identity as a Rembrandt copy, because not Rembrandt, but a copyist, was its author. Even a forgery of a well-known masterpiece has its own truth, namely that of being a forgery. The content or meaning of truth is, in all these cases, singular, unrepeatable, and therefore individual.

Second Case

Close to the above is the interpretation of an object's truth as a value conditioned by a set of conventionally selected features, or by its origin. In this way only some objects are accepted as 'true', while the rest are 'untrue'. As before, the object's truth (or, its untruth) is ontological, that is, it is intrinsic to the object and may be identified. Analysis may, as before, detect the object's truth. If wrong, the analysis may negate the object's truth, or leave the object unevaluated. On the other hand, the object's truth (or untruth) is dependent on the act of cognition so far as it is based on some a priori definition, norm or standard, which may be conventional or even arbitrary. Two main variants arise.

In variant (a): the object's truth is identified with its authenticity. An a priori assumption determines what should be understood as the object's authenticity. For instance, if an artistic masterpiece is taken as the output of a certain artist, the a priori norm for its authenticity is that it should be completed entirely by the author himself (i.e. without the help of the author's assistants). Many works which have been only designed by their authors, or only finished by them, would thus qualify as non-authentic. Another example is when an original object becomes modified in some of its features but because of its origin and the preservation of the features regarded as essential to its authenticity, is still regarded as authentic and a bearer of truth. For instance: a work of art which, as the result of the conservation process, becomes modified in some of its features (even to the extent that the whole of its individuality becomes change, for example, when its authentic, dark varnish has been replaced by a new one, when old canvas has been relined, etc.) still qualifies as 'authentic' (sometimes paradoxically, 'more authentic' than it was before). Its authenticity is recognized because the object's features which are considered essential remained unchanged. The list of features is, of course, assumed conventionally; for instance it does not matter that in such cases the object after conservation 'looks' differently, or that it becomes physically a different thing. In restored objects this sense of authenticity becomes reduced; one already distinguishes the 'authentic' and the 'restored' parts.

Variant (b) occurs when the object's truth is regarded as a value independent of the object's authenticity, or when truth is limited exclusively to that of selected features, irrespective of their physical nature. In such cases the whole physical substance of the given object can be replaced with a non-authentic one. For instance, the Hammurabi stele in the Vorderasiatisches Museum in Berlin is a plaster cast of the original. Although only a reproduction, it functions as a valuable exhibit, for it contains and transmits the same amount of scientifically essential data as the authentic object (shape, size, engraved inscriptions and so on), even accidental damage to the original. The circumstance that its physical substance is of plaster and not of stone, and the manufacture by a contemporary museum technician rather than a Mesopotamian sculptor, is of no importance. Satisfactory concordance of some features with the original is the single factor which is essential for the exhibit's truth. Untruth would appear in such a case only if somebody tried to erase some parts of the inscription, or replace one text with another, in other words to change the content of the exhibit or its artistic form.

Third Case

The features of an exhibit may in some cases be of heterogeneous origin. This happens when they are introduced into the exhibit as a novelty to communicate a scientific concept, and visualized through the communications media. The truth, untruth, or probability of the concept consequently determines the value of the objects which take part in its 'materialization'.

As in the previous cases, the object's altered content is intrinsic to it and can, at least, be known and evaluated. The analysis of the object may therefore reveal its heterogeneous structure; distinguish the elements which belonged to it primarily and those which have been secondarily introduced; and determine which ones convey truth, and which are hypothetical or evidently imaginary or untrue. Thus the Ishtar Gate in the Vorderasiatisches Museum contains some untruth as regards size and proportion of elements, because the exhibit is installed in an interior which cannot take the object at its original size. Explanatory text added to the exhibit corrects these deformations and help visitors understand the restoration.

The role of scientific concepts is important when the exhibits are intended to represent or illustrate not individual things, but concepts, classes of objects, notions and so on. In such cases the objects which are represented, symbolized or illustrated by the exhibits are creations of scientific ideas and are thus determined, in their ontological type, essence, degree of generalization and defining features.

The truth of the exhibits depends mostly in such cases on the satisfactory concordance of their features with the features of what they are illustrating. Only some selected features are taken into consideration; the rest, in particular the features determining the uniqueness of the given exhibit, are suppressed and play no role in the presentation. The features which are selected, are intended to be understood as general ones. There are several variants within this third case.

(A) This variant applies when the role of the exhibit is limited to the representation of some general class of objects, and when the representation is not connected with any material changes to the exhibit. The simplest case occurs when the object's meaning is limited to its class, for example when a natural history specimen is exhibited as a representative of the species to which it belongs or when a work of art is presented as an example of a class, for example as a 'Renaissance' painting, as a piece of 'Mycenian' pottery. In such cases the individual features of the exhibit (i.e. those which identify it as a single thing) are of minor or of no importance at all; they are intended to be postponed in the process of understanding the exhibit's content. On these grounds the choice of an exhibit within its class is free: not a singular, definite object, but any object from the given class will do. The sufficient condition of its choice is that it actually belongs to its class and can represent it satisfactorily. For example, in a geological exhibition a piece of granite rock may be used irrespective of individual features (e.g. size or shape). Similarly, in an archaeological or historic exhibition, any example of Minoan pottery will serve to give the visitor an idea of Minoan pottery. Sometimes, when the type which is intended to be visualized comprises examples of very diversified character, a selected group of exhibits (each representing a typical sub-group) may be chosen.

More complex cases occur when an object in the exhibition has to represent an inferred idea or process. For instance, when a geological specimen is used to illustrate say, sedimentation, nothing of this process is actually present in the exhibition; it is inferred from the features of the specimen on display. The most complex cases arise when the concept illustrated by the exhibit becomes an interpretation of a scientific idea concerning the origin, function, mutual relations, evolution, etc. of particular objects, processes or events. Such an interpretation may have a scientific or non-scientific origin (although usually presented under the aegis of science). Most of the cases represent some hypothesis (e.g. how did the Carpathians emerge?). Exhibits stand as documents or proofs of scientific concepts: their content and, consequently, their truth may, in some cases, not be concordant with the value of the idea they are intended to illustrate; for example, well determined (true) objects may become illustrations of a hypothesis which is completely wrong. Conscious falsifications of scientific truth can occur where exhibits, instead of being vehicles of scientific information, are converted into instruments of 'ideological' indoctrination.

(B) In the second variant of the third case, representations of general objects may lead to changes introduced into the material substances, or the objective structure, of the exhibit. The representation becomes, therefore, a visualization of a general scientific idea or concept. An example is the palaeontological restoration, intended to represent not an individual fossil organism but the entire species. These restorations characteristically preserve some authentic features; but they can also contain an element of scientific creation, based on the data of research and on reasoning, but sometimes inspired by free imagination. Palaeontological restorations are sometimes free of any new elements: everything in them is authentic. In such cases, it is only the configuration of the constituent parts that is the novelty, for example, in the way the bones – correctly or wrongly – are mounted in a skeleton. Truth and untruth in a palaeontological restoration is dependent on the results of research, and on the probability or non-probability of the proposed hypothesis, for all restorations are to some extent hypothetical.

(C) In the third variant of the third case, a class of ideas may be represented by artefacts materially and structurally different from the documentary material on which they are based. These creations are executed mainly as artworks, that is, as models, sculptures, reliefs, paintings or graphics. Here there must be concordance between a selected set of features and the general features of the designates. The more general the represented objects, the smaller the number of necessarily concordant features in the artefact. For example, the 'mammal in general', or the definition of the group Mammalia, would need fewer of such features than a model intended to represent a certain mammalian species. The model of a whale exhibited in the British Museum (Natural History) is naturalistic to such an extent that it can illustrate a definite whale species. Features which would identify it with any particular specimen are unnecessary, and even if included (e.g. because of the artist's accuracy in representing animals), would be of no importance to the correct understanding of the exhibit. Untruth in such cases would appear only if the representation were provided with features that were not concordant with the definition of the reference object, for example if the whale were painted red, or had three tails instead of one.

The model of an orthopteran (a group of insects) in the Senckenberg Museum, Frankfurt am Main is made of brass: although its colour is that of metal and none of the orthopterans are of that colour, it is correct in its content and truth, because the morphological feature of colour does not exist in the definition of Orthoptera, and consequently it can be ignored in its representation *ad libitum*, as the artist wishes.

Disinformation (and hence untruth) may, therefore, appear in artworks which are 'too detailed', for example when the degree of realism is much above the message they are intended to transmit. This is the case when a designer fills in the lacking elements of the object he intends to represent with naturalistic, but completely imaginary, features. Marginal cases exist among creations representing general cases when the class of objects is represented by a single specimen, for example as with the coelacanth

Latimeria chalumnae when only a single specimen was known. Very naturalistic models were made and displayed in many museums. Formally they resembled a reproduction (partly a restoration) of the single specimen that was given as a model. Here a highly naturalistic representation was fully acceptable.

In relation to the scientific concept, the didactic concept of an exhibit is always secondary; it presents a means of interpreting the exhibit's basic scientific idea. Didactic reasons influence, for instance, the statements to be visualized in the exhibit; sometimes they introduce a special structure into the exhibitions as a whole, for example the sentence-like organizations of its elements, each of them becoming the bearer of special meaning to be decoded according to a special 'key'. The semantic structure of the exhibition resembles, in such cases, that of a textbook and is essentially linear. Although such exhibitions are intended to become conveyers of scientific information they can, through oversimplification, become a source of untruth.

Fourth Case

The reason for the heterogeneous structure of an exhibit may lie in its design. The design itself becomes an expression of the scientific message; in other cases, however, it is independent of it. In either case the design may convey information which is not programmed in the exhibit's script. Information may carry some untruth which needs neutralizing in the process of understanding. For instance, Coptic columns exhibited in the National Museum, Warsaw were received in fragments and had to be restored. The restoration was conceived schematically, that is, the missing parts were suggested in their main shape, but not according to size, and were deprived of detail. The most characteristic feature was, however, the arrangements of the columns as a 'bunch', close to one another, as never occurs in the original architecture. This schematic arrangement of Coptic columns is indisputably untrue and is so self-evident that it practically excludes any misunderstanding of the exhibit; the exhibition merely presents a collection of restored columns and not a restoration of their arrangement, or their architectural space. Misunderstandings may however arise when the visitor is not able to distinguish an exhibit convention, which is intended to be meaningless, from the message. Many palaeontological exhibitions combine the principle of a diorama with that of a collection. In such cases quasi-surrealistic scenarios are created, where skeletons are placed against painted, more or less realistic, landscapes, and the restorations are included into the scenery as models reduced in scale. This approach excludes any misunderstandings of the exhibits. However, the artistic conception can be misunderstood and interpreted by the visitor (especially if the visitor is a historian of art) as an intention to create a surrealistic work of art. Finally, numerous exhibitions are strongly influenced by abstract or pop art. In the University Museum of Zoology, Copenhagen, there are no restorations, but all the exhibitions are strongly influenced by abstract art. Colour has in some cases the function of an iconic sign, but in other cases it is meaningless.

Fifth Case

Truth or untruth in museum exhibitions may, finally, depend on the way in which the exhibit conditions will affect the appearance of objects. We perceive real objects through their form and appearance: museum exhibits present merely one example of this. The way we perceive things is not conditioned by any intellectual concept, or scientific message, which is encoded in them. Appearances are always changing: they may last for a shorter or longer time, but irrespective of how long they last, one second, one hour, or one year, they are always ephemeral.

Because objects in museum exhibitions are mostly detached from their natural surroundings they look different in the exhibition milieu. Aesthetic qualities (all of which are of a typically phenomenal character) founded on the basis of the object's appearance, change correspondingly. For instance, a painting created in an artist's studio looks different when installed in the exhibition hall with different lighting, space, etc., and presented against a different colour background, so much so that it often becomes an astonishing discovery, a 'new' work of art: it reveals qualities which could not be seen in the conditions of the studio. A specimen of a deep-sea fish is deprived of any appearances and consequently of any aesthetic qualities when it is in its natural environment: living in complete darkness it is 'nothing'. Observed in daylight it astonishes us by its bright, often vividly red, colour – 'illogical' for the conditions in which it lives. In a museum display we see it in its 'illogical' colour. A fragment of Mediterranean architecture which, in its natural surroundings, presents aesthetic qualities connected with the natural lighting for which it was designed, becomes aesthetically neutral when installed in a museum interior under diffuse top lighting. Summing up, one can say:

1. Any surroundings in which an object is amenable to our perception affects the object's appearance and, correspondingly, its aesthetic qualities.

2. The influence of the surroundings act on any kind of object, man made or natural. In works of art the changes of appearance are especially important as regards their aesthetic values, but the same rules and the same phenomena can be observed in all other kinds of exhibits, even those which in their origin, function and meaning have nothing in common with aesthetics. In museums, where the aesthetic factor is neglected or deliberately suppressed, the conditions under which particular exhibits are presented are regularly provided with negative aesthetic qualities.

3. Regarding the changes in an object's appearance, especially in works of

art, it is often difficult to say which of these appearances should be defined as the 'true' ones. In many cases, one can speak exclusively about different objects' appearances, all of which are equally valuable as regards their truth. One can speak, at least, about more or less favourable conditions for presenting things, or about better or worse appearances as regards their effectiveness – and these differences are sufficiently important for us to look for the optimal design solution.

4. Modifications of the exhibits' appearances mostly occur as a result of twofold relations: (a) those between particular exhibits and (b) those between exhibits and their background. These relationships never occur separately, but are always combined.

An object's appearance may carry some extra novelty which may be a strong emotive factor in modifying the intended meaning of the object. Emotive expression may raise the visual quality of objects presented in museum displays: ordinary 'everyday' objects, when installed in well-arranged exhibits, start to function as if they were authentic works of art. Irrespective of their being objects of cognition, they become objects of aesthetic experience, amenable both to our feeling and to our understanding.

Many examples from artistically advanced archaeological exhibitions, where exhibits are presented as treasures, may be quoted as typical examples. This bi-functional character of exhibitions (cognitive and emotively aesthetic) is of great significance in contemporary culture. The role of the museum, especially that of presenting and interpreting cultural heritage, achieves it in concrete form.

References

Ingarden, R. (1958) '*Studies on Aesthetics*, PWN, Warszawa, Poland.
Swiecimski, J. (1974) 'Scientific information function and Ingarden's theory of forms', *Analecta Husserliana*, Reidel Publishing, Dordrecht, Netherlands.

24

Heritage Revisited: A Concluding Address

David Lowenthal

How should we assess the Second World Congress on Heritage Presentation and Interpretation. One way is to compare it with its predecessor (Lunn, 1988). What distinguished the Second from the First Congress, Conventry from Banff? Salient differences emerge in at least three realms: culture, conservation and concern for truth.

The balance of subject matter noticeably shifted from an emphasis on natural to cultural heritage. Both figured in Warwick as in Western Canada, but it is not surprising that in the heart of England, encircled by steel and Shakespeare, coal mines and cotton mills, castles and cathedrals and country houses, the concerns reflected an Old World heritage more markedly man-made than that of the Canadian Rockies. This shift notwithstanding, we need to ponder Kenneth Craik's (1988) insight that appreciation of cultural and natural heritage involves strikingly similar psychological dispositions; individual tastes for 'pastoralism' and 'antiquarianism' embody many of the same preferences. Nor should we stress too much the dichotomy of nature and culture, since Kenneth Olwig (in Volume I) had alerted us to their profound and complex interconnections. Indeed, the very idea of nature as heritage is itself a product of cultural imagination.

If 'culture' at this congress in any sense overshadowed 'nature', it was not for want of ecological commitment. The conservation ethos animated discussion not simply as a background motif but as an impassioned explicit concern. The urgency of global environmental problems, if not of local ones, has enormously heightened over the three preceding years. Heritage interpreters, as Adrian Phillips (Volume I) noted, face a public now better informed and more alert than ever before.

If preservation is sometimes at odds with interpretation, as Neil Cossons (Volume II) suggested, other contributors emphasized their essential conjunction. They viewed the material culture in their charge as especially at risk. Apprehension of physical damage caused by visitors has mounted with the expansion of that clientele. Heritage managers expressed concern not merely about the impact of hiking boots and beach buggies but about the derangement of entire ecosystems by the growing tourist and leisure industries.

But delegates' concern was not limited to threats to physical fabric. They were equally dismayed at the loss of immediacy and ambience at heritage sites owing to over-visitation and over-interpretation. On the eve of our meetings, the rising popularity of art museums was reported to have turned viewing into a treadmill, with an endless queue of visitors pushing past paintings seen mainly at a distance, behind bubble glass, and surrounded by armed guards. 'The greater the public's desire to make pilgrimages to art's ever more holy body, the more it has to be protected from public contamination' (Brenson, 1988). With heritage generally, as with works of art, it becomes ever harder to retain the sense of mystery lauded by Don Aldridge (Volume I) and others, or to keep something free of interpretation for venturesome visitors to discover unmediated.

Concern for truth and authenticity was another dominating theme. Participants were responsive to the irony underscored by Robert Hewison (Volume I) and Peter Fowler (Volume I): the more popular and successful interpretation becomes, the more it sacrifices historical realities for heritage images, truth for illusion. Sophisticated representations can be brilliantly effective, as Jorvik demonstrates. But as many emphasized, only close and continuous connection with the physical reality they portray can prevent such presentations from emulsifying heritage into demeaning falsehood. Instead of a genuine exploration and explication of the past, heritage then degenerates into little beyond an evocation of the taste of the present.

The public overwhelmingly trusts that heritage interpreters are telling them the truth. How well that reputation is deserved, in Cossons' phrase (Volume II) is what this congress was all about. How typical was the heritage entrepreneur cited by Hewison as saying, in defending Plymouth's Armada hype, 'what's history if you can't bend it a bit?' (Peek, 1988). Between Cossons' ideal and Hewison's exemplar the gulf seems unbridgeable. Brian Redhead's faith that it 'never does any harm to know how things really happened' (Redhead, 1988) is not shared by many who are fearful of or angry at the past. The 'passionate objectivity' Peter Rumble (Volume I) called for is a contradiction in terms: indeed, even *dis*passionate objectivity is unattainable. We all bend history at least a bit, and as one participant observed, the older the heritage site, the easier it is just to mow the lawn and avoid the truth.

The debate over truth bears closely on the issue of 'hot interpretation' raised in David Uzzell's keynote paper (Volume 1). Lack of passion was a complaint several foreign participants levelled against their British hosts in particular and Anglo-American interpretation generally. History elsewhere is more often a burning issue, historical identity bound up with issues of immediate import. In such circumstances, 'hot interpretation' is unavoidable; like the curator in Siegfried Lenz's novel, *The Heritage* (1981), interpreters confront emotionally charged responses to sites and relics. Custodians and interpreters in much of the world are not only paramedics who need to keep alert for audience distress but combatants in the trenches of historical warfare.

The British sense of heritage was once more similarly *engagé* than it now is. Half a century ago, the historian Herbert Butterfield contrasted English with other ways of incorporating the past:

Because we in England have maintained the threads between past and present, we do not, like some younger states, have to go hunting for our own personalities. We do not have to set about the deliberate manufacture of a national consciousness, or to strain ourselves, like the Irish, in order to create a 'nationalism' out of the broken fragments of tradition, out of the ruins of a tragic past . . . . Our history is here and active, giving meaning to the present. (Butterfield, 1944)

English history no longer fulfils so active a function. But many in Britain today similarly value their beleaguered old museums. Having grown 'piecemeal from the passions of private collectors', as a museum defender puts it, 'in their haphazard way they have become valuable repositories of reference material that can never be matched by the sanitized and neutered new museums of America (Sewell, 1988). Yet to embattled curators elsewhere in the world, British museums sometimes seem, if not sanitized, perhaps remote from reality.

The rest of the world had little voice, however, at this congress. The paucity of delegates from overseas, even from beyond the Channel, was perhaps our gravest disappointment. Three years previously Banff attracted delegates from a wider range of countries, notwithstanding its greater remove from most of them. At Warwick, the virtual absence of Asians and Africans was sadly apparent. Nor were we much better supplied with continental Europeans. Distinctive individual voices, especially from Fenno-Scandia, contributed substantially to mutual understanding, but the mainstream expressions of heritage interpretation were essentially Anglo-American. Yet Britain did not invent heritage, nor have Anglophone nations any monopoly of interest in it. It is crucial to our global enterprise that the heritage concerns of the rest of the world, whatever the status of heritage management there, be seriously addressed when the Third World Congress meets in Honolulu.

For heritage managers in many countries, as Spanish colleagues especially commented, lack of confidence seems an overriding concern. Yet few if any accepted Cossons' charge that they lacked confidence in the value of their product. Quite to the contrary, most delegates felt convinced that what they had to offer was of vital importance. What they lacked, instead, was confidence that they could, or even should, persuade the public of the value that they themselves perceived in heritage. But too many delegates seemed ready not only to plead guilty to the inadequacies that others ascribed to them, but even to beg critics like Hewison to provide a blueprint for correcting them.

No such blueprint seems to me either necessary or desirable. Heritage interpreters are their own best critics. Their experience and surveillance offer better guides for corrective action, whenever that is needed, than any academic or journalistic dialectics.

But we and our critics alike need to realize that heritage is much more than what interpreters choose and shape and present, more even than what the public may want or can cope with. Heritage is also what we are stuck with; it is the Roman concept of *damnosa hereditas*, the legacy you would rather not have but must accept because it is part of what has been left to you – your just desserts. This sense of 'heritage' in English usage goes back at least to the fourteenth century (Gower, 1390).

Such awareness also reminds us that aspects of heritage which our generation spurns or mocks may be wanted later. Future needs matter as much or more than today's market place. Against pressures to cater for immediate wants, many delegates reiterated our duty to that future. We cannot predict how our successors will define their heritage, but it is bound to include, besides some of our own and of subsequent creations, a rich and representative array of currently existing relics of nature and culture (including some as yet undiscovered or whose importance is not now recognized). Those who follow us should not expect to inherit these things unaffected by ourselves. They have a right, though, to see us as stewards, not as final owners, of that heritage. Neither zealous salesmanship nor self-righteous exclusion, simplistic interpretation, mass visitation, or self-conscious admiration should be permitted to vitiate the substance of that heritage or wholly to subvert its meaning.

In his opening remarks, John Foster (Volume I) held up three worthy aims: to learn from each other; to forge practical links; and to make identifiable contributions to heritage matters. Those who came together at Warwick, like most heritage interpreters, showed their dedication to such self-improvement. Among other admirable traits interpreters today exhibit: growing tolerance and genuine appreciation of their audiences. Heritage sites where visitors are talked down to, once the rule, are now the exception. Gone for good is the interpretive exemplar of H.M. Bateman's horrific cautionary tale, *The Boy Who Breathed on the Glass in the British Museum* (1971), the heinous crime for which he was jailed for life. Bateman's Boy is superseded in real life, if not quite as an ideal type, by the small child in a hushed New York gallery, cautioned by her mother: 'Now, remember, what is the first rule when we are in a museum?' 'Yes,' says the toddler, at the top of her lungs: 'NO YELLING!'

References

Bateman, H.M. (1971) *The Boy Who Breathed on the Glass in the British Museum*, Pordes, Cockfosters, Hertfordshire.

Brenson, M. (1988) 'How museums turn you off', *International Herald Tribune*, 27–28 August, p. 7.

Butterfield, H. (1944) *The Englishman and His History*, Cambridge University Press, Cambridge, p. 114.

Craik, K. (1988) 'Personality and sense of history', paper presented at the Second

World Congress on Heritage Presentation and Interpretation, 30 August–4 September 1988, University of Warwick.

Gower, J. (1390) *Confessio Amantis*, R. Pauli, 1857; Eng. Works, Early English Text Society, 1900, Vol. II, p. 364.

Lenz, S. (1981) *The Heritage*, Hill & Wang, New York.

Lunn, J. (ed.) (1988) *Proceedings of the First World Congress on Heritage Presentation and Interpretation* (Banff, Alberta, Canada, 1985), Heritage Interpretation International and Alberta Culture and Multiculturalism, Edmonton.

Peek, B. (1988), quoted in W. Greaves, 'Sir Francis fights again', *The Times*, 30 January, p. 13.

Redhead, B. (1988) 'Keynote address', presented at the Second World Congress on Heritage Presentation and Interpretation, 30 August–4 September 1988, University of Warwick.

Sewell, B. (1988), 'A case of arts for oblivion', *The Times*, 2 April.

Index

Contents

Volume 1: The Natural and Built Environment